PRAISE FOR

RICH BITCH

"Stressing over money can harm your overall health.
Let Nicole be the doctor for your financial health and
you will feel better in more ways that you'd think."
—DR. OZ, HOST OF *THE DR. OZ SHOW*, AND LISA OZ, HOST OF *THE LISA OZ SHOW*

"*Rich Bitch* should be mandatory reading for every young professional
woman who wants to take control of her financial destiny."
—MINDY GROSSMAN, CEO OF HSN

"Nicole's advice is a swift kick in the pants to the young, ambitious, upstart
women out there who want control over their lives, debts and careers."
—WENDY WILLIAMS, HOST OF *THE WENDY WILLIAMS SHOW*

"*Rich Bitch* is the manual for a new generation of women who want
both job stability and financial peace of mind."
—STACY LONDON, HOST OF TLC'S *WHAT NOT TO WEAR*

"Nicole does a fabulous job educating people about money
while always keeping it fun and entertaining."
—ALEXIS MAYBANK, COFOUNDER OF GILT GROUPE

"Lapin's unfiltered, energetic advice speaks to anyone
taking aim at their own career destiny."
—MIKE PERLIS, CEO OF FORBES MEDIA

"*Rich Bitch* is essential reading for 21st-century women
wanting to rise to the top of the economic ladder."
—REBECCA TAYLOR, DESIGNER

"If you're a woman and you like money, you need to read this book.
Immediately. You can't afford to miss this one, ladies!"
—ALLI WEBB, CEO AND FOUNDER OF DRYBAR

"Nicole delivers expert financial advice straight up, no chaser,
in a tone that's as lively as it is likable."
—NEIL BLUMENTHAL AND DAVE GILBOA, FOUNDERS OF WARBY PARKER

"Nicole brings to life in a highly readable way the real pitfalls and
solutions of financial life in a more complex world."
—NIGEL TRAVIS, CEO OF DUNKIN' DONUTS

"A financial diet is like a regular diet: if you allow yourself small indulgences, you won't binge later on. Nicole offers you a plan you can stick to."
—SANJAY GUPTA, CHIEF MEDICAL CORRESPONDENT FOR CNN

"Whether you want to take over the world or just balance your checkbook, Nicole gives you the tools to save, spend and succeed."
—RANDI ZUCKERBERG, TECHNOLOGY EXPERT

"I wish I'd had Nicole's book when I was starting my business. She makes business and finance feel accessible but does it in a sassy, humorous way. It's a must-have for any budding entrepreneur."
—KRISTI YAMAGUCHI, OLYMPIC GOLD MEDALIST, FOUNDER OF TSU.YA

"Women will talk about—and ask for—absolutely anything, except money. Time with Nicole and her no-nonsense advice will change that for good."
—TORY JOHNSON, HOST OF *GOOD MORNING AMERICA*'S "DEALS & STEALS"

"At last! A finance book that's cool enough for my kick-ass teenage daughters, and smart enough for my CEO self!"
—JULIE CLARK, FOUNDER OF BABY EINSTEIN

"Having the life you want isn't just about managing your career brilliantly. It's about getting control of your finances—starting RIGHT NOW. Nicole's sassy, smart and super-easy-to-digest book will help you do exactly that."
—KATE WHITE, FORMER EDITOR-IN-CHIEF OF *COSMOPOLITAN*

"What I love about Nicole is that you don't need a dictionary to understand her advice. It's crystal clear, straight up and spot-on."
—ALYSSA MILANO, ACTRESS AND FOUNDER OF TOUCH BY ALYSSA MILANO

"*Rich Bitch* gives a brash tutorial for women looking to take their share in today's bleak economic climate. Lapin leads the way brilliantly!"
—KAREN FINERMAN, PANELIST ON CNBC'S "FAST MONEY"

"Nicole is the money expert with sensible advice to help you be the CEO of your own life."
—FRED DELUCA, COFOUNDER AND CEO OF SUBWAY

"You don't need Google search to understand Nicole's advice. It's crystal clear, straightforward, shameless and spot-on."
—JANE PRATT, EDITOR OF XOJANE

RICH BITCH

A Simple 12-Step
Plan for Getting
Your Financial Life
Together...*Finally*

NICOLE LAPIN

RICH BITCH

Rich Bitch™ is a trademark used under license from Nothing But Gold Productions, Inc.

ISBN-13: 978-0-373-89317-1

Library of Congress Cataloging-in-Publication Data
Lapin, Nicole.
 Rich bitch : A simple 12-step plan for getting your financial life together...finally / Nicole Lapin.
  pages cm
Includes index.
 ISBN 978-0-373-89317-1 (hardback)
1. Young women—Finance, Personal. 2. Women—Finance, Personal. 3. Finance, Personal. 4. Investments. I. Title.
 HG179.L2662 2015
 332.024'01082—dc23
                  2014038162

www.Harlequin.com

Printed in U.S.A.

To my former self,
who has finally stopped smiling and nodding.

And for all my Rich Bitches—
the women who understand that
you don't have to be either to be both.

CONTENTS

There are people who have money
and then there are people who are rich.

—COCO CHANEL

INTRO

CHOOSE YOUR OWN
MONEY ADVENTURE

So you picked up a book about money. You? Yes, *you*! Well, you didn't pick up just *any* book. You picked up the first finance book that... swears! And is written in plain English! Yes, it's true. This. Is. Happening.

And I think I can guess why you picked this book up. You want control of your life and your finances; you want to live a rich life. Am I right? You want to understand the language of money. I thought so. Well, then, yes, you're in the right place. Don't freak out. Think of it as an adventure.

Remember reading those "Choose Your Own Adventure" books as a kid? I loved them; still do (shh... don't tell). As you will find by the time you finish this book, I'm a huge proponent of taking control of your own destiny—yep, choosing your own adventure—whether in life, love or finance. There is no set way to do this; it's all about what works for *you*.

In that spirit, while I've set this up as a 12-step program, you can read this book and its 12 steps in whichever way you want—it's your choice. You're a big girl. In need of some serious budget reform? Start with Step 3, "Your New LBD," and learn all about how a Little Budget Diary can keep you on track. About to have a panic attack because you are drowning in debt? Go to Step 6, "Get That Monkey Off Your Back," to lose your debt load and keep it off. Jonesing to be your own boss? Step 8, "Work It, Bitches," has you covered. Feel like you're *never* going to have enough money to retire? Head to Step 9, "Aging Gracefully," and find out how to save for the long term without depriving yourself or sacrificing fun in the short term. Looking to take your hard-earned money to the next level? Yep, there's a step for that: Step 10, "Make It Grow, Baby, Grow," where you'll learn that investing just isn't that serious.

If you're in the market for a complete financial overhaul, I'd suggest starting at the best place to start…you guessed it, Step 1. That's where we take stock of your current financial situation (the real one, not the one you've told yourself is real). After that, I'm going to guide you through setting up a badass savings plan, and then suggest some ways to maximize your money and your lifestyle now.

I've broken this book up into steps, because it's easier to digest that way. If you read it sequentially, each step builds on the last, but each step also stands on its own if you want to map out your own journey instead. After all, this is your book; you bought it. This is your life; you live it. I'm just here to help you discover the one you want to get out of it.

However you choose to read this book, I *do* have one requirement: that you read the whole thing, even if out of order. Then I have a humble suggestion: that you keep it. It will never go out of style.

Maybe you're thinking, "Hey, Lapin, I already know everything there is to know about money and living a rich life."

I doubt it. Chances are, other so-called financial experts have drilled all sorts of truisms into your head that might not be, well, true. Like: "You should invest in a 401(k)" or "You should work toward buying a house," which I disagree with, mostly because nothing in finance is for everyone. Or, that you can't treat yourself to a latte while you're trying to get out of debt, which I also think is BS. (Much more on all these topics later.)

It's time to rethink convention and learn to think for yourself. Stop being brainwashed and start making financial decisions for *you*, for your own personal adventure.

Finally, before we get going, I need you to embrace one thing: being a Rich Bitch is *good*. It can be the ultimate source of power if you choose to make it yours. It's confidence in knowing your stuff, knowing what you want and grabbing it by the balls. It's time to get it together and get it all. It's time to be a Rich Bitch.

STEP

1

STOP SMILING AND NODDING
Embrace the Rich Bitch Attitude

Every single story goes back to money. I learned that being in the news world for so long. If you want to get to the heart of any story, you just have to follow the money trail. So, let's follow the money trail of your life.

Yes, that will take us through the nuts and bolts of hard-core personal finance. Of course. But it also means going down paths of topics like shacking up and taking care of yourself. "Wait, say what, Lapin? *Those* aren't money issues," you might be thinking. Well, sure, they're just topics about men and wellness at first blush, but they are absolutely money topics, too. Actually, to me, those are the best kinds of money stories because you don't *feel* like you are talking about money. And that's how I like to talk about money: in a sneak-attack way, like mixing spinach into a chocolate brownie. You don't taste it, but you still get the nutrition.

Throughout our adventure together, don't forget *why* we are following the money trail. We want to get to the heart of your life story, the one you have lived so far and the one you'll continue to write. So I will do a lot of storytelling: my money stories, your money stories, the ones that we can all relate to and link us all.

It's that simple: financial lessons are more easily digested through brownies and story time. Who said learning had to be boring? So here we go. It's time to learn everything about money that you need to know but don't—or *think* you know but don't.

Now, before we start, let me make a confession: I wasn't always this confident.

CONFESSIONS
OF A RICH BITCH

Stop smiling and nodding

I was sure I nailed it. When it came time to interview for my first-choice college, I was beyond prepared, like the star student I portrayed myself to be (but I was really kind of a wannabe). I studied up on the history of the school, practiced saying the names of the important alums and remembered the titles of the courses I thought would be impressive to say I wanted to take. I did almost everything to look and sound the part but wear the school colors, and trust me, I thought about it. My test scores weren't stellar, and I had no family connections to the school, but I wanted to get in so badly. I was convinced that going there was my ticket to the television news career I had dreamed of. So when the admissions officer asked me what else I wanted to know about the university, I pounced on my time to shine, asking my rehearsed, well-researched, confident-sounding questions.

Then she started asking me more about my proclaimed love for journalism and media. She asked me which papers I read, and I said something like, "I love the *New York Times*, skim *USA TODAY* for good digests and am a closet politico junkie with the *Washington Post*." She said, "Oh, great. And I'm sure you're like me and can't get the morning started without the *Journal*." I smiled and nodded. I had no idea what the *Journal* was.

A few years later, I was at that school I so intensely craved to attend as a high school senior: the Medill School of Journalism at Northwestern University. By then, I thought I was done with the "fake it 'til you make it" shtick of doing cursory research and focused on really nailing my work once I was there. In fact, I thought I was the bee's knees of broadcast journalism when I received a big award while I was a student. It was a big, fancy shindig with bubbly and bow ties—my chance to meet some of the people in TV news whom I looked up to and admired, including the legendary Helen Thomas. Eek, Helen Thomas!! As in, the first woman ever to sit in the front row of the White House pressroom. I wanted to be like her with her badass red suit. She frequently got to ask the President the first question he would take. This was akin to meeting the biggest celebrity you can imagine. She was my idol. I worked up the courage to introduce myself in front of the people she was chatting with. I proudly said my name, shook her hand and told her what an honor it was to meet her. And then the group proceeded to talk about shorting the stock market.

I smiled and nodded. I was embarrassed that I couldn't join the conversation, because it was a topic that totally stumped me.

It wasn't until after I graduated from college that I finally snagged my high school crush. He was the chisel-jawed, blue-eyed editor of the school newspaper and the only person I knew who'd scored a perfect 1600 on his SATs. He was the geek-chic guy who quoted Tolstoy and Dave Matthews in the same breath. He was brilliant, and I was absolutely smitten. We talked about a future together. We talked about the home we would share and the kids we might have. He was the only person with whom I could wax poetic about almost anything (I thought at the time)—politics, music, history, philosophy, you name it. Then he told me his dream of becoming a hedge fund manager.

I smiled and nodded. (I thought a hedge fund had something to do with gardening.)

You get the point: there was a lot of ignorant smiling and nodding going on in my teens and early twenties. My younger self thought she knew a lot. But hedge funds, shorting stocks and the *Journal* were definitely not on the list, and I was too scared of looking dumb to admit it. So instead of asking a question when I didn't know what someone was talking about, or actually looking it up later, I continued to smile and nod, too nervous to confront the topics that scared me the most.

And I pretended all the way until our breakup, when my boyfriend told me that we couldn't date anymore because I wasn't smart enough to get along with his finance buddies. Okay, he *dumped me* because I was clueless about the subject he loved most.

Getting dumped by Mr. Future Hedge Fund Manager was equal parts devastating and motivating: I became determined to be a person who could hang out with those Wall Street guys. It wasn't so much about the fact that I had been dumped by a boy, but that I had been exposed as not knowing or understanding such a crucial topic. It was like Elle Woods possessed me. I began by reading the *Journal* every day. At first it looked like complete gibberish. Then it started to look like Chinese, and after a few months it morphed into something quasi-understandable. I was still speaking only broken Wall Street when I got a great and super intimidating TV job offer to be an on-air business reporter for a national show on the floor of the major stock exchange in

Chicago. I was beyond freaked out, but I took the job because I knew I could—and would—learn the language. And I did.

Fast-forward about five years, and I was named the anchor of the only global show on the most popular business network in the world, CNBC. (And yes, that means that it covered pretty hard-core financial news.) By then, I not only understood the language but also spoke it fluently—to the world.

STOP THE BS AND JOIN THE CONVERSATION

Looking back, I wish I could talk to my younger self, whom I would have told that some guy shouldn't be the motive for coming out from behind her cowardly smile and nod. I would have told her to figure out that the *Journal* means the *Wall Street Journal*. I would have told her that Helen Thomas probably would have respected her more if she had just asked what shorting the market was instead of acting like she knew that it meant you were betting that the market would go down.

Tell yourself earlier than I did that it's enough already. You need to learn the language of money—and don't think you don't because you aren't on TV talking about it. Money speak comes up in *all* aspects of life: from jobs to social situations to relationships. So the sooner you can understand and speak it, the sooner you'll be able to accomplish what you want to accomplish and the sooner you'll be able to live the life you want to live—that's what being a Rich Bitch is all about.

WHAT IS A RICH BITCH?

Let me be clear. Being a Rich Bitch is *good*. (Rich Bitches are the good kinda bitches, like Glinda in *The Wizard of Oz*, not the bad bitches like the Wicked Witch of the West.) It's about empowerment. It's about taking control.

Being a Rich Bitch means going after what you want in life by getting the financial part in order. Because let's be honest: you need *money* to live the life you want. And that's what this book is going to help you do. You're going to set your goals, and then together we're going to figure out how to achieve them. My mission is to make you so financially fit that you're confident to call yourself a Rich Bitch.

A Rich Bitch has the self-awareness to know exactly what she wants from her life—whether it's buying a house, chasing her dream career, having three kids or none—and she is fluent in the language of money that is the key to achieving those goals.

The dirty little secret is that at some point in our lives, we're all scared when it comes to money. You're not the only one. I am proud to admit that I've been in your shoes. And I am proud to talk honestly about my setbacks along the way, because I made it through a very bumpy journey. And you can, too. I promise each and every one of you aspiring Rich Bitches, I've got your back. I'm going to tell you exactly what you need to know, straight-up without any jargon. *Rich Bitch* is your Rosetta Stone for finance.

I didn't work at a bank or get my MBA, and I'm not going to pretend like I did. I just figured it out the hard way. This book is everything I have learned about money, warts and all.

Just to warn you: I'm going to admit to some embarrassing stuff in this book, so feel free to laugh at me; in fact, I want you to. I want you to be able to smile when you think about money issues. So if I have to be teased for my personal and financial foibles, I'm happy to take one for the team, as long as you remember one thing: learning about the financial world is not as bad as it seems, and once you learn the language I'm about to teach you, you will be able to join conversations I couldn't back in the day. It's only then that you will no longer feel left out. It's only then that you will feel truly empowered.

Let's get one more thing straight before we begin: you're not going to read this and then all of a sudden make a million bucks. This isn't financial boot camp. It's a sustainable financial diet, one that encourages small indulgences to keep you from binging later on. I wish there *were* a magic potion but, as we've all seen from those protein or grapefruit or master cleanse diets, the extreme short-term diet ultimately just keeps us in terrible shape. And when you don't get a six-pack after a day, what happens next? You quit because you feel like a failure.

And we are in it to win it, bitches.

THE FIRST STEP: ADMIT YOU HAVE A PROBLEM

I like using steps for anything I try to accomplish, especially in the realm of money stuff, because it prevents you from having an anxiety attack when you don't accomplish everything all in one day. Like with learning any new skill, things need to be broken down into steps so that you're doing one thing at a time. When I did my taxes for the first time, I didn't set aside one day to do them. I set aside an entire month. Day one: uncrinkle my receipts. That was it. Success! If I had told myself I needed to sit down and do all my taxes and not get up until they were done,

I would have panicked and found myself on the couch with a pint of Häagen-Dazs, taxes incomplete.

This is not going to happen to you on my watch. Baby steps, baby. And the first one, affectionately borrowed from our friends at other 12-step recovery programs, is, all together now: ADMIT YOU HAVE A MONEY PROBLEM.

There, we've said it. You have a problem. I had a problem. We've all got problems and this is just one of them. Maybe it's a HUGE problem for you right now, but it's one that I can help you cross off your list. And now, with feeling: I HAVE A MONEY PROBLEM.

Okay, phew. Step 1: done and done! Now let's move on.

CONFESSIONS
OF A RICH BITCH

Growing up with that cash money

My approach to money has a lot to do with how I grew up. I was raised in an immigrant household where there was no discussion of money, ever. There were no finance books in my home. There was definitely no *Wall Street Journal* at the breakfast table. The TV was never tuned to a business channel. But there was a lot of…cash.

It sounds kind of awesome, like suitcases of hundreds, mob-style. Not so much. Living a cash-only existence meant you bought what you could afford. It's that simple: if you don't have the money to buy something, you don't buy it. No credit cards. No car loans. No any loans. No mortgages. No fancy investments like bonds. It was just green or checks.

In my older, wiser years, I realized that this was actually quite sound from a personal finance perspective, but it wasn't fun growing up. It embarrassed me. Not so much because I couldn't buy things out of my reach (although that did suck a little), but because it wasn't practical and made me seem weird. But the thing was: I didn't realize I was weird until, one day, I did.

I can actually pinpoint my epiphany. It was time to go to college, and I needed to buy a plane ticket from Los Angeles to Chicago. This was back in the day when buying a plane ticket online was cool, but still confusing. Sure, I wanted to be cool and say I bought it online. But I couldn't—because the internet didn't take, um, cash.

So there I was: a wannabe hip college student in this new internet generation with a bundle of cash at the ticketing counter. And the look I got from the airline rep? EM-BAR-RASS-ING.

IT'S NOT ABOUT THE MONEY; IT'S ABOUT YOUR LIFE

I'm not going to start telling you how perfect you need to be with your money, how you should start clipping coupons and stop buying your latte, how saving for retirement should be your main goal and how you've been doing it all wrong. What made me fall in love with talking about money and figuring out how it worked wasn't about what would happen to me in fifty years. It was about what was happening *right then*. It was being disappointed in myself for not being able to join basic money conversations and interactions, not being able to fit in (which I realized later wasn't always the right thing, but a normal desire, nonetheless).

CONFESSIONS
OF A RICH BITCH

Check, please!

I was having dinner with a group of girlfriends at a great French restaurant. When the check came, everyone kept talking and laughing as they threw down their credit cards. Except…I didn't have one. (Remember, I was the weirdo cash-only girl.)

I went into my wallet to put down some cash on top of the pile of cards when I noticed I had only a $20 bill. Eek… I thought I had more than that with me, and I didn't realize the meal would be so expensive! I quickly went over my options in my head. I could:

A. Put down $20 and look like a jackass if the bill was more than $100 for five of us.

B. Ask for the bill to see how much it was and then run to my dorm room (in the middle of winter, in Chicago, wearing heels) if it was more than $100 total.

C. Pay with a check. Seriously, I didn't even have a debit card until midway through college. At that point, I still took out cash from the teller inside the bank, not at the ATM, or used checks.

D. Try to get the waitress's attention and ask her to help a sister out.

I chose D but failed miserably. I tried to be cool about it but ended up drawing more attention to the situation. The waitress didn't come over despite my nervous little waves and chin nods. After a few minutes, there were four cards in the middle of the table and then me clutching $20 under the table. I got the "Hey, Lapin, throw your card down" looks (they felt like dead stares to me).

So now I had to be the awkward girl who stopped the convo and made up some story about forgetting my card and needing to use…a check! I vetoed the option of walking in the freezing cold to get more cash, and I thought it was better to say that I had a check than to look like a cheapskate by having only $20 in case it was more than $100 total. Which, of course, it was. It felt like that moment in the movies when the music stops and everyone at the restaurant turns to stare.

Me: "Um, so what should I write the check out for?"

Girlfriend #1: "I dunno. I didn't look at the bill."

Girlfriend #2: "I guess just split it evenly like we are."

I start trying to figure out how to divide $120 by five girls. At that point, my brain is not going to cooperate with me to do even simple math in front of a crowd.

Me to the waitress: "Excuse me, ma'am, do you mind dividing this? I'm so sorry, I just have to pay with a check. I forgot my…"

Waitress: "Sure, one sec."

Me: "My bad, ladies, but what an amazing night. What were we talking about before?"

Waitress: "Your portion is $20, and I charged each of the others' cards $25."

OMG, no! I meant it should be divided *equally* by five, not how much what *I* ordered was! Now they have to pay $25 instead of the $24 if it had been split evenly. It's not about the $1. It's about the weirdness of me getting out of paying the same. But that, of course, wasn't my intention! "How do I fix it now?" I think. Their cards are already charged and I've already caused a hullabaloo. I can't ask the waitress to change it. Oh, dear God. Now I *do* look like a cheapskate, and that totally isn't what I meant to do at all.

It was right then and there that I knew I needed to put my big-girl undies on and make a change. I *finally* got a debit card. It was a baby step, but a step nonetheless. I used my grown-up debit card to buy the next plane ticket I needed. It was immensely satisfying to get an electronic receipt. And it would feel awesome to throw down my card the next time I had a girls' dinner.

It wasn't just the fear of being weird or awkward that motivated me to understand money. It was also fear of the debt I found myself in and all of the things I wanted—a dinner out tonight, a car soon, a house someday, maybe even a child—that I saw no way to afford. I was afraid of the path I was on. I needed to talk to someone about how to get on the right track.

Still, the more I finally started to want to have these conversations, the more I realized that no one really wanted to have them with me. Let's face it. Women will talk about *anything*—from blow jobs to diarrhea—before we will talk about money, even with our close friends. We will share the number on our bathroom scale before the number on our pay stub. Try it as a social experiment. Ask people both. They will address the weight one first, albeit reluctantly, then hem and haw over the salary one. Would you do the same? Be honest. Back then, I would have, too. Now it's time to put my money where my mouth is.

CONFESSIONS
OF A RICH BITCH

Let's put it all out there

Okay, I'll go first.

I made $26,000 per year at my first television job. I made incrementally more as I worked my way up to a network job at CNN, where I made $75,000 per year. Not a bad living, especially for someone my age, but not exactly rock-star money, either, especially after agent fees and taxes.

At that point in my life, I felt like I was an adult and needed to upgrade my debit card to a credit card. Okay, okay, there was another reason—namely, clothes. I had landed my dream job, and I wanted to look the part when I arrived, but I hadn't gotten paid yet. I figured I'd just go on a little shopping spree and then pay it off when I got my paycheck. I felt as though I *deserved* it.

What I forgot about were all the initial expenses I would have when I moved to Atlanta to start my job at CNN: rent, a car, furniture, not to mention insurance, gas and electric bills, groceries, etc. Then there was a dress for this event or that event and all of a sudden, during the whirlwind of a new city and job, paying it off didn't seem to be a priority. What was the worst that could happen? The move, the clothes, the other expenses were all important and, while my father would have been turning in his grave, I thought it was all worth the debt.

It didn't take long to run a balance of about $5,000. Stupidly, I had allocated all of my salary to rent, my car and some savings. There was nothing left after that. What would I cut back on to pay off my credit card bill? I couldn't think of anything. I *needed* all that stuff. In hindsight, spending almost double what I should have on a two-bedroom apartment just for myself wasn't the wisest decision.

I was stuck. My apartment was too expensive, but moving would have been too expensive, too. I felt as though I had no way out of the hole I'd dug for myself.

I was torn up about it, because deep down I was still my parents' child, and having debt wasn't how I was raised. I was programmed to save money, and I was so staunch about sticking to it that I did so to my own detriment. For what seemed like the right reason, I kept pulling money out of my checking account every payday to stash in savings instead of paying down my credit card, where the double-digit interest meant I was racking up even more debt.

To make matters worse, I took my savings out in green cash. *Seriously*. I had a checking account at the bank, but I put my savings in a real safe under my kitchen sink. My family didn't trust banks. Banks closed or collapsed. So I kept my cash where I could see it. I knew it was there. It was in a safe. But I didn't earn a penny of interest. Over the couple of years it took me to pay off that credit card balance, that safe cost me real money. I only realized later that, had I paid off the debt more quickly with the cash in the safe, I would have had *more* savings. But for no other reason than being a creature of habit and upbringing, I actually went into *more debt* in order to save. Cuh-razy.

It's easy to get in trouble with your finances. Every time you turn around, there's some ad telling you what you really need to have. And I'm not saying you shouldn't spend—it's your life to enjoy, and, yes, even indulge when it's appropriate—but to do that, you need to know what you're doing with your money. It's why you picked up this book.

Yes, breaking news: here is a financial expert who doesn't tell you you're stupid if you don't make your own coffee in the morning. Financial health isn't about deprivation. That's not a ticket to knowledge or power. It's a scare tactic that makes you feel bad about yourself and keeps you out of the money conversation. It doesn't need to be that way.

Money lingo is actually not that tough to learn. I know it's meant to sound complicated and make outsiders feel all intimidated and, thus, not want to talk about it. You might be thinking, "All those numbers and math, shoot me now!" But, I pinkie swear, the math part is easy. It's the humanities part of money that's tricky. Money is cultural. It's filled with conflict. And in the end, it's about character. *Your* character.

Most of us value honesty when it comes to character. When it comes to money, you have to be open and honest with yourself, too. It's like cheating on a workout. You're only cheating yourself, and you'll never lose weight. A quick fix here and now will not solve the problem in the long run.

I've always said the best diet is the one where you only eat looking at yourself naked in a mirror. Will you eat the chocolate cake then? Same goes for money: look at the real version of yourself. Once you've looked into the financial mirror, would you rack up five grand in clothing debt? Didn't think so.

So let's get naked.

BOTTOM LINE*

Conventional wisdom: Finance is complicated and difficult. You need experts to talk to you about things you don't understand, because this is all over your head.

False. You can do this! Everything you need to know and do to take control of your financial life is right here in this book. Yes, there will be times when it is wise to seek out expert advice, but you can be the chief financial officer (CFO) of YOU. In fact, you're perfect for the job.

Conventional wisdom: Money is about math, and, if you can't do math, you're screwed.

The truth is that when it comes to personal finance, any third grader can do the math. What truly matters is knowing how you want to live—and then translating that knowledge into smart, swift and strategic financial action. That's right: it's not about math. It's about *you*. Who you are and who you want to be. Put another way, how you handle money is an expression of your character.

Conventional wisdom: You have to change your bad financial habits all at once.

Hardly. We're going to conquer 12 steps to getting your financial shit together in this book, one at a time. This isn't a crash diet. It's a sustainable long-term plan to get you where you want to be. And as with any sensible diet program, don't beat yourself up if you slip—just pick yourself up and keep moving forward, your eyes focused straight ahead at the fabulous life that will someday be yours.

Oh, and BTW: This isn't meant to be school. Still, a little review never hurts, and so at the end of each step, I'm going to debunk some of what you might think of as financial advice. Ideally it serves as a chance for you to rethink conventional financial wisdom—and begin to think for yourself.

---

* I've put a handy dandy glossary at the end of the book as a cheat sheet for finance terms you might think you know but don't or just want to admit you don't know at all. (You'll see them noted with an * in the text.) FYI: the concept of "bottom line" actually comes from a finance term. Decoded, it just means how much you or a company are making when all is said and done. There you go! You've already got a finance term in your quiver.

STEP

2

HELLO, IT'S A MARATHON *AND* A SPRINT

Get a Grip on Your Future

I can answer almost any question you throw at me, but the one that always gives me pause is also the simplest: "What do you want?" It seems so basic, but it can also fill me with a ton of anxiety. I'm guessing it makes you squirm a bit, too. Am I right?

"Where do you see yourself in five years?" "What do you want from your career?" "Do you want to have kids??" AHHHH!!!

The questions seem harmless, but they can freak anyone out. I'm here to tell you, those freak-outs can stop pretty easily. How? By *actually* answering the questions for yourself.

Remember, the hardest part of getting what you want is figuring out what you want in the first place. Which brings us to Step 2: ask yourself what really matters to you. This might sound stupid, but, right now, ask yourself the question. Do you have an answer?

CONFESSIONS
OF A RICH BITCH

Every girl should have a (professional) girl crush

I bet that at some point in your life you've had a girl crush. Oh, c'mon. Who doesn't love them some Gisele? But beyond supermodels married to football players, you've likely had a few girl crushes at work. I have.

A professional girl crush, to me, means you like what another woman has going on. You look up to her. You respect her and kinda sorta want to be her, or have certain things she has, or do certain things she does or has done. If you're lucky enough, you get to meet or talk to her. I did.

One of my most significant girl crushes became one of my mentors. She was, and still is, a superstar in the media world. I'm not going to name her because that's not the point of the story, but she anchors one of the most respected network shows and is famous for negotiating her own contracts, demanding the same pay as her male counterparts. She also made headlines for refusing to report on Paris Hilton going to jail. When her producer kept putting it in the show script, she literally shredded the script on live TV. She was one ballsy chick—and I was totally taken by her.

One day she emailed me to say that she had seen me on TV and she wanted me to call her. OMG! I was excited but even more nervous. I practiced saying "hello" a few times and primed my pipes with a few sips of water to make sure my voice sounded relaxed. She told me that she had seen me on the air the previous weekend and thought that I was good—not great, but good. She said she wanted to bring me on her show as a test to see if I might be a good fit to contribute to their team. (I thought "eek" and "yippee" in my head almost at the same time.)

Before long, I was a regular on her show, so we talked frequently, on-air and off. One day she called with a more personal agenda.

"What are you doing?" she asked.

I remember her telling me not to lie to her, so I didn't. "I'm drinking a glass of Cabernet on the couch."

It was two o'clock in the afternoon. I know, not normal. But I'd been up for work since 1 a.m. I was in a fog of fatigue and barely knew my name or what day or time it was.

She asked, "Are you dating someone?"

Oh boy. "Yes."

"Is he the one?"

I said, "You're joking, right?"

"Is he?"

"Maybe," I said. "Okay, probably not."

"You need to make a concerted effort to find a husband," she said. "If you're going to have babies, you need to get on that right now."

"Oh…um…" Beyond that, I was speechless.

"If that's what you want, you need to do it now."

"Yeah, I guess you're right."

"Is that what you want?"

"I don't know. Probably? I'm focused on my career now. I guess I haven't thought much about it."

I felt weak and wishy-washy and totally unprepared.

I spent a long time thinking about that call. What was she trying to tell me? Not having an answer to my mentor's question, or even a basic narrative for my life, made me feel out of control. The lack of focus made everything seem chaotic.

The truth is, that wasn't the only time someone has asked me a question like that. I got bombarded with questions like this from all sides in my twenties, and I quickly realized that the more you hem and haw, the longer the awkwardness lasts and the shittier you feel about yourself. If you can answer confidently, it will project a lot more positive energy than a blank or panicked stare.

It could be your mother asking when you're going to make her a grandmother, or your supervisor trying to suss out whether you're management material, or a potential spouse trying to gauge whether you share compatible dreams. But trust me, you will be asked, and you'd better have an answer. For your own sanity's sake.

There's actually some science to this. Studies have shown that women who create cohesive narratives for their past and their future are most likely to be successful. Having a confident story about your life, saying specifically what you want from it, is the key to having it all.

Are you getting the idea? Being a Rich Bitch means living the life you want, but you're not going to get what you want until you figure out what that is. You might think you know what you want, but here's a little exercise to see if you really do.

See if you can answer these big-picture questions confidently.

1. What do you hope to get out of your career? What's more important: the money or the work you do?

2. If you're at the beginning of your career now, or even well on your way, what does your job look like in five years? In ten years?

3. Do you see yourself settling in one spot and buying your own home someday, or do you imagine a globe-trotting life of travel and adventure?

4. What do you like to do in your off hours? Alpine skiing every winter, karaoke with friends on Friday nights, or does a monthly book club float your boat?

5. Do you see yourself being married? Having kids?

Raising a child can cost between $250,000 to $2 million over your lifetime, depending on where you live, how much you contribute to that child's education, etc., so you'd better be ready. Sure, you might think your kids are priceless (and of course they are), but they're also *price-y*.

Can you answer these questions honestly and in "elevator pitch" style—i.e., simply and concisely, in the time it takes to get from the lobby to the tenth floor? I couldn't for the longest time. I thought I was a confident woman, but the questions made me wonder: do I really know what I want? and when I want it?

These are big, serious questions, I know. Let's break them down into the basic components, or what I call the Three F's: Finance, Fun and Family.

FINANCE

Fact: you want to improve your finances. But, as we discussed in Step 1, the first question you really need to answer is, "How do I want to live?" After that, making wise financial decisions gets a lot easier.

Let's say your answer is, "I want to teach kindergarten and make a real difference to young kids. Oh, and I also want to retire by the time I'm 50."

Uh, no, because, unless you were born wealthy or marry someone with a lot of money, that's not going to happen. Hey, I'm not judging. It's just that some careers, like teaching, don't pay a whole lot (even if they should). These are careers that people tend to pursue for the love of the job, not the size of the paycheck. So pursue your dreams, but decide which dreams are most important. If, for you, it is more important to retire young than to teach children, select a career in, say, a big-bucks industry that allows you to make enough money to check out of the work world before your hair turns gray. This isn't rocket science. It's common sense—which often gets thrown right out the window when the conversation turns to money.

Here's another question: what do you want to do for a living? I'm going to assume that you have a career or are at least working toward one. No matter where you are in your career trajectory, you still have to give yourself goals.

BITCH TIP I suggest you sit down with a notebook or a diary with a colored pencil, or start a spreadsheet on your computer—whatever you're most comfortable with—and write down your goals, divided up into increments of one, three, five, seven and ten years. This allows you to make plans in easily digestible chunks so that you're not overwhelmed by the five- or ten-year ginormous ones. It breaks those down into small milestones on the road to the biggies.

Year 1: What is your career objective right now? Is there a particular job in a desired industry you currently have or hope to get?

Years 3 and 5: Where do you want to be in your career in a few years? Is there a promotion or job switch in your sights?

Years 7 and 10: What do you want your job to be a decade from now? Do you want to move up or sideways or do something else altogether?

Keep the notebook or document somewhere you can access it—your desk or home computer, for instance. You'll want to go back to it from time to time, perhaps once a year, or even every six months, so you can check your progress against your goals. Are you getting to where you want to be in the time frame you hoped for?

I slacked off writing down my goals for some time. Then, whammo, I randomly had the urge to do it. I wanted to do it right then and there before the urge went away. As Harry said in *When Harry Met Sally*, "Once you figure out what you want for the rest of your life, you want the rest of your life to start right away."

I had one minor problem: I had no paper. I am a tech junkie, so I had an iPad, a BlackBerry (back when people still used them), an iPhone and a computer but, seriously, no paper. I really wanted to write my goals down on a physical piece of paper rather than typing them out. It felt more real, more official that way.

Then, an idea! I had plenty of books. I grabbed one, my fav, *Anna Karenina*, and I wrote my goals down on the back of the last page of the book. I didn't mean to do it in a cheesy way. It was just the only blank piece of paper I had around. I knew I'd keep that book for a long time, so even if I changed my goals, I could always look back at where I started. And here's what it said:

Year 1: Stay at current job. Work hard to advance, but don't stress much about doing it.

Year 3: Look at other jobs for more leverage or a jump.

Year 5: Start laying the foundation for my own show.

Year 7: Have my own show.

Year 10: Start a production company.

At the time I wrote this, I was working on the early morning show at CNBC. And by early, I mean 4 a.m., so I needed to leave my apartment at 1 a.m. I knew it was something that I (or anyone) couldn't sustain. It wasn't that I didn't want to work my butt off; I did. I just didn't want to lose my mind being a vampire forever.

I ultimately knew I wanted a big change, a new challenge. I wanted to start a production company at some point. I wanted to be my own boss eventually. But I wanted to be realistic and honest. (I couldn't lie in front of Anna!) I needed *money* to start a company. At least more money than I had then. So I put that as a goal way in the future toward which I would work over the next ten years.

AND NOW IT'S YOUR TURN, BITCH

Face it and own it: you'll probably work at different places of employment within your chosen field, or you may well have more than one career. Heck, maybe you'll go out on your own and want to be your own boss like I did. There are no good statistics on how many careers an average person has—the US Bureau of Labor Statistics doesn't track it—but people switch careers all the time. In fact, you may have picked up this book with just such an intention in mind. So think about that when you're listing your goals.

That said, don't dilly-dally. If you're even thinking about a big move, write it down, even if it's ten years away. If you stay too long in the wrong career and/or accumulate financial obligations (like a mortgage or a kid's tuition) or debt (like credit card bills or student loans), then switching careers can become a lot more difficult. Remember: making that switch can be expensive if you have to relocate, learn new skills or take a pay cut to start over. So it's important to make this choice carefully, but as soon as you do, start prepping for it. You need some foresight to research it, plan for it and spend some time with people actively pursuing the career you think you might want.

Over time, your life circumstances will probably change, requiring some changes to your original goals. After all, life isn't predictable; you need to have a plan, but you also need to be ready to make a new one.

STRIKING OUT—ON MY OWN

Over the next year, my yearning to start a production company grew. I couldn't deny it, and I couldn't wait ten more years to have it realized. I felt an urgency to produce accessible financial content. As you can probably tell by now, I love financial news, and I love storytelling. So that made sense for me.

Aside from my own drive, a couple of other things changed: the landscape and the logistics. The world was going through the

Great Recession, and money news was, for better or worse, more popular and needed than ever. So the landscape and timing were ripe for what I wanted to do.

Logistics also shifted: entrepreneurialism was democratized. Being your own boss was a winner of the recession. Why? For one thing, people were frustrated with the jobs picture and wanted to go out on their own, finding their own dream versus the American dream.

Being "funemployed" beat the status quo; even if it meant a more precarious income, it meant being paid in happiness. In addition, people wanted to be Mark Zuckerberg. Well, not literally, but he and a few other rock-star entrepreneurs made it look easy, prompting people to think, "Hey, I can do that!" Because of that demand, starting a business no longer took a boatload of money. Tools cropped up online to "Fake It 'til You Make It" (we will get into that more in Step 8). They were cheaper, more ubiquitous and easier than ever before. The logistics of being your own boss worked in people's favor, including mine!

With those systemic shifts, I shifted my goals. I opened up the back of another book (this had now become my thing), wrote the date down and then listed this:

Year 1: Start a production company.

Year 3: Produce original content on-air, online and in print.

Year 5: Write a book series and create financially related products.

Year 7: Lay foundation for my own show.

Year 10: Have my own show.

I haven't changed my goals since, and I am actually on track to fulfilling them. I am more laser-focused than ever before, because I can, for the first time, articulate exactly what I want to do.

BITCH TIP

Before I wrote down my goals, employer/friend/ random person would ask: "So, what are you doing with your career? Where do you see yourself in ten years?"

Me: "Well, I want to, um, do it all. You know, I just love work and love all media stuff. I am passionate about it and, well, I want to do great things. You know, like take over the world. You know what I mean, right?"

Okay, looking back, I wasn't a total bumbling idiot, but I totally skirted the question like any politician doing a news interview. I *was* passionate. I just wasn't focused. At all. And because I never actually answered the question for myself, none of the people who might have been able to help me achieve my goals could. I didn't blame them: none of us knew what I wanted to do.

After I wrote down my goals, employer/friend/random person would ask: "So, what are you doing with your career? Where do you see yourself in ten years?"

Me: "I love business and media, so I want to marry those two things by laying the foundation for my own production company. I'm hoping to produce business-related content online, in books (!) and on-air. Ideally, in ten years, to answer your question, my production company will be rockin' and I'll have my own show."

Now, I try to keep it real. Who knows if this is actually going to happen? I mean, I chose a hard-as-hell

> business, but now no one can argue with my answer or say I'm not at least answering the question.

Excuses, like not having a piece of paper, are dumb. Figure it out. Don't give yourself any excuses. Stop telling yourself "Oh, it depends on the opportunity" or "Someone else has that position." Whether it's a stretch or not, be specific. Pick goals and be clear about when you're going to achieve them. Putting dates on things keeps you focused and allows you to track tangible results.

A friend of mine who teaches at a rough school in a big city recently shared her goals with me:

Year 1: Start interviewing at charter schools.

Year 3: Move from teaching second grade to teaching high school.

Year 5: Become a principal at the school or another in the area.

Year 7: Start my own tutoring company.

Year 10: Start my own product line for lesson plans and school supplies.

What I loved about her timetable was that she was ambitious but not totally unrealistic. She was specific and real. She didn't make the goals either ridiculously easy or impossible, but she wasn't afraid to stretch, either. She often recites this quote to me and her class: "A man's (woman's!) reach should exceed his (her!) grasp." I couldn't agree more.

Other things to consider for your Financial goals, beyond career:

- Do you want to own your own home?
- Do you hope to retire early, or not at all?
- Do you need to fund your children's college educations?
- Do you need to provide for your aging parents?

How much money do you have to put away to get to the end objective, and how much do you need to have at each yearly increment to accomplish those plans? Just make an estimate. Whatever your goals are, open up a Word document or a spreadsheet, or you can even steal my idea about doing it in the back of a book, and write them down.

FUN

I wouldn't confuse this category with frivolity, although I'd like to think that some frivolity is part of every happy life. ("Everything in moderation, including moderation" anyone?) What I'm really suggesting here is that we live to maximize our understanding of what makes a rich, fulfilling life.

Maybe you want to take flying lessons or become a black belt in jujitsu or simply spend more time with your family. No judgments on the goals, but let's lay 'em out there. (We'll talk about how much of your salary you should spend on this in a bit; just make a plan for your dream now.)

You want to go on a first-class, around-the-world trip once in your life? Write it down. Feed the poor? Write it down. You want to own a Chanel bag for every day of the week? Meh, that's my first value judgment. Don't write that down. Preserve the park where you played as a child? Write it down.

FUN AND FUNCTION

My first stab at a Fun goal list looked like this:

Year 1: Never order more than I can pay for myself on a date. Go out for drinks with girlfriends once/week.

Year 3: Have a $500 clothing budget/month.

Year 5: Get a two-bedroom apartment I can afford with new furniture.

Year 7: Start a charity organization with enough money to hire one staff member and cover legal fees for setting it up.

Year 10: Take two vacations/year—in first class (either with miles or fully paid for).

Here's a little explanation of my goals:

Year 1: Maybe it's my cash-based upbringing, but being able to afford my own meal has always been important to me. In New York City, it's totally normal to take yourself out to dinner and a movie, even if you don't have a date. Why make your fun dependent on someone else? Anyway, that's my own independence thing. You may feel differently about it, and that's totally cool.

Year 3: And while it's true I get a small clothing budget from my job, I want to be able to buy my own duds for my off-hours.

Year 5: Ever since that two-bedroom apartment debacle in Atlanta, I remained focused on getting one I could actually afford.

Year 7: One aspect of a fulfilling life is public service. We don't tend to think of this as fun, per se, but when you get right down to it, service to others is one of the most fulfilling things a person can do. If you think you might be so inclined, add charitable work to your list. But remember, this is my list. It's not for everyone.

Year 10: Well, this is self-explanatory.

So, What are your Fun goals? Fun doesn't have to be leisure, and maybe it doesn't have to be fun in an obvious way. Maybe it's simply good for you or for your career.

Here are some things women have told me they like to do and/or spend their money on:

- Work on a political campaign
- Foster stray dogs or cats
- Take a class or workshop
- Attend an industry networking event
- Start a blog
- Join a support group

Once you've figured out what your goals are, think about how much money you'll need to make them happen. Know exactly what it's gonna take you to get there, considering money but also your time. Repeat after me: Time. Is. Money. My mission is that you don't lose any of either and take control of both.

CHANGE ISN'T GOOD OR BAD; IT JUST IS

When I revamped my Finance goals, I also revamped my Fun goals to look like this:

Year 1: Never order more than I can pay for myself on a date. Go out for drinks with girlfriends once/week.

Year 3: Start a charity organization with enough money to hire one staff member and cover legal fees for setting it up.

Year 5: Get new furniture and move into a bigger apartment.

Year 7: Contribute $15,000 annually to a retirement account.

Year 10: Take one vacation/year—in first class (either with miles or fully paid for). Take one staycation/year.

I don't want you to go back and cross-reference, so I'll just tell you I moved my charity goals up, which then warranted a little reshaping of my clothing and vacay goals. The rationale stemmed from the same landscape shift that was at the root of the rejiggering of my Finance goals. When the Great Recession kicked into high gear, twenty- and thirtysomething women found themselves struggling to find full-time work in their chosen fields. These young women were part of the "lost generation" competing for fewer and fewer jobs; some were tempted to drop out of the race altogether. That's where my idea for a charity came into play. I wanted to call it "Lost Girls" to reflect the landscape.

I'll quickly tell you where this idea came from and why it was important to me. When I first started my career, I could afford only one black blazer from J. Crew. I wore that blazer to death, trying to make it look different every day. I finally cut my losses when the white pit-stains were too nasty and it was fraying at the edges. It sounds superficial, but a new blazer made me feel more confident going to work. So I wanted to offer young women gently worn career attire and advice to give those ladies the self-assurance and motivation to stick with it. I don't want to sound Pollyanna-ish, but the current economic conditions at the time made me want to make the charity happen sooner.

That also meant that I had to rearrange the rest of my list. You'll notice that I had to scale back or push other goals into the future. Doing a ton of research on starting charities, I was shocked to learn that making such a good thing happen can cost so much. It's surprisingly expensive to set up a 501(c)3 organization: there are attorney fees, accountant fees and an application fee, not to mention day-to-day operating costs and time consumption. All of that didn't deter me, and in fact I found a creative way to get my charity off the ground by incubating it under another similar charity to cut down on operating costs. It just meant that I needed to make a decision about what was/wasn't a priority and rejigger accordingly.

FAMILY

It's such a personal question, but you'll get it all the time. And even if you hate being asked, you'll probably end up answering anyway: "Do you want to get married?" And if you are already married or in a serious relationship, there's this one: "Do you want to have kids?" Then, if you have a kid, it's "Do you want to have more kids?"

Remember, I'm the girl who had no idea what to say when my mentor asked me these questions. So along with my goals for Finance and Fun, I wrote out my goals for Family. I knew they were going to change, depending on whom I met (or didn't meet). Yours will, too. And that's okay. In fact, it's good motivation for revisiting your goals often, whether you feel cornered into it (in a good way) by a mentor or not.

My first stab at these answers wasn't right or wrong, but it was a starting point. It was something, I thought. And something to organize my thoughts on the uncomfortable conversation of love, marriage and kids was better than nothin'. Here's how mine started:

Year 1: Make time for dates, even if I'm exhausted or want to be working.

Year 3: Date one person seriously.

Year 5: Consider getting engaged/married.

Year 7: Consider having a kid.

Year 10: Consider having more kids.

Yep, those were my Family goals when I was twenty-five. And yep, Betty Friedan would be turning in her grave. I'm not going to get into what you should and shouldn't put on your list; it's yours, and whether you want to tell anyone about it is up to you. But make one, even if you have no plans for change. Look your destiny in the eye. Again, this isn't about deciding that you are going to be married at twenty-five—it's about gaining some semblance of control, even if your goals change.

When I first did this exercise, I wondered, "How do I put a date on a goal like 'I want to find the love of my life and have children with him'?" Well, of course, you can't. While it's true that you can't have children forever, and plenty of people who do find the loves of their lives decide not to have kids at all, you can be proactive about finding love and creating opportunities to meet new people. Having a deadline motivates you to seek love actively rather than sitting around, waiting for it to fall into your lap—whether you want a family someday or not. So whether you want to put a ring on it or not, you gotta put a date on it.

CONFESSIONS
OF A RICH BITCH

Friends don't let friends live without tangible goals

Here's how the conversation went the next time I spoke to my mentor. I said, "You know, I thought about what you said, and I would like to be on the road to marriage by the time I'm thirty."

"Good girl, now that's a goal."

"Yeah, I don't know how realistic it is."

"But from one goal-oriented woman to another, have the goal—you have goals for other parts of your life, so why not the most important one?"

"But how do I work toward a goal like that? It's so different from choosing a career path or saving for a vacation."

"It's still figuring out what you want. Only you can answer that, but now that you have, yes, you have to work toward it."

I wasn't the eager-beaver girl who "had to get married"—oy, we all know those girls. I wanted to actively take advantage of opportunities to come across someone I could reach those goals with. And, if I didn't—that was okay. I would change my goals. And I did, many times.

A lot of women I talk to say, "Maybe such and such female CEO can 'have it all,' with a ton of kids, a major company, flying around in a jet with a fabulous husband…but how am I supposed to do that??" Yeah, maybe you're right, or maybe she just has a great publicist, or more likely a lot of help. I'm not saying that you or I couldn't be that woman, but the chances are slim. So for the rest of us mere mortals, "having it all" is a little different. It needs to be more realistic. Even Meryl Streep's seemingly invincible boss lady character in *The Devil Wears Prada* broke down crying over her divorce.

Keeping it real means you need to consider stuff like this: are you willing to be away from your kids for long periods of time? No? So you'd like to go on every school field trip and be at every after-school sporting event? Would you give up, or seriously hamper, your career for that? Because, let's face it, these choices are tough, and they're going to come up.

A healthy dose of realism will set you up for a greater chance of success with your version of "having it all." Your goal can't be to be a full-time parent AND a trauma surgeon. I'm sorry, it just can't. Your goals *must* be compatible.

Once you decide what's important, phrase it in the affirmative: "I'd like to have children," not, "I don't want to be childless." I know it sounds silly, but we're talking about what you want from your life. Be positive.

LIST, EVOLVE, ADJUST, REPEAT

A year after my first batch of Family goals, I was head-down in my career and a little jaded by my many first dates and sparse second ones. I looked at my list, and I couldn't help but think about how my Family goal sheet would factor into my career or the rest of my life. At that point, I wasn't willing to give at all on my work life, then or in the immediate future. Realistically, I knew that family requires time and money—two things I didn't have.

So here's what my revision looked like. It was similar to the first list, just pushed back a little:

Year 1: Make time for dates when not working or exhausted.

Year 3: Make time for dates, even when working or exhausted.

Year 5: Date one person seriously or live together.

Year 7: Consider getting married.

Year 10: Consider having kids.

Five years after writing the second list, I was in love and living with someone. But that someone had been married before and already had a child. He wasn't opposed to doing those things again with me, but there was no rush for him. He had his own goals, and syncing those with mine was something we, like every couple, worked hard on.

Let's face it: relationship shit is complicated and weird, and every relationship is different. No one's priorities are right or wrong. It's all about reconciling and reassessing your goals to achieve balance among all of them as life happens. And if your first list doesn't work out, don't stop having goals—just change your list. I have tweaked mine a ton and will likely continue to tweak them in order to keep myself positive and moving forward, and you should, too.

SCREAM AND SHOUT AND LET IT ALL OUT

Now that you've established your goals, talk about them! Don't keep them to yourself, and don't wait for someone to ask you one of those dreaded questions we went over before. You have specific dreams and a plan to make them come true, so tell your friends. Tell your family. Scream about them from the rooftops to anyone who will listen. While you don't want to be the Reese Witherspoon character from *Election* and spout off your list like a dissertation (that's weird), bring good energy to your goals. Don't feel compelled to share every detail, but feel compelled to share every chance you get.

Good energy begets good momentum, and you should take all of that you can get—after all, it's free! That's why you need to be able to get your dreams across in that elevator pitch. Those ten seconds could make all the difference. You never know how the person you're sharing that ride with to the tenth floor might be able to help you, now or in the future. Talking about your goals out loud also holds you accountable to others (they will remember) and to yourself. A Rich Bitch is proud of who she is and who she wants to be. Own it.

BOTTOM LINE

Conventional wisdom: Focus on the big goals first.

Um, this is so unrealistic it makes me want to crawl out of my skin. You'll hear that you should focus on your important goals like buying a house and a car. Those are awesome goals, but what about the rest of your life? Is it going to be one of austerity? It shouldn't be. The more you deprive yourself of a well-rounded life complete with small sacrifices and small rewards, the more likely you are to botch your goals.

Conventional wisdom: Your first goal should be financial security.

Okay, your financial goals are going to need to be broken down somewhat after you get a handle on what your future might look like. But what kind of goal is "financial security," anyway? That's like saying, "My goal is to live life." Cool...but what does that mean? Imagine a full-fledged lifestyle instead of just the numbers, like debt and savings. We will get there, young grasshopper; we will get there.

STEP
3

YOUR NEW LBD
Create a Little Budget Diary That Fits YOU

You lie. I lie. We've all lied to ourselves about money at some point. My lies would go something like this: "I need this LBD for such-and-such event. With this bomb dress, I'll look the part." I know, I know, it's confidence that makes you shine in a room. But if you're like me, you can convince yourself of anything in crunch time, even the things you know are wrong or stupid.

C'mon, admit it: you have spent money on stuff you don't need or that's more expensive than you can really afford, and you've told yourself a lovely little fairy tale about why you absolutely have to have it anyway. Sometimes we need those little lies to move forward, to propel ourselves to seize the day or night.

Sorry, bitches. This is not one of those times.

In Step 3, I'm going to teach you about the only LBD you really need: the Little Budget Diary. I told you we were gonna get naked; now we're going to take a good long look at what we see in the mirror.

TO HAVE OR NOT TO HAVE: THAT IS THE QUESTION

In Step 2, we established what your goals are and worked out a timeline for when you hope to achieve them. Now it's time to get the lay of your financial landscape and take a careful inventory of what you actually have and what you owe.

Time to get out that notebook or spreadsheet you've already started, since your budget is linked directly to and intertwined with your goals. If you started old school on a piece of paper like I did, it's probably a good time to switch over to this decade and put it on your computer. You're going to create your very own personalized LBD; it's a classic piece you're gonna want to keep.

Start your LBD with two columns. Everything you have (a.k.a. your *assets**) goes on the left and everything you owe (a.k.a. your *liabilities**) on the right. (BTW, subtracting your liabilities from your assets will give you your net worth, which is nice to know, but at this point, don't be too concerned with that sum. Just make a little mental note.) You can draw a line down the middle of one page or do it on separate pages. You can do it in a metallic color or in a code only you understand—whatever way does it for you, just as long as you do it.

The goal here is to give you an accurate snapshot of where you stand financially. Here's a true statement an unnamed person made to me when talking about her financial standing: "I have money…I have checks!" Yep, that happened. So, your snapshot might not be pretty, but I doubt it's *that* bad.

Promise me you'll never make a statement about your finances like that. Instead, here are some general guidelines so that you can talk about your situation in an intelligent way. You can and should tailor them to your particular circumstances. You may not have some, or any, of these particular items listed, and that's totally cool. Maybe you've got gold bars and a string of polo ponies instead of a savings account and an old VW bug. This is just a template to organize what you've got going on.

So here's roughly what your two columns should look like:

ASSETS	LIABILITIES
CURRENT ASSETS	**SHORT-TERM DEBT**
Cash	Credit Card
Checking Account	
Savings Account	
Money Market Account	
Short-Term CDs	
NONCURRENT ASSETS	**LONG-TERM DEBT**
Long-Term CDs	Mortgage
Stocks & Bonds	Student Loan
Retirement Account	Car Loan
Owned Home	
Owned Car	
Art, Jewelry, etc.	

Bravo, you just made a "balance sheet," which is basically just that: a list of what you have and what you don't have. And, yep, I'm going to start springing some other jargon on you, because you can handle it. Get excited—shit's about to get real.

THE BRIGHT SIDE: YOUR ASSETS

The first subcategory in your asset column is what the money geeks call current assets, which is just a fancy way of saying cash and anything that can be turned into cash quickly.

CASH: Under this heading, list cash you have in the bank, whether it's in a checking account, savings account or both. If you've got any actual cash stashed in a cupboard or, God forbid you're like me, in a safe, add that to the list of current assets as well. Don't add money you are promised for work or otherwise but don't have yet. You might think, "Duh!" But seriously, cash is cash only when you have it. You'd be surprised to see how many balance sheets are mucked up because of that.

INVESTMENTS: Then, if you've got a money market account, which is like a regular savings account but typically earns more interest, or certificates of deposit, a.k.a. CDs, which are basic investments you get at the bank that pay you some interest if you don't touch the money for a set amount of time (could be one month, six months, one year, five years, etc.), write these down under current assets, too.

The next subcategory in your asset column is for your other assets, the ones that aren't current assets, which are called, you guessed it, noncurrent assets. This is stuff that can be turned into cash but not anytime soon or not for a predictable price.

LONG-TERM INVESTMENTS: These might include things like stocks and bonds, and anything held in a retirement account like an IRA or 401(k), which are off-limits until you reach 59½ years old (we'll talk about exceptions to this and whether or not a retirement vehicle like this is even right for you in Step 9).

REAL ESTATE: If you own a home, add its value to the list. Note: your home's value isn't what you paid for it or what you wish you could sell it for. I know, I know, if it were up to me, it would be. But it's the value you could get for it right now, minus a realtor's commission (usually 5-ish % of the price). You can check out real estate listings online for similar homes in your area that have sold within the last year to get a sense of the market value of yours.

STUFF: If you own a vehicle—a car, truck, motorcycle, snowmobile, jet ski, tractor, whatever—check the Kelley Blue Book value (kbb.com) and add that to the asset pile. If you have other assets that have and will retain value (collectibles like art, say, or real jewelry like Grandma's pearls or your diamond engagement ring), list their value here as well.

Don't worry if you don't have anything to write down for some of these categories yet. Just write down whatcha got.

THE DARK SIDE: YOUR LIABILITIES

Your liabilities are whatever you owe. Like assets, these are divided into two categories as well—short-term and long-term.

Your short-term debt, a.k.a. current liabilities in money speak, includes credit card debt. Go online or call your credit card company (or companies) to get your most up-to-date balances. But don't go crazy: as I said before, this is a snapshot of where you are, not a test of your accounting skills.

Then you've got your long-term liabilities, like a mortgage, or a student or car loan. If you don't own a home or a car, cool— that's just debt you haven't accumulated, so leave that blank. If you do, though, keep trying your bestest to be as thorough and accurate as you can: dig out your bank, brokerage and mortgage statements, etc., to get the most up-to-date numbers. Remember, there's no need to get everything down to the penny. You just want a reasonably accurate picture.

AND...I don't want you to get overwhelmed by lots of phone calls and paper. If it seems more manageable to do one thing per day—savings one day, credit cards the next, and so on—then, please do it that way. I'm gonna keep reminding you: it's all about baby steps. And sanity.

YOUR FINANCIAL REPORT CARD: YOUR CREDIT REPORT

So, here's the deal: we are looking at ourselves financially naked. The good, the bad and the ugly. Your credit report is like not only looking at yourself naked but also doing it under fluorescent lighting.

If your credit report is your financial report card, then your credit score is the actual grade. As we are creating your LBD, we need to take both your credit report and your credit score into consideration, because they both influence a number of items in your budget:

- **Credit card rates.** The nastier the score you've got, the higher the interest rate you'll pay on your cards. Yes, sadly true, and it really sucks.

- **Your ability to buy a home.** Your score will dictate your mortgage rate (and closing costs), and it can be the deciding factor in whether you can get a mortgage at all.

- **Getting cash.** Banks use your score to determine how much quick cash you have access to if you need to borrow it—whether it's to go back to school, renovate your home, upgrade your car, invest in your business, or something else that's worth going into debt for.

Your credit report isn't everything, but as you can see, it is very important. It's basically supposed to tell people who are looking at it—like a lender—how trustworthy you are, or how likely you are to pay them back. The better your credit score, the lower the rate you'll usually get on a loan you apply for because you are seen as more trustworthy. But if your score is low and you're thus not considered trustworthy, your interest rate will be higher, making your monthly payments higher (and your overall loan more expensive), which will mean less cash on hand to pay for other things, which is obviously not good.

Don't open any new lines of credit and chill on the big purchases, like a big-screen TV or computer, a few months before you are trying to refinance or get a mortgage. It could screw with your credit score and lead to a higher interest rate.

Unlike real school, there's no final credit report, nor do you get to graduate out of getting one. You will always have one, and it will always be changing based on what you're doing with your money, which means that you are really only as good (financially, anyway) as your last credit report. So if your credit score all of a sudden goes down, the interest rate on credit cards and loans you already have can go up without warning (even if you were an A student at one point). And other things could be affected, too:

- **Your insurance rates.** Insurance companies use it to determine the kind of risk you pose.

- **Your employment.** Yes, employers look at it to determine if an applicant is responsible.

- **Renting a place.** Landlords use it to help them decide whether to let you rent an apartment or how large a deposit they require before they'll let you in.

Now you see why the C-word is so dreaded. The slight difference in interest rates you get because of your score can make or break a Spending Plan. On top of that, other businesses and organizations you might not even need money from are judging you based on it. And that's not superficial judging, because getting a good job or an apartment can also make or break your Spending Plan.

A broken Spending Plan is not a helpless Spending Plan. It's just one that needs a makeover. Let's first find out if it's broken before we get our makeover on.

SO WHAT'S YOUR SCORE?

So what, exactly, does your score…score? Here are the major factors contributing to your credit score and how much each factor contributes:

1. Payment history: 35%
2. Debt load: 30%
3. Credit history: 15%
4. Number of times you've checked your credit: 10%
5. Mix of credit you have: 10%

And, you guessed it, these factors are all outlined in your credit report. Here's what to note from this list. The two major factors, payment history and debt load (how much debt you are carrying), are totally in your control *now*. That's 65% of your total score. The last three factors might haunt you from your past habits, and that is what it is. But you can change that last 35% by being more mindful of those factors later on, too.

Your credit score—a.k.a. FICO score (named after the Fair Isaac Corporation, the data company that dreamed up the equation for calculating the score)—is graded on a scale between 300 and 850, with 300 being the worst and 850 being the best. Assume an A average in school is kind of analogous to a 750 credit score. In general, those with scores of roughly 750 and above tend to qualify for whatever access to credit they want. If you don't have that, you're not doomed. You just might want to know more about how the class is graded so you can do better in it.

We saw that your score is mostly calculated using a combination of your record of paying bills and taking out debt and paying it off (or not). With that in mind, here's a cheat sheet of ways to get a higher score:

1. **Pay your bills on time.** Not to sound patronizing, but it's worth repeating: pay your bills on time. It's the best way to get your score up where you want it.

2. **Don't cut up unused credit cards.** This one might be a little surprising, but bear with me. Let's say you have some random gas cards or department store cards you don't use anymore. Maybe you opened a store card to take advantage of the extra discount you get when making a purchase that day, then never used it again. A C-word misconception is that you should cancel those

cards if you want to improve your credit score. Wrong. You want a record of being able to pay your credit card bills, not being a serial card opener and canceler. The best way to keep up steady payments that you can sustain is to put one regular bill, like cable or utilities, on each card. Set that bill to autopay on your credit card so you are technically using your card but not thinking much about it while racking up good payment points.

3. **Build a credit history.** Remember that safe I used to keep my cash in? My credit score was crap because of that. It took me a few years of disciplined use of the plastic to get it somewhere respectable. It was all well and good to try to use cash or a debit card until I started thinking about the idea of buying a house. Because my credit history wasn't as strong as it could have been, getting a mortgage was a challenge. It's not fair. It's just the way it is.

4. **Don't max out your cards.** Keep the balance at no more than about 20% of your limit. So if your limit is $5,000, don't spend more than $1,000. A big factor in determining your credit score is the ratio between what you are borrowing and your access to credit. If a bank thinks you owe more than you can pay back, your score will feel the backlash.

5. **Limit how often your credit is checked.** Any time you look for a loan, which includes applying for a credit card, a credit check is done on you. So what, right? Wrong. Every time your credit is checked (by someone else), your score will actually go down. Why? Because the perception of having too many accounts or trying to borrow too much (called overleveraging yourself) can work against you. This piggybacks on my rationale for #2: if you've done

it a bunch already, fine. It's done. You can't undo the credit check they ran on you. But stop the cycle of impulsively opening cards and having credit remorse. Your score won't improve by taking it out on your past mistakes by impulsively snipping up the old cards. Even if it feels great to do, that "snip snip" won't help. Your score will only improve by your being mindful of what you are doing from here on out. You don't have to/shouldn't accept every credit card offer that comes in the mail. Open accounts you need, but only accounts you need, and your credit score will eventually show you love in return.

BITCH TIP

While your credit score ranges from 300 to 850, there is one exception to the rule: a credit score of 0. Yep, goose egg. Nada. You get one of these from having no credit history: no lines of credit, no debt, likely paying for everything with just cold hard cash. Sure, you get the "I just use cash" badge of honor, which is great in theory. But that's a pretty unrealistic goal. It really just means that creditors don't know what to do with you. You're a financial anomaly, and that makes them nervous. They want to see you take on some debt to see how you can handle it when you do want credit—and you will, for one reason or another in your life. Some financial experts will say that you should aim for a "0" because carrying debt in general is a bad money practice. I say, that's admirable…until you become human. Then, call me.

CHECK YOURSELF

Checking your own credit is a once-a-year thing. It's an annual financial physical. And when I said that your score is docked the more it is checked, I should be totally crystal clear: that is by *others* (a.k.a. banks), not by you. Go to town if you want, but you shouldn't be that hypochondriac who is in the doctor's office every day. Once per year is fine. And free!

There are three official credit reporting agencies: Experian, Equifax and Transunion. Each one provides a yearly free report by law. Note, however, that the report doesn't tell you your numeric score. If you want the separate agencies' scores, or your overall FICO score—an average of the three—you have to pay for it.

BITCH TIP If you apply for a loan, you can ask the lender for a copy of the report and FICO score they pulled so you don't have to pay for them yourself.

You've probably seen a ton of gimmicks—catchy commercials or random pop-up ads—or a ton of confusing, seemingly official sites when you do a Google search for "credit report." But there is only one that offers truly free reports. Uno. One. It's annualcreditreport.com. (Just keep in mind that while you can always get this yearly *report* for free, most of the credit bureaus charge a one-time fee of $5 to $15 to give you your credit *score*. Ugh.) Again, you don't really need more than the free official reports you get yearly. But continuing with my doctor analogy, if something bad happens, you should go back in for a visit. That means if you've had your card stolen or you shopped at a place that was hacked (like Target was in late 2013, putting an estimated 40 million customers' credit info at risk), then go back for another credit check to make sure everything is kosher.

When you get your report, check it super carefully for accuracy. If there's a mistake, you could be hurt without actually having done anything wrong yourself. So if you see people you don't know claiming you owe them money, dispute it. Sometimes it's an honest mistake, like having the same name as someone else, or the result of a disconnect in a company's billing department. If there's a mistake, send a letter and call the company or person filing the complaint against you. You also then have to follow up and *keep* following up with the credit reporting agency to make sure the problem is fixed. Be a dog with a bone about this; if you let it go, it will get worse.

CONFESSIONS
OF A RICH BITCH

You never forget your first…credit report

I was freaked out to open my credit report for the first time. Truth be told, I didn't open it for about a week after signing up for it. I just assumed it would be terrible.

But when I finally did open it, it was 720, which wasn't that bad. There were a couple of lines that I didn't recognize, though, including some doctor's office in Texas. It claimed that I had a missed payment of $250. Um, I had never even been to Texas! I had two options: 1. go through the credit bureau and dispute the claim through them (now there is an online way to do this, but it takes a lot of verification) or 2. go directly to the source.

So I called the doctor's office. I explained that something showed up on my credit report from them but I had never even been there, so I couldn't possibly be their delinquent patient. I was patched over to the billing people, and they had me fax them a copy of the report (quick tip: make sure all personal info like your name and Social Security number are blacked out if you do this) so they could verify it, which they did after "investigating" for a couple days. Then, after it was all verified, they were the ones to drop the claim with the credit reporting agencies.

It took a few months before the line actually disappeared, but it did go away, and dealing with that one doctor's office was much more pleasant than going through the credit agency itself. So if you find a straggler like this on your report, it might be worthwhile to start at the source.

And one more thing: while I was in my credit-report-self-discovery phase, I did a ton of digging into the so-called "credit fixer upper" companies. There's nothing harmful about them per se, but you're paying for something you can totally do yourself, and you'll care way more about it anyway.

THE B IN LBD

Here's where we are: we've got a balance sheet and a credit report. Props. Those are the things we need to have to get to the B in the LBD: the budget.

URGH...I know, the worst. But stop your bitchin'; budgets get an unnecessarily bad rap. You think budget and you might think austerity. Get that out of your mind. From now on, I'm going to affectionately call it a Spending Plan because that doesn't have the same connotation as a big bad budget does. All we are looking at is how well (or badly) what you've got and what you're spending are playing together. Your Spending Plan is just about making those two things friends.

Think of your Spending Plan as the first step toward achieving your goals. You determined how you want live in the future; well, your Spending Plan is how you are living *now*. Here is a sample budgeting worksheet that you can use as a template:

INCOME			CURRENT MONTHLY INCOME	PROPOSED MONTHLY INCOME
EARNED INCOME*				
INVESTMENT INCOME*				
OTHER INCOME*				
* net, after taxes	TOTAL MONTHLY INCOME			
EXPENSES			CURRENT MONTHLY EXPENDITURE	PROPOSED MONTHLY EXPENDITURE
THE ESSENTIALS	Living	Mortgage or rent		
		Real estate taxes		
		Home repairs/ maintenance/ HOA dues		
		Home improvements		
	Utilities	Electric		
		Gas		

EXPENSES			CURRENT MONTHLY EXPENDITURE	PROPOSED MONTHLY EXPENDITURE
	Utilities	Water/sewer		
		Communications (all phone/ internet)		
	Food	Groceries and take-out		
	Transportation	Car payment		
		Gas		
		Fees/routine maintenance/ repair allowance		
		Public transportation/ taxis		
	Insurances	Health (ins. premium, out-of-pocket, gym)		
		Life		
		Home/renter		
		Auto		
	Appearance	Necessary clothing/ accesories for work and life		
		Necessary grooming (hair and beauty)		
	Home Requirements	Misc. household items (light bulbs, cleaners, etc.)		
THE ENDGAME	Retirement			
	Home	Upgrading/ downgrading home		

continued on next page

EXPENSES			CURRENT MONTHLY EXPENDITURE	PROPOSED MONTHLY EXPENDITURE
	Education	Master's degree, continued education		
	Career change	Networking events, seed money		
	Children	Basic expenses		
		College education		
	Other			
THE EXTRAS	Restaurants/ Bars			
	Entertainment			
	Vacations/ Travel			
	Non-Essential Clothes/ Shoes			
	Beauty	Mani/pedis, salon visits, cosmetic surgery		
	Extra Fitness	Yoga, spin classes, beach bootcamp		
TOTAL MONTHLY EXPENSES				
Check the total against your monthly income. Are you in the red or black?				

If you want to make yours more detailed, by all means, go for it. In fact, you probably should. We all spend differently; our Spending

Plans will be as individual as we are. Nothing wrong with that. The idea here is to make it make sense to you. So create categories or buckets of spending that you will relate to and remember. However you organize and whatever labels you assign to the categories, you need to account for all the money that's coming in and all the money that's going out each month. All of it. Think hard. It's not just rent and utilities. Um, what about that Netflix or *New York Times* subscription? A daily road toll on your commute? That impulse "other" LBD? Well, those add up, too. So create as many categories as you want to—just as long as no dollar is left behind.

7 BITCHES WHO ARE ALWAYS BROKE
ARE YOU ONE OF THESE PEOPLE, OR KNOW SOMEONE WHO IS?

1. **Bitches who try to keep up with other bitches.** If you always have to have the latest gadget, most expensive clothing label, or nicest home, this one's for you. You're driving yourself straight to the poorhouse trying to outspend everyone in your life in order to convince yourself and others that you are making it. Keep it up, and you *won't* be.

2. **Bitches who don't have a Spending Plan.** I've said it before and I'll say it again: *write it down.* Having a mental Spending Plan is about as good as having no plan at all. Jot down every single little thing you spend your money on so you can really get a feel for the bigger picture.

3. **Bitches who don't have savings (in the, ahem, bank).** You might think you're making bank, but if you regularly blow your entire paycheck and have no savings to back it

up, guess what? You're back to zero. We will get to more about how to set up an emergency fund in Step 7, but for now, reframe the way you think about savings as being part of your Spending Plan. Yes, *savings* is really just *spending* on your own future well-being.

4. **Bitches who don't pay on time.** Making late payments isn't just idiotic for the way it impacts your credit score; it also comes with a price tag. Whether it's your credit card bill, phone bill, utilities, rent—you name it—there is almost always an additional fee for late payment. So now that "low" monthly phone bill of $39.99 is more like $59.99 with the late fee. Not so much of a great deal anymore, huh? Smart bitches know that being late to the bill-paying party is never fashionable.

5. **Bitches who lack ambition.** I will elaborate more in Step 8, but start freeing yourself from the anxiety of saving so much by…making more. Yes, I know, that's easier said than done, but if you start coming from a place of aspiration instead of desperation, you will change the way you look at your money. Whether it's finding a job you love, an employer you admire, or a lucrative job on the side, think of making *more*, not spending less, as your best weapon against going broke.

6. **Bitches who are unhappy.** Women joke all the time about retail therapy, but it's really just a euphemism for overspending. Bitches who are unsatisfied with their careers are more likely to impulse spend to try to fix it, which—of course—only leads to more unhappiness once those bills add up. Whether at work or in your personal life (or better yet, both), find therapy in something else you love to do: reading, running, crafting, whatever! And focus your leisure time on that instead.

7. **Bitches who care too much.** This is a tricky one. You
    know how I feel about charity work, and I want nothing
    more than for my bitches to be compassionate members
    of society. But this becomes a problem when you put
    others' needs before your own. The brutal reality is that
    you need to help *yourself* financially before you can help
    others (like they say about the oxygen mask on a plane).
    So instead of dumping a disproportionate amount of
    your paycheck into your favorite charity (not to mention
    the scores of emails you likely get from friends and
    family or your alma mater asking for the same thing),
    volunteer your time and energy. Spending the day
    cleaning up a community garden or volunteering at your
    local animal shelter makes you feel good, has an impact
    on your community and costs *zero* dollars.

History repeats itself, and that applies to your financial history as
well. You're predisposed to do what you know and have practiced
growing up. So if you grew up going out to dinner four nights
a week, you're more likely to continue to do that in college, and
even after you are financially independent—even if you have
a lot less money on your own than your lifestyle afforded growing
up. So if your mom bought a new dress for every family function
growing up, you might be programmed into thinking that you
can't wear the same thing twice and buy something new, too. Or
if your family bought a new car every five years, you might think
that older models are to be avoided and trade yours in more often
than you need to. This can also become an issue postrelationship:
those date nights out to dinner that you are conditioned to block
out every Wednesday night add up more quickly when it's just
you footing the bill, unless you break the cycle.

I'm not judgey about what you spend, because I've been there. I've spent on ridiculous things, fallen into predispositions and told myself lies for the longest time. The only thing I'm judgey about now is the lying to yourself part, because I don't want you to waste the time I did. Don't leave anything out. Get down to the truth, whatever it is. Look at your habits and see which are actually good habits and which are the dumb ones that you stick to just because that's the way it's always been. You're not a little girl anymore. Nothing needs to be any way other than the way you make it.

EASY COME, EASY GO: INCOME

Money might not be so easy to earn, but it is easy to calculate. What comes in is your "income" (duh). But, as you've probably noticed from your pay stubs, the money you bring home isn't the actual salary you signed up for.

WHAT DO "NET" AND "GROSS" MEAN?

Not all income is created equal. *Gross income** is the whole she-bang, before Uncle Sam takes out a bunch of taxes. After that, it is called *net income,** or whatever you actually take in. (A synonym for net income is "earned income.")

BITCH TIP

If you make money in an unpredictable way—maybe you're a real estate broker or a freelancer who doesn't know when her next deal will close, or for how much—try to come up with an average, preferably based on what you've earned over a multiyear period. If you're just starting out and can't do that, make your best guess, but be conservative. After all, earning more money than planned is a high-class problem, not to mention a much easier budget issue than having less.

INVESTMENT AND OTHER INCOME: DEFINED

Income doesn't have to come only from your paycheck. You might have investment income, which is money that comes in from stocks and bonds and investments like that. Maybe you have what's called "other income," like regular cash gifts (from your parents, say), or things like alimony and child support. Include those, too, but only if it's *ongoing*, not a one-time thing. One-time income is called "nonrecurring income" or "windfalls." That just means that it is a one-time gift, bonus, or any other kind of money that you can't necessarily depend on receiving again.

You should have the number that represents all your income right now. Of course, it may change in six months or a year as you get raises, get promotions, change jobs or make extra money on the side. Your Spending Plan will shift around a little, too. And that's okay. You're gonna revisit your income often. And that can truly be a good, a great, thing.

Do me a favor, though, and try to forget the negativity of budgets you've previously had in mind. Focus on the possibility. Focus on the potential of great things that could happen with your income, not the harbinger of cutting back and saving to death. This is an important philosophy of mine: the more you earn, the more you have to spend. It's obvious, but it's a mental shift I want you to take away from the doom and gloom of budgeting your income, as we now move on to your expenses.

EXPENSES: BROKEN DOWN

Spending your money is normally the fun part. But your expenses encompass *everything* you are paying out, from the nonfun stuff like your rent to your retirement to, yes, the fun stuff, too, like a night out. That's why I'm going to break down your expenses into three E's (yeah, after the three F's, I think I have a thing for alliteration): the Essentials, the Endgame and the Extras.

THE ESSENTIALS: SPENDING TO LIVE NOW

THE ESSENTIALS

FYI

What's included: Basic expenses of your life/stuff you typically have to pay every month: rent or mortgage, utilities (including cable, internet and cell phone), food grocery and takeout), transportation (a car and/or public transportation), insurances (health, life, car).

Percentage of expenses: 70%

The Essentials should account for no more than 70% of your expenditures. It sounds like a lot, but it goes pretty fast. To see how much you're spending, the easiest place to start is to go through your statements online (if you've gone paperless, which ideally you have). Or you can go through your credit card statements if you've paid that way, or just do it the old-fashioned way by going through old mortgage, utility and car bills, etc.

Gathering this info is tedious, I'm not gonna lie, so, as usual, I suggest you don't do it all at once. Start with the big kahunas first. The biggest kahuna of them all is housing. Keep another figure in mind here: your housing bill should be half of what you're spending on the Essentials, so 35% of your expenses (half of 70%). If your pad is costing you 50% of your paycheck (remember my stupid two-bedroom in Atlanta?) then you should reconsider, because you're leaving yourself just 20% of your Spending Plan for things like food and transportation, which just isn't realistic. (I'll get into more detail about what percentages your different expenses should be in Step 4, when we talk about living within your means.)

BITCH TIP

If you're a cash-only person and you don't hang on to old bills, stop it! Ask for receipts to help you track where the money is really going. And don't crumple them and toss them into your bag, only to find them smooshed up with gum at the bottom of your purse (not that I would know anything about that …). At the very least, keep your receipts in a container or a large envelope. Even better, set up a filing system to separate the different categories of expenses: one folder for food, one for rent—you get the idea. Keep it on your desk or anywhere you can get easy access to it. Once a week, or even once a month, go through the receipts you've collected and drop 'em in the folders. This may sound a little old-school, but it works for me. If you want to be more new-school, there are lots of websites and apps that will scan and organize your receipts for you, too.

And while you're getting a handle on your expenses, organize your paper trail moving forward, too. You will thank me when your favorite time of year rolls around: tax time! You don't have to save *all* of your receipts for deductions and whatnot, but those related to business, charitable donations, mortgage, student loans, and medical *are a must*. Here are a few scenarios and the types of receipts you should save for each:

- **If you work out of your home**: utilities, cleaning supplies, office supplies
- **Travel expenses for work**: hotels, flights, car rentals
- **All work-related things**: cell phone, internet, trade books and magazines...pretty much anything you purchase for your work (it could be paint if you're an artist, dog treats if you're a trainer, wigs and big shoes if you're a professional clown)
- **Business meals/entertainment**: meals, games, shows, wherever you take clients to do business (but FYI, there are a lot of restrictions for deducting these, so be sure to document who, where and why for each receipt)
- **Anything medical-related**: premiums, prescription drugs, contacts, medical tests (not over-the-counter stuff or "preventative" treatments like...spa days)

The easiest things to overlook are those expenses that don't necessarily occur on a regular basis, or occur just once or twice a year:

- **Real estate taxes:** If you own your own home and pay your own real estate tax, as opposed to paying into an escrow account as part of your monthly mortgage, you may pay that bill quarterly or even just once a year. (I'll talk more about mortgages in Step 4.) Add it all up and divide by 12 so you can list it with your monthly expenses.

- **Out-of-pocket medical expenses:** They can come at any time, but you *can* estimate what you're likely to spend in a year and, again, divide that number by 12 (the point of this is to come up with a monthly estimate) to assume a monthly expense. Factor in your best guess, ideally rounding up, 'cause chances are, you're not coming into a bunch of extra money in the same month a big medical bill hits to offset it then and there.

- **Car insurance:** If you have a car, you may have a monthly loan or lease payment (more on whether this is a good idea in Step 5). That's easy enough to track. But auto insurance may bill only twice a year, so add up the total amount you pay in a year and then divide by 12 again to figure out your monthly cost for that.

- **Car maintenance:** Oooohhhh…forgot about that car maintenance? Four oil changes a year? Add up the total cost and divide by 12, too. Do you have an older car? Figure out what you've been spending on repairs each year, add that in and divide up.

 You may think your gym membership or spin class is an Essential, but unless your physical fitness is part of your job, it isn't. Sorry, that's an Extra. After all, you can be the chick version of Matthew McConaughey: run outside, do push-ups on park benches, lift water bottles instead of free weights. For free.

Once you've sorted through all of your outgoings and figured out how much you're spending, start comparing this number to the amount of cash you're starting with. Can you account for how much cash is flowing through your fingertips? I've probably jogged your memory on a few, but keep thinking hard since (pardon the cliché) the devil is in the details. Gaps in your spending plan because of, say, the dog-treat-of-the-month club you signed up for but forgot about will give you a false perception of what you've got going on. And inaccuracy, even the smallest bit, can lead to a hellish overspending cycle. So show the details who's boss. The good news is that once you've thought of everything, you won't have to come up with these categories again and can get into an easier plug-and-chug mode.

SHAMELESS PLUG ALERT

CASH™ Smartwatch, invented by yours truly, is the first ever financial smartwatch that calculates everything you spend throughout the day so that no dollar spent on stuff like a newspaper, highway toll or snack is forgotten. It's like a calorie or step counter you might wear...except it calculates your cash! cashsmartwatch.com

THE ENDGAME: SPENDING FOR THE FUTURE

FYI

THE ENDGAME

What's included: Things for your future like savings accounts, investment accounts, retirement accounts.

Percentage of expenses: 15%

I hear ya. All this subtracting from your hard-earned money can get any bitch down. And when it does, remember all those big life questions we addressed in Step 2. Let's channel those.

Remind yourself what you want, what you really, really want. (Sorry, I couldn't help myself.) Why are you saving for the future? What do you want to get with that money? It may be taking that great trip, or having a sweet retirement, or buying a home, or saving up to start a new career, or supporting a child. Think of the Endgame as being the lovely stuff you get from this 15%, not the burden of having a 15% "bill" every month.

I like to put aside 15% of my total Spending Plan for the Endgame, which I'll talk about in more detail in Step 9. So if you are doing any Endgame-ing now, write it down. Or maybe you're not saving a damn penny. Well, this is where you admit it. Put a big fat zero in for this category. (But it won't be that way for long, my pretty!)

THE EXTRAS: SPENDING FOR FUN

THE EXTRAS

What's included: Whatever does it for you.

Percentage of expenses: 15%

FYI

Save the best for the last bucket. Here you add up all that other stuff, like restaurants, bars, clubs, vacations, nonessential clothing, mani/pedis, entertainment, random retail therapy, pets, whatever it is. There's nothing to be embarrassed about, but fess up.

I like to keep this category to no more than 15% of my total Spending Plan. Maybe you're a workaholic who spends next to nothing in this category. You might also find that what you're spending in the Extras category isn't, well, all that much fun. Hey, it's entirely possible you're not having enough fun; it's also possible you're having too much. Is that how you said you wanted to live when you listed your goals in Step 2? Keep checking back in on your plan to keep from veering off course.

BITCH TIP

Once I figured out my goals in Step 2, it was time to figure out how far my money could legitimately go. In other words, I needed to reconcile my salary with my expenses into something realistic. Breaking down my expenses into our three categories looked like this, after taxes:

HOUSING 35% (Essentials)

TRANSPORTATION 10% (Essentials)

HOUSEHOLD BILLS/INSURANCES 15% (Essentials)

FOOD 10% (Essentials)

SAVINGS 15% (Endgame)

FUN 15% (Extras)

I started with my gross income, an empowering six-figure $150,000. But then the net income was more depressing than I thought. Taxes in New York City are some of the highest in the country, because the city helps itself to a whole extra chunk of your money on top of what the IRS and the state get. Don't get me wrong. You get a lot for your tax bucks—it's a big city, with a huge subway system (722 miles of it!) and tens of thousands of cops, firefighters and teachers—so I get it, but still… ouch. So, after all those taxes got taken out of my paycheck, my annual take-home pay was about $95,000.

Breaking that down monthly, my take-home was approximately $7,900. So applying the guidelines I set for myself, my budget should have looked like this:

HOUSING 35% of $7,900 (Essentials) = about $2,765/month

TRANSPORTATION 10% of $7,900 (Essentials) = $790/month

HOUSEHOLD BILLS/INSURANCES 15% of $7,900 (Essentials) = $1,185/month

FOOD 10% of $7,900 (Essentials) = $790/month

SAVINGS 15% of $7,900 (Endgame) = $1,185/month

FUN 15% of $7,900 (Extras) = $1,185/month

Now that I had the big picture, was it accurate? After all, we're talking New York City, where a decent apartment in a convenient neighborhood for less than $3,000 is the stuff that urban myths are made of. (Greenpoint, Brooklyn, may be uber hip, but it's a pain in the ass to get to work in Midtown from there.) My budget was more than $200 short for housing.

But there was good news in the transportation department. I didn't have to have a car as I had in Atlanta, so no gas, maintenance or insurance to pay for. Subway rides are relatively cheap; cabs and car services not so much, but I wasn't going to need anywhere close to 800 bucks per month. That meant I could move $400 into housing.

Likewise, my health insurance was largely covered by my employer, which allowed me to move another $350 into housing. Hey, suddenly I've got a housing allowance of around $3,500. A lot in most places, not huge in Manhattan, but within my budget!

And as a TV anchor, my wardrobe and beauty needs (which are typically large expenses for news anchors) were mostly covered by work (which, with backcombs for my hair, mile-long fake eyelashes and shoulder pads for my blazers, was not the blessing you may think it was). That allowed me to take some of my fun money and move it over into my Endgame savings. Sure, it was a small amount—sometimes just $200 per month—but every little bit counts (and compounds!).

Here's where the revised budget stood, give or take $5–$10:

HOUSING (Essentials) = $3,500/month

> **TRANSPORTATION (Essentials) = $390/month**
>
> **HOUSEHOLD BILLS/INSURANCES (Essentials) = $835/month**
>
> **FOOD (Essentials) = $790/month**
>
> **SAVINGS (Endgame) = $1,190/month**
>
> **FUN (Extras) = $1,190/month**

Up to this point I was within my budget guidelines, more or less, but then reality got in the way…again.

Let's have another look at some of my short-term goals from Step 2:

1. Start a production company.
2. Contribute $15,000 annually to a retirement account.
3. Drinks with girlfriends at least once a week.

There was a disconnect between those goals and what I wanted for myself in the long term. There was no way I could swing a retirement contribution and put up the scratch to get my production company going. Then, it turned out that starting a company was really a lot of work (on top of a full-time job, thankyouverymuch), which, frankly, made it tough to find the time, let alone the energy, to have dinner out with friends.

So I went back to the budget. I scraped together $1,000 per month for a retirement contribution (which was less than my goal, but all I could handle), and I scaled back drinks to every other week. Not the exact goal I had written down, but still something, as it allowed me to see my friends and maintain the important relationships in my life. And by making these friend-dates just drinks instead of dinners, I was able to stay within my budget while contributing a more modest amount to my retirement. So here's what all of that rejiggering added up to, for me:

HOUSING (Essentials) = $3,500

TRANSPORTATION (Essentials) = $390

HOUSEHOLD BILLS/INSURANCES (Essentials) = $750

FOOD (Essentials) = $700

SAVINGS (Endgame) = $1,000/month

FUN (Extras) = $1,335/month

SHORT-TERM GOALS = $225/month

In other words, I needed to reconcile the Essentials, the Endgame and the Extras. We all do. I'll tell you honestly, I've never felt more out of control than I did during the time I was working to reconcile my goals. I felt totally fine (in ignorant bliss) before I tackled them, and I felt totally fine (in empowered bliss) after. But the budget purgatory is the worst. Knowing you have to fix something but feeling overwhelmed that the problem is bigger than you is admittedly the most painful part of this process. All I can say is that I feel your pain. I'll also say that once you're in purgatory, there's no going back to hell. It will never feel like as much fun as it did before.

CALLING BULLSHIT

I've read advice book after advice book that suggest there's a limit to what you should spend on fun. I call bullshit. If you're covering the Essentials, and the Endgame is well taken care of, then you have my full permission to go wild with the Extras.

Here's the beautiful thing I learned from heads of major companies: if it's in your Spending Plan, even if it seems random, it's accounted for, and you have every right to spend it.

From here on out, consider yourself a small business, whether you have one or not. You, {INSERT NAME HERE}, are in charge of your profitability and losses. You are in charge of your balance sheet. So if you think of yourself as a small business, look at a traditional small business for cues on spending. If a little company needs staplers, it's in their Spending Plan and accounted for, so the founder is allowed to buy staplers. Or, if the company accounts for the founder to buy cupcakes every Friday for employees, she doesn't need to sneak cupcakes in or feel guilty about it. But if there's no room in the Spending Plan for the founder to pay for business lunches, and if she does anyway, it screws up the balance sheet. If it happens all the time, it puts the whole business on shaky ground. So, as your own business, you have trade-offs. You have staples and cupcakes but no lunches. But guess what? It's your money; you make the rules. You want staples and lunches and no cupcakes, great, whatever works for you, just put it in your Spending Plan and then it's all aboveboard.

In the words of one of my favorite poets, Jay-Z, "I'm not a business[wo]man, I'm a business, [wo]man."

BITCH TIP

So I've knocked the cash thing a lot so far, but I'm not a hater across the board. In fact, when you are adjusting to the Extras number you came up with in your Spending Plan, I suggest that you take that exact amount out in cash at the beginning of each month. Yes, physical cash from the ATM. This is your Extras money. I'm not going to tell you how or where to spend it, and I'm not going to judge you, but you get *only* this amount of cash, and when it runs out, show's over until next month. As you'll soon find out, it's much harder to spend green, physical cash you don't have than to keep swiping that credit card and guesstimating what you are spending. Creative rounding will never work to keep you on budget. When you feel comfortable with what you can get with that amount, you can graduate to a debit card (which, remember, is still cash—just in plastic form) for your Extras.

THE BS TEST

Okay, you've laid out everything you spend, and the numbers are all in your worksheet. But is that worksheet telling the truth? There's only one question on your pop quiz: do the sum of the three sections (the Essentials, the Endgame and the Extras) equal your net income? Yes is the only possible answer.

Let's use an example with real numbers to show what I'm talking about. Let's say your worksheet shows you spend your money like this every month:

The Essentials..$1,500

The Endgame $1,000

The Extras..$500

Total outgoings $3,000

On the opposite side, it says this:

Your net income............................$30,000, or $2,500/month

Well, bitch, there's $500/month unaccounted for, or $6,000 per
year. Go back and figure out where that money is going. Take
your dog to the groomer to get his nails trimmed? Bought your
mom flowers for her birthday? It all counts. No matter how trivial
the purchase, it's still crucial that you make a note of it. It could
make the difference between achieving one of those goals you
worked so hard to figure out in Step 2 or not.

Don't be discouraged if you aren't getting this right away. After
all, a Rich Bitch isn't born, she's made—by taking careful control
of her goals and organizing her money in a way that will get
her there. Become obsessed. Track everything you are making
and spending, stick to the guidelines you set for yourself and
remember your priorities. But then, reserve the right to adjust
your guidelines, change your priorities...it's all good. Learn and
grow: that's how we Rich Bitches roll.

BOTTOM LINE

Conventional wisdom: Budgeting means having less fun.

Hardly. Budgeting means making conscious decisions about
how you're going to deploy your money based on how you want
to live. It means more choices, not fewer. It makes your finances a

lot less scary when you know exactly where your money is going. And it gets rid of the buyer's remorse because you've accounted for it.

Conventional wisdom: Your Spending Plan is fixed, and you have to stick to it.

Absolutely not. Your Spending Plan is only your Spending Plan until you change it. You find a higher paying job or move? Great, time for a new Spending Plan. Your goals will change, and so will the way you spend or save. Stay obsessed with the rules even when the game changes.

Conventional wisdom: You need to save more.

Well, frankly, you might, but that really depends on what your goals are and whether your actions are aligned with them. Saving needs a purpose behind it. Also, call me Captain Obvious, but if you make more money, you won't stress over the penny-pinching. Focus on the positive—the potential of making more money—not on the burden of saving so much that your life sucks.

PUT A ROOF ON IT
Home Is Where Your Stuff Is

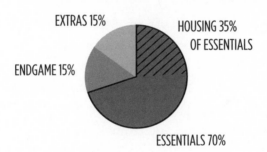

'm not so much of a bar hopper. But there is a specific bar night I will never want to miss if I can make it work: trivia night! I recently went to trivia night at a fun bar in my neighborhood, and the question was, "What is the mother of the arts?" A friend of mine blurted out, "Painting!" Every drunken person high-fived her. It was a great answer, and it sounded right…right? Wrong. The real answer was "architecture." My girlfriend, always the witty, outgoing one in any crowd, said something like, "Oh, right, of course. What's the point of having a painting if you don't have a wall to hang it on?"

Oh, how I love bar wisdom: we all need walls to hang our paintings on. Yes, duh.

So how are you going to afford your own four walls? That's where Step 4 comes in.

THE ESSENTIALS: HOUSING (35%)

As you'll recall from the Little Budget Diary we made in Step 3, the Essentials include your essential expenses, such as living space, utilities, basic food, transportation and insurance (health and home). *Again, these should account for no more than 70% of your expenditures.*

And the biggest chunk of your Essentials budget—as much as half of that 70%, or 35% of all expenses combined—goes to housing. This is where you need to get your shit together first.

Home base: it's where you can strike out or knock it outta the park. Yes, housing will make or break your financial foundation. And I'll tell you from all of the time I've spent helping people untangle their financial messes that housing is one of the top three things people go to financial planners to figure out.

LOCK IT UP

Where you live is important (obviously), and we all have different ideas about what—and where—home, sweet, home should be. On the one hand, we all want to live in a nice place. On the other hand, because a home is one of your largest expenses, what you decide to spend will have the greatest impact on the rest of your Spending Plan, a.k.a. what else you can do in life.

I usually like to think of myself as the cool chick who tells you to loosen up, but I'm going to be a hardass right now. You might be tempted to stretch for a killer loft or a sweet bungalow, but if it pushes you over 35% of your net income, fugheddaboudit.

Look, I get it, there are "special" circumstances. Maybe you want to live closer to work, which is more expensive but also means you don't need a car. That can work. Maybe you want to live where you like to be when you're not at work, by an ocean or park, for example. That's okay, but you'll probably need to cut back someplace else to afford it. At the other end of the spectrum, if you're comfortable living in a fixer-upper that hardly dents your paycheck at all, you go right ahead. You'll have spare cash for the fixing-up.

BITCH TIP

Note to freelancers and entrepreneurs: if you work from home and have extra space, perhaps an office within your home, a little more money in the housing budget makes sense for you. 1. You could get a tax deduction, and 2. you reduce the amount you spend on commuting—because, well, you're not.

Keep in mind the 35% guideline for housing is just that, a guideline. It's a tough one, and I *strongly* advise you to stick to it, but it's not the hard line. Our hard line is 70% for ALL Essentials. As you creep up to that percentage, you flirt with disaster. There's wiggle room, for sure, but it's gonna be pretty tough when you've got 50% going toward housing alone. Even if you're the homebody of all homebodies and all you want to do is nest, never promise yourself you are going to spend nothing on the Extras so you can nest your brains out, because it's not going to happen. What you spend won't be in check until you have a reality check. It might feel awesome to get an insane place that's half your salary, but it's not so awesome when you're there eating ramen with no electricity.

This guideline holds whether you own or rent. That decision— to own or rent your home—is the most important Essentials question you're going to have to answer. Burn that 35% guideline into your brain and keep reminding yourself that going over it leaves you vulnerable to busting your Spending Plan. And "busting your Spending Plan" is another way of saying "busting your dreams."

CONFESSIONS
OF A RICH BITCH

Movin' on up

The Big Apple. New York F-ing City. I was 25 years old and, after living in Atlanta for a few years, I was jonesing to be in the center of the universe—trash strewn on sidewalks, subways jam-packed with all flavors of humanity, the Naked Cowboy in Times Square (!), the whole shebang. It was tough and competitive, and if you weren't already, it made you those things. Honestly, I wanted to be Carrie Bradshaw. Um, I mean, who doesn't?

But after the initial wide-eyed wonder, the romance began to fade. The city was everything I dreamed of—greasy cabs and the like. I knew what I was getting into and loved it just the same, except for the part I didn't think much about: money. Namely, the amount of it it takes to live in The City.

When I moved there, I was making a six-figure salary. Albeit it was a low six-figure salary of $150,000, but it felt good to say "six figures" nonetheless. I felt like a BFD (Big F-ing Deal). That is, until New York City knocked me on my financial ass.

I moved to New York from Atlanta, remember, where I had made less money and still had a two-bedroom apartment (even if it was more than I needed). Surely if I was making more money now, I could actually afford a two-bedroom no problem, right? Ha! Yeah, right, very funny. When I started looking for a place, I almost hyperventilated at the prices, and this was during a brutal recession when rental prices had supposedly belly flopped. Talk about sticker shock to the extreme. A two-bedroom apartment in a so-so neighborhood was $7,000?! A month?! One-bedrooms I looked at ranged from $3,000 to $5,000! Oh. Dear. God.

On the upside, I'd accomplished one of the goals I made for myself in Step 2: I was making more money. But now I was living in a way, *way* more expensive town, so I could afford even less than I could before on a smaller salary. And, using my Carrie Bradshaw voice, I wondered: was I really moving forward? Or, was I, God forbid, taking a step back? (Cue *Sex and the City* theme music.)

Who can forget the *Sex and the City* episode when Carrie comes up short for a down payment on a home, only to do the math in her closet and realize where all of her money has gone?

"I've spent $40,000 on shoes and I have no place to live? I will literally be the old woman who lived in her shoes!"

Yes, Carrie and her shoes are famous and fabulous. But this was a pretty big "ah-ha!" moment for me. It was the moment when I thought that while it might be nice to walk a day in her fictitious shoes, who wants to walk in five-inch heels to a friend's couch? Not moi.

QUICKQUOTE

TO BUY OR NOT TO BUY?

When it comes to financial planning, that *is* the question. The relative merits of buying a home versus renting one are one of the biggest debates out there right now. So, we gotta tackle this sucker first.

If you haven't already noticed, owning a home is almost universally considered a good thing. You'll hear it touted by your favorite spewers of conventional financial wisdom. After all, they say, it's the American dream! It's the white picket fence, keeping up with the Joneses shit. It's the apple pie of money advice. Who argues against apple pie? Well…this girl does.

Hey, I love apple pie; sometimes, at the proper temperature and with the right amount of whipped cream or ice cream, it can be amazing. But you know what? I don't want to eat it every day, for any number of different reasons: it could be nasty quality; or I could feel full, fat, bloated; or I could just be in the mood for something else. Same goes with buying a home. When it's good, it can be a great thing. It also might not be right for you at this particular time in your life.

So, get control of your pure, knee-jerk cravings, and get smart about your consumption. Here are the three things you need to say "hell yes" to before even considering buying a home:

1. You are gonna live in it for a while.
2. You can afford it.
3. You have a steady job that you love.

Okay, now for another bullshit test. First, are you really, in full faith, going to stay in a home for an extended period of time? Let's say five years. Sure, things change…people move, get fired, promoted, hitched, preggo, etc. Yeah, life happens unexpectedly, but if you know or have a strong hunch you're going to need to move soon for whatever reason, you should not buy. Period.

Sorry, that was a little harsh, and you deserve an explanation. A home is not just about playing house. It's an asset, and it's an illiquid one, which means it's hard to "melt" into cash when you need it. And if you need to move, you're going to be thirsty for money, but that home is going to take time to sell. Nothing is more annoying than trying to drink from a frozen water bottle when you're parched. So you might not be hungry (or thirsty) for money now, but there's probably a good chance you will be in the future.

Next, can you really afford it? I mean, *really* afford it. Almost everyone needs a mortgage to be able to buy a home, especially first-time buyers. Typically you need about 20% of the total cost of the house in cash for a down payment, although in some cases you might be able to put down less in exchange for a larger mortgage loan. Do you have that? You can sometimes take out a second loan to cover the down payment, but that just means you actually don't own *any* of the house, at least in the beginning, and your monthly payments will be a lot higher. (As you can probably tell, I don't love this option.)

And finally, do you love your job and want to keep it for a long time? If you're unhappy about your job and looking into new opportunities, you can forget about buying. Job uncertainty makes for *terrible* timing to make an investment this enormous. You should also leave the door open (pun intended) for any opportunity that might come up...which, should you take the job, might demand moving.

The zinger beyond having the money for the house itself, whichever way you go on the down payment, is closing costs. You'll also need to set aside approximately 3% of the purchase price (as much as $10,000 on a $350,000 house) in closing costs *on top of the down payment.*

WTF ARE CLOSING COSTS?

- **Lawyer's fees.** Depending on how complicated the sale is (or how savvy your realtor is), you may need to hire a real estate attorney to draw up contracts and negotiate terms with the seller (or the seller's attorney) as well as explain what all this stuff below is.

- **Home appraisal fees.** You should know the worth of your new home *before* you buy. Have a third-party appraiser to check it out and determine the actual value.

- **Property survey fee.** Gotta know where the property line is so you don't piss off your new neighbor when you inadvertently build a fence on his property.

- **Home inspection.** This is to make sure the property is in the condition the seller says it is, and to uncover any potential problems before you sign on the dotted line. Once you close, anything wrong with the house is your problem.

- **Pest inspection.** Termites and other house-wrecking varmints. Yep, all part of playing house.

- **Local property taxes.** Varies widely based on where you live.

- **Local sewer fees (unless you have a septic tank).** Romantic.

- **Homeowners insurance premium.** Just like a car, you can't complete the purchase without proof of insurance.

- **Title insurance.** It's insurance for the amount of the mortgage loan, and it protects the lending financial institution's investment. It can also protect you as the owner for the price of the house. But really, this is why you need a real estate attorney. Mo' potential problems, mo' money.

- **Realty transfer fees and clerk fees to the local municipality for merely recording the transfer of deed and mortgage.**

- **Miscellaneous weird fees like potentially being charged for heating oil the seller left in the tank.**

BITCH TIP

I think of mortgage "points" as being like prepaid interest "fun bucks" where you can basically pay cash up front to get a lower interest rate for the long run. You might be *required* to buy points if your lender feels your credit or assets aren't up to snuff. But you can also *choose* to buy points at closing to reduce your interest rate, which is a smart way to benefit from having a lower rate down the road if you have cash now. Here's a point cheat sheet:

- A point is basically prepaid interest on your mortgage loan. Each point costs the equivalent of 1% of the mortgage loan. So if you got a $250,000 loan, a point costs $2,500.

- Each point you pay at closing lowers your interest rate 0.25%. So in exchange for paying more up front, you can lower your interest costs over the life of the loan (typically thirty years). So if you paid, say, two points at closing, you could bring down a 5% rate to 4.5%. That's a lot

> of scratch over thirty years, but you'll need to stay in the house a long time to reap the benefit.
>
> • If your credit score isn't great, the bank could peg your interest rate at a higher level than they would for another girl whose credit score is stellar. You might be quoted 6% because you have too much debt already on your credit card, and she might be quoted 4.5%. Unless you want to hold off buying until you can improve your score (by paying down debt, using your credit cards, and all that stuff we talked about in Step 3), the only way to bring down the rate is to pay points. In this example, you would need to pay six points (6 x 0.25% = 1.5%) to get the same rate as that other girl (6% - 1.5% = 4.5%).

BITCH QUIZ

If you're still dead set on buying, here's a quiz to see if you are considering everything. And I might be belaboring this, but this is the first chapter on spending for a reason. It's damn important to the success of your whole financial life.

Let's assume you are looking at buying a $250,000 house (I used that figure for quick math, but you can easily gauge your particular numbers based off it.)

1. Do you have $50,000 in the bank for a down payment?
2. Do you have roughly $5,000 to $10,000 for other stuff like real estate taxes and insurance?
3. Are you totally cool with about a $1,500 monthly payment (assuming low interest rates)?

4. Got $3,000 to $7,500 for closing costs?

5. You all set with moving costs and other big expenses when you move in (furniture, renovations, appliances)?

6. Are you down with maintaining all those appliances? Hiring plumbers, landscapers, exterminators, snowplowers and whomever else for work to be done on your property? Do you look in the mirror and see yourself as a superintendent? I would account for about 1% of the home value in maintenance costs per year— so got another $2,500?

7. Have you shopped around the neighborhood and couldn't find a similar house or apartment for less rent than what you'd be paying for your mortgage?

If you answered yes to EVERY single question and will live in your home for a few years, then you're looking like a good candidate for buying.

Let's go back to question 7 again. What if you found a similar house/apartment for $1,500? Same rent as the mortgage: what do you do? Rent or buy? All the psychological stuff aside, here are the strictly financial pros/cons to buying:

PROS

1. **Money will come back to you later.** Your mortgage payment includes a small amount of principal repayment, so some of that money will come back to you when you sell. When I say *some*, though, I mean *some*: don't expect to get rich selling your house. If you rent, the money you pay every month doesn't come back.

2. **No big surprises.** Your mortgage payment will not go up much (the real estate tax and insurance parts of your mortgage tend

to rise, but the principal and interest parts of the payment are fixed, provided you have a fixed loan—more on that below). If you rent, you could either get kicked out or gouged on rent later on. Renters are at the mercy of their landlords and the local real estate market. Renters can and often do get priced out of neighborhoods.

3. **Tax savings!** The interest you pay on a first mortgage is deductible up to $1 million. Yep, ONE MILLION DOLLARS. The amount you could be saving using our example could yield close to $500/month if you're in a state with high personal income taxes and you're in a higher income tax bracket (if you're not, you will be! At least, think that way...). Renters usually don't get tax love.

CONS

1. **If anything goes wrong with the house, you pay; if you're renting, you're usually off the hook (unless you actually caused the damage, of course).**

2. **You're tying up $50,000 (based on my example of a $250,000 house).** That money can be put to work in a ton of other ways, namely investments (which we will get to in Step 10), ideally making you more money than the amount you would have used as your down payment. When you rent, you don't have to tie up or even have $50,000.

3. **The home can lose value.** At the start of 2013, for example, homes in Las Vegas were on average worth only 75% of what they'd been worth in 1987 (yikes!), adjusted for inflation. A ten-city US index showed that over the past 25+ years, US real estate increased in real terms by less than 1% per year. What kinda "investment" is that?! Put simply, there's

no guarantee your house will increase in value. Many don't, so don't bank on it; in fact, assume the opposite. When you rent, you don't have this risk.

The list is for you to mull over, and the questions are yours to answer: is this the home you're really going to want and love for the long term? You can't change houses like you can outfits. Ask yourself: can you be happy in a rental? What's more important to you: not having the headaches of repairs and upkeep or being totally in charge of what happens to your place? And finally, whether renting or buying, ask yourself if you're taking on expenses you can comfortably afford. Any home that sinks you financially is a prison, no matter how nice it is.

BITCH TIP

Thinking about shacking up with your friend or sig-o? We'll get into this in detail in Step 11, but just know that it's risky business whenever someone else's name joins yours on the lease or mortgage. Sharing home goods and maintenance responsibilities, not to mention legal/financial obligations, can be tricky. The process can get jammed up if one of you has poor credit, which could inhibit you from getting a lease or mortgage in the first place (or saddle *you*, just assuming you'll be the one with the better credit in this scenario, with the bulk of the financial commitment). You're better off with the flexibility of renting unless you're 120% sure. At least you can bail more easily in a year or two when the lease is up if you need to.

LAPIN, I PASSED ALL YOUR TESTS AND I'M BUYING

Mazel tov. But be super smart when it comes to setting your mortgage up. A quickie cautionary note on fixed-rate mortgages (*FRMs**) versus adjustable-rate mortgages (*ARMs**): they sound similar but are very different. Be careful what you're getting yourself into.

FRMs are just what they say: fixed. Whatever rate you get is the rate you pay for the duration of the loan. That's it. Even if the market changes and rates go way up, yours will stay the same. The thing to keep in mind is your timing: get in when interest rates are high and they stay high; same goes for low rates. You're stuck with whatever you get, good or bad. But, it's predictable, and you can factor your payment into your Spending Plan easily.

ARMs are, well, adjustable and therefore unpredictable. They are tempting because they are usually much lower than the equivalent FRM (if you can get a 5% FRM, you can usually get a 4% ARM). But the rate will rise when market rates rise, which makes them very risky (especially since as of writing this book, interest rates seem to have only one direction to go...up). The amount you pay could change yearly, quarterly or even monthly, which makes it really tough to budget properly.

You might go for what's called a "hybrid ARM," which is a fixed rate for a certain period, like five or seven years, and then is free and clear to adjust. If you know you can pay the house off before the rate adjusts, then kudos—go for it. If not, you are just kicking the unpredictability down the road. (P.S.: I know you're not going to tell me that you'll just put the house on the market then, because if you are even thinking about selling, you shouldn't be buying.)

And (another) word of caution about ARMs: some ARMs have teaser rates that are low for a few years and then jump up…even if interest rates don't increase. You might think you found a trick by *refinancing** into an FRM then, right? Not so fast. Refinancing an ARM to an FRM is really expensive. During the financial crisis, the housing market crumbled because many people had taken out ARMs thinking the same thing: "When interest rates rise, no problem, I'm going to game the system and just refinance into a fixed-rate mortgage then." Yikes, were they wrong. The problem was that many of them ended up *underwater** because of tanking home values in a lot of housing markets, which left them unable to refinance at all because their homes weren't even worth the amount of the loan!

BITCH TIP

Don't let your bank tempt you to borrow more than you can afford. Just because your bank approves you for a mortgage of a certain amount doesn't mean you have to take it; in fact, in many cases you should opt for taking considerably *less*.

And the same thing goes for "interest-only" loans. Do not let me see you taking one of these out. Yes, I know, the monthly payments are often lower than for regular loans…but *none* of that goes to paying off the principal! You're basically a homeowner in name only: all of the responsibilities of being a homeowner but without getting any closer to actually owning the home. You just have a fake label of being a homeowner, and people who need that label are not Rich Bitches. They are Loser Bitches.

> Just like you don't want to max out your credit card, you don't want to get your financial butt handed to you in housing loans. Taking on debt can be very helpful when you are strategic about it. If you maintain a minimum balance on a credit card, you build a credit score. When you take out a reasonable mortgage that you can realistically pay and ultimately pay off, you can build wealth. If you're a drunken sailor about it, the banks win. I'm rooting for you, not the banks, so sober up.

STOP BELIEVING THE LIES YOU'VE BEEN TOLD ABOUT HOME VALUES

"Wait," you say, "I thought real estate was a *good investment.*" Well, that's what you've been told over and over again, and I don't blame you for believing it. But it's wrong.

One of the biggest sources of the misconception is inflation, a.k.a. the amount prices go up over the years and what makes movie tickets $15 today but only a couple of bucks in your childhood memory. If you bought a house in 1970 for $50,000 and it's worth $300,000 today, you may think you made a killing, right? Not. So. Fast. You've made nothing when adjusted for inflation. You'd basically be breaking even on that $50,000 house. BUT, if you add in repairs, taxes and other home expenses, you are probably in the hole.

Yes, on the surface it may seem like a simple case of making money by subtracting $50,000 from $300,000 and thinking you're making $250,000, but if making money were *that* simple, *everyone* would do it.

Contrary to what you might think, home prices historically remain unchanged if adjusted for inflation (in fact, they've stayed flat since the turn of the twentieth century). The idea that your home could get you stock-like returns is bananas, a holdover from the go-go days of the housing bubble that you should remove from your brain immediately.

Case in point: let's say we both have $100,000 right now. I go buy a house for $100,000, and you rent and put $100,000 in the stock market (I will tell you how to do that in Step 10). Assuming that inflation and stock return rates are predictable, after twenty years, my home is worth about $80,000 and your stocks are worth $165,000, adjusted for inflation.

Your home is a place to live, not a place to get rich. If you want to buy a home, buy a home, but don't try to convince yourself that it's a good investment.

PLAY FOR KEEPS

From an investment standpoint, homeownership is somewhat of a crapshoot due to all of the variables involved, like timing and location (buy in the right place and you could do great; own in the wrong one and you could get killed), not to mention *macroeconomic** and *microeconomic** factors. We all hear the stories of people who won the lottery or made a killing at the casino. But you also hear about people who lost their life fortunes gambling. I've heard the same stories about the housing market.

I met a woman whose grandparents lucked into a house back in the 1960s for just $20,000. (That was equal to about $150,000 in today's money, which is still a bargain.) They planted a garden, raised a family, the whole nine yards. Forty-five years later, long after the mortgage was paid off, they sold that same house for $650,000 in cash—more than four times what they paid for it, adjusting for inflation. Not great savers during their working years—they had six kids to raise—the windfall from the house ended up becoming a retirement lifesaver.

There are two key things to take out of that success story. 1. This happy couple bought their house with the goal of living in it for the long term and raising kids. 2. It's a once-upon-a-time kind of story because it happened, well, over a long time, i.e., *decades*.

Another woman who came to me for advice bought a little house in rural New Jersey in 2006 for $360,000, thinking she could make money because housing prices had been quietly going up in her area for years. She thought it seemed like a good bet. Then whammo, 2008 rolled around, and you could hear the flushing sound as the market went down the potty. Now that house wasn't even worth the money she'd borrowed from the bank to buy it. Yes, she was underwater. She stuck it out for a couple of years in the hopes that the market would rebound, but then she met a guy and got married. The house wasn't big enough for both of them, so she put it on the market. And it sat there. And it sat there. The price kept dropping. She couldn't get a single offer even with an asking price less than half of what she paid for it. As I type this sentence, it's been more than three years, and that house is languishing in a weedy yard, no takers.

Notice a couple of things from this failure story. 1. She bought the house because she thought she could make money off of it. 2. She thought "sticking it out" meant over a couple of years, not decades.

Don't base your home-buying decision on hearsay stories but pay attention to the overall themes of the success stories and failures, because they surround the basic question everyone should ask themselves before buying a home: am I going to live in it for a long time? I'll tell you that whatever success stories I hear usually come from people like the grandparents I just told you about who answer yes to that question. If the investment factor is anything but a side benefit, it usually doesn't turn out well. So stick to the basic question and get the "I'll get rich" idea out your head.

I know that a house is not just a financial decision. It's safety, security. It's psychological. I hear you. But for financial safety and security, you do not *need* a house. It doesn't need to be in your goals outlined in Step 2. If it is, great. Just know this is a choice, not a requirement. If you want to own your nest, I totally understand that. But you don't *need* a house for a nest egg; in fact, you should consider the possibility that your dream house will crack the nest egg you do need to have.

BITCH TIP

If you're thinking you can buy a house and flip it fast, keep one thing in mind: you're going to have a lot of expenses at the outset—closing costs, moving costs, fees, taxes, maybe points. So that means you need to sell the house for what you paid plus all those costs and then some to even make money. I'm not totally pooh-poohing the idea *if and only if* you are experienced at this. If not, you should buy only if you plan on staying put, not try to get your own HGTV house-flipping show.

SO YOU WANNA RENT

Buying is not for a lot of people. What scares me is that we are so brainwashed into thinking it's what we *should* be working toward. Absolutely not. It's just maddening when I hear young women tell me, "Yeah, but renting is like throwing away money." Well, then buying is, what? Throwing away *more* money? It's death by a hundred cuts or a thousand cuts. How do you want to dig your financial grave?? I mean, c'mon.

My favorite one is hearing that you should "skimp on the latte so you can buy a house." I mean, what?! I usually say back to that, "Buy your latte. Rent a place!" You'll hear more on this argument from me, but I use it here only to say this: rethink what you've been told or think you know about buying. Maybe you'll come to the same conclusion, but take no advice as gospel, even mine.

Yes, buying makes sense for some people, absolutely. Just not everyone, and don't think for a second that it's a blanket rule or something. Ask yourself the tough questions. If you are still raring to buy, then buy! If you're not, rent. And I would say that if you're not sure, definitely rent. Does your job require you to relocate from time to time? Or do you simply have wanderlust and want to try living in different places? Getting yourself in a buying trap you're not ready for will be financial suicide. I know I'm stressing it, but I'm doing it for your own good.

BITCH TIP

Think renting is just for those who can't afford to buy? Think again. Lady Gaga pays $25,000 a month to live in her Bel Air mansion instead of purchasing the home, which is valued at $4.475 million dollars. Okay, okay, that's a LOT of money. But her constant tour schedule means she is only there a few months of the year, so buying just isn't worth it. And considering that she makes $2 million plus per show (yes, *per show*), she could definitely afford to buy—but it makes no financial sense.

Oh, and she's not alone! Tim Tebow rented a place in Hoboken, NJ, while he played for the Jets to save money instead of getting an expensive place in downtown NYC. And after her infamous split from Russell Brand, Katy Perry opted to rent instead of jumping back into another property. Okay, sure, their rentals make most people's dream homes look like cottages, but the point is this: they can afford to buy, and they still opt for renting. Maybe we can learn something from these celebs, after all: the rich stay rich because they don't do things just because they *can*.

Renting isn't some consolation prize. It's not failure, and I don't know why it's given that connotation, ever. Let's bring sexy back into renting. After all, renting can free up money you could have invested elsewhere, like in yourself and your career (more on that in Step 8), ideally making you more money in the long run. That's what people mean when they say having the ability to "put your money to work," which you can't do if it's tied up in something like a house. Also, it's definitely a renter's market. The recent housing mess forced a ton of coveted houses and condos that couldn't sell into rentals, so there are some amazing deals out there to be snagged.

So, "own" your renting decision. Here are the basics of what you've gotta get down. Even if you're not in the process of renting a place now, assume you will be in the future:

1. **Most landlords require proof of employment, one or two bank statements, and a photocopy of your driver's license or passport as part of the lease signing process.** You should also have a check ready to make the security deposit, should you decide to rent. (And BTW, a check is better than cash because you have a record of it; if you lose the receipt from the landlord and you paid in cash, you're SOL.) Make several copies of these documents ahead of time and bring them with you while you look at rentals. If you see a place you like, you'll be a baby step ahead of anyone else vying for it and, yes, sometimes it's that competitive.

2. **If you're looking for an apartment, don't skip over the less desirable units.** You can often get a good deal on a lower floor, say, or a place at the back of the building, that you can "deal" with not having a view.

3. **No matter the location, take a close look at all of the rental's fixtures, tiling, AC/heat units, floors, paint, and all that jazz to make sure they're in tip-top shape before you sign.** Turn the shower on to check the water pressure (especially on high floors). Count the electrical outlets (some smaller or older apartments might have only one or two, and you'll find yourself dangerously overloading your extension cords). Landlords are more likely to fix any problems—and fast—if they think that not doing so might be a deal breaker on signing the lease.

4. **Get your negotiating on.** If you think you'll stay in one place for a while, ask your potential landlords if they will lower the monthly rent if you sign for longer than twelve months. An eighteen-month or two-year lease means less work for them trying to find a new tenant, touch up the apartment or home, and market the property at year's end, all of which could translate into major savings for you. If you plan on staying for a while and there are improvements you're willing to pay for, such as installing a dishwasher, ask the landlords if they'd split the cost with you (usually by forgiving part of your rent). They may go for it; after all, they ultimately get to keep the improvement.

5. **Don't sell yourself short by skipping over listings for newer developments or high-rise buildings.** That's right: look for the grand opening. Management companies often want to fill a building as quickly as possible after opening to boost its profile and exclusivity. It's simple: empty apartments don't turn a profit. Pay attention to when new apartment buildings hit the market, and you may be able to sneak in under the listed price. Yes, sometimes newer can be cheaper.

CONFESSIONS
OF A RICH BITCH

Breaking the lease

A few weeks after I moved into my first apartment in New York, I discovered my neighbors across the hall hosted frequent parties that got out of control with noise and hallway damage. (Call me an old lady, but keep in mind that I needed to *wake up* at 1 a.m. to go to work while people were still going strong partying.) To make matters worse, the landlord wouldn't return my calls. And then, to add insult to injury, my plumbing broke. I was fed up and miserable. You would be too if you had to use the bathroom in the laundry room and shower at the gym for two entire weeks!

I wanted out…which meant attempting the impossible: breaking the lease.

Once I left a message for the landlord informing him I was leaving, he was all of a sudden able to return my calls right away. Funny how that happens. As expected, he threatened to penalize me for breaking the lease. But all that time I had while I couldn't sleep because of the noise allowed me to do a little digging into the city's rental laws. I found out that in NYC, there was no penalty in instances of gross neglect on the part of the landlord—which definitely applied to my situation, since my landlord was violating two rules: fixing the plumbing efficiently and in a reasonable amount of time AND not ensuring the "quiet enjoyment" of the apartment.

I attached a highlighted copy of these rules to my lease termination and moved immediately. I was never charged a dime. Moral of the story: know the rules so you know when you can break them.

BITCH TIP

Don't be a bad bitch. Remember, Rich Bitches are good bitches. If you rent or even own an apartment, add a little extra into your budget for tips—for the super, the elevator guy, the doorman, the handyman, the mailman—anybody who works in the building who can make your life easier. Certainly tips at holiday time are appreciated, but smaller tips for any special favors—changing a light bulb, carrying a bag, watering your plants, etc.—will buy you a lot of goodwill and make your apartment living experience a whole lot smoother. Heck, even a smile and a hello to the building workers you pass in the hall will make them more inclined to help you out the next time you need something.

Where you live is undoubtedly the biggest and yet most personal part of your Spending Plan. It's complicated, for sure. But as long as you stick to the 35% housing guideline as closely as possible, you can be as personal and choosy about the rest as you want. Go back to Step 2 and ask yourself, "What do I want from my life?" And whether you choose to buy a home or rent, own your decision. The world has changed since your parents and your grandparents were coming up. Decide for yourself. Create your own American dream, and that doesn't have to include the cockamamie picket fence and 2.5 kids. The one-size-fits-all quintessential American dream is dead. It is your dream. Your destiny. Your foundation. So pick your place, because we've got some art to slap on those walls.

BOTTOM LINE

Conventional wisdom: Paying rent is just money down the drain.

Saying that is like saying that buying food is money down the drain. I mean, you eat it and it's gone! Well, hey, guess what, it costs money to live. There are costs associated with a home, no matter what. The interest you pay on a mortgage, for instance, is money down the drain—the bank gets it. Yes, there are some tax advantages to paying mortgage interest, as we've discussed, but the after-tax number you pay is still gone. In the end, there are serious expenses to owning a home that don't come back, either.

Conventional wisdom: Homeownership should be your ultimate goal.

Um, no. Owning or renting is a highly personal decision that also requires serious financial examination. There is definitely no one-size-fits-all answer.

Conventional wisdom: Buying a house is a safe investment.

That may have been true once upon a time, but since the housing crisis began in 2008, there's no such thing as a sure thing in real estate. Buy a house only if you can afford it and you really want to live in the place for a long time. Don't fantasize about trying to *make* money off it.

Conventional wisdom: If a bank preapproves you for a mortgage, you can afford it.

No way. That's like saying just because a guy wants to marry you, you should marry him. Crazy talk! Don't forget, during the subprime mortgage scandal of the housing crisis, banks were offering mortgage loans to people no matter their creditworthiness, which led to a lot of people losing their homes to foreclosure. You need to work out your own budget—including all the costs of owning a home that aren't included in the mortgage, like utilities, repairs and maintenance. Oh, and the bank doesn't care how much money you might need for other parts of your budget, like food! Remember: no financial institution knows you better than *you* know you.

STEP

5

EAT, PRAY, DRIVE

Transportation, Food, Insurance and Other Essential Expenses

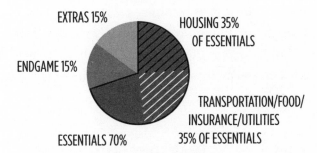

EXTRAS 15%

HOUSING 35%
OF ESSENTIALS

ENDGAME 15%

TRANSPORTATION/FOOD/
INSURANCE/UTILITIES
35% OF ESSENTIALS

ESSENTIALS 70%

'd never seen anything like it. In college, I took a Russian lit class that caused so much hoopla that kids who didn't even go to the school snuck in for the last lecture. The professor said he would reveal "the meaning of life." Makes sense that it was such a draw, right?

So, here's what he said was the meaning of life: to focus on the little things. Yep, that's it. *That* was the meaning of life. "Living a life rich in love and joy," he said, "is about the little things: the way you smile at someone or thoughtful gestures you make, they make all the difference."

If I were in that class today, I would blurt out, "Yes, but we need to pay for that life!" Instead, I'm just going to tell you my thinking has evolved since I took that class (which was also when I first read *Anna Karenina*, by the way, the book I wrote my first Spending Plan in). So here goes: in order to focus on the little things in life, you first have to focus on the big ones—with your money.

My master plan for Step 5 is to finish knocking out some of your megaexpenses so that your biggest Spending Plan percentages are in check. We've done our biggest one—where you're going to live—so it's time to move on to the rest of the Essentials: transportation, food, insurance and bills.

That way you don't sweat the small stuff (like a latte). And not sweating the small money stuff is really what will let you focus on the little things in life that matter. And that's what *I think* the meaning of a rich life is: the ability to focus—with your time or money or both—on whatever you want.

TRANSPORTATION
BABY, YOU CAN DRIVE MY CAR

For many of us, cars are pretty important. Depending on where you live, a car may well be the only way to get to work, or anywhere else for that matter. For those of you who'd like—or really need—a car, what can you afford?

The conventional rule of thumb has always been that you should limit your all-in car expense (payments, insurance, maintenance, gas, parking) to 20% of your monthly income. Sounds fine if you don't really think about it for yourself, right?

Well, kind of, but again, this is why you need to think about it for yourself.

So let's look at it together: spend 35% on housing and 20% on a car and you're at 55% for the Essentials, and you haven't paid a single utility bill, not to mention your health insurance premium. I say, take that traditional rule of thumb and put it on the high end of the range (you thought I was going to say "and shove it," right??). Keep transportation costs from 10% to *no more than* 20% of your income. And when I say "no more," I'm not joking. (Remember, we are trying to budget fun in here, people!)

Aside from a car lease or loan payments, you need to factor in the following:

1. Gas
2. Insurance
3. Maintenance costs
4. Parking

You can actually calculate the dollars and cents per mile for those things on sites like edmunds.com.

SHOULD I LEASE A CAR?

Hell no. I might blow your mind right now, but leasing a car is the biggest scam ever. Sit with that for a second, because it's not a typo.

You want a fancy car but can't afford one? Let's lease one so we can lie to ourselves that we *can* afford it! Terrible idea. Lying gets you nowhere, fast. You don't have money to buy the car? Don't get it. Makes complete sense in theory, but obviously hasn't clicked since leasing a car is more popular than ever.

Yes, falling into a lease trap is normal, because you think that's what you're supposed to do. It's so much a part of our culture to lease that it's not even questioned. But that doesn't make it right for you. "But it's SO convenient," you say. I say: how convenient is it to be broke? Do you want convenience or do you want to be broke? Exactly.

Consumer Reports backs me up and says leasing is the MOST expensive way to get a car. Why? Because you're essentially buying a used car at its new car price!

Let's assume that you are leasing a car for $500 a month (which is higher than the national average but easy for math). Let's say you get a fifty-month car lease. That means you are spending $25,000 before giving it back after those four-ish years. Now cars depreciate *a lot*, but the car company will estimate that it will depreciate less than what you paid, say $20,000, which is a lot but not the $25,000 you paid. So that $5,000 is their profit.

Why do you think car companies do this? Because they are making a ton of money off it—ahem, it's why they came up with the idea! They are actually making more money renting their cars to you than they are selling them.

FYI

New cars depreciate 15-20% the second you drive them off the lot. And they lose 70% of their value in the first four years.

The most common transportation faux pas is dumping too much money into leasing when you could have used that lump sum to buy a car a couple of times over. Calculate how much you are spending on a lease and think of that full amount as your *opportunity cost*,* or the potential value of your money over time if you were doing something else with it like paying off debt, building savings or investing (all of which we will get to in Steps 6, 7 and 10). Is tying up $500 a month or $25,000 over five years worth it? Would that $25,000 be better spent buying a cheap car, with the rest going toward something else? Get the idea out of your head that leasing is cheaper. It's not.

We talked about this opportunity cost concept in Step 4 with regard to renting a house or an apartment. In this step, I want you to look at your opportunity cost to argue *for* buying a car, whereas before I showed you the opportunity cost to argue *against* buying a house. It might sound contradictory for me to lean toward buying a car and not a house, but they are obviously different beasts with vastly different prices, and their values act differently over time. I mean, there is no situation in which the decision to buy a $25,000 car and a $250,000 home should be treated the same way, anyway.

You can say, "Whatever, Lapin, I can handle a lease, thank you very much." Cool, but remember it is nearly impossible to get out of leases, and you'll be stuck with the duration of payments. If you do get into a lease, you have to be 100% sure you want to do this and know what it's costing you.

1. **Add it up.** A lot of the car business is designed around making that monthly payment *look* good. What they don't show you is the total cost you're *actually* paying. Car salespeople usually quote you a price without sales tax or licenses, so factor that in before you sign so you know exactly what you're signing up for.

2. **Be up front about what's "up front."** "No down payment" doesn't mean no payment is due up front. Most leases make you pay fees for tag, title, acquisition, registration and dealer documents. Some leases also require a security deposit. Okay, so all that is not called a "down payment" per se, but it is normally due along with your first payment, so it might as well be one.

3. **Don't fall into the term trap.** One of the oldest tricks in the lease book is manipulating the term of the lease to make you think you are getting a deal. Let's take an example of you thinking you're doing good by getting a $277.77 thirty-six-month lease down to $250. The salesman might huff and puff and give you a "you're getting away with murder this deal is so good" look and tell you he can do $250 payments but it has to be a forty-month lease. Well, sister, that's the exact same deal—you're just spreading it out a little more.

4. **Care about the price of the car.** Just because you are leasing and not buying doesn't mean you can ignore the sticker price of the car. The price is a big factor in determining the lease payments, so haggle for that, too. The lower the price is, the lower your lease payments will be.

5. **Beware of early termination hooey.** Don't get bamboozled into thinking a dealer will "take care of" getting you out of your old lease early. You technically can get out of a lease early, but you will pay A LOT to do so. Don't ever let them convince you to "wrap" those costs into the new lease, because you will end up eating them; after all, you are financing over a longer period.

6. **Don't comparison shop.** Sometimes car salesmen will try to show you what an amazing deal leasing is by comparing your lease payments with your car payments if you bought the car. Well, yes, of course the lease payments are lower, because you don't actually own the car in the end.

There is a lot of stuff dealers don't tell you about leasing a car…shocking, right? If you get into a lease, make sure, sure, sure it is a "closed-end lease." This is the lease where the dealer, not you, absorbs the loss if the value of the car when you turn it in is less than the market value. This is in comparison to an "open-end lease," in which you absorb the costs at the end if the residual value of the car is less than the market value. A quick example of this would be the HUMMER fad. Imagine if you'd leased one five years ago. What do you think happened to the value of that tank? It plummeted as gas prices skyrocketed. People who leased one via an open-end lease were screwed when they handed that big boy in.

You *must* ask about this. The sales folks at a dealership are obviously not jazzed about offering up this information, so you need to ask up front. Dealers have to disclose it by law, but only if you ask.

OKAY...THERE'S A BUT

There *are* a couple of cases in which leasing might make sense. If you are relocating temporarily, say across the country or over-seas, it might make more sense to sign a short-term lease than to buy a car and deal with the headache of selling when your time there is up. Or if you own your own business, you can write off the lease payment. But you need to make sure you nail this from a tax perspective, so if you go this route, talk to your accountant before you step foot in the dealership.

WHAT ABOUT AN AUTO LOAN TO BUY A NEW CAR?

I'd really prefer it if you don't. Because you are borrowing to buy a *depreciating asset*.* A depreciating asset refers to stuff that's worth less the older it gets. This includes most goods like furni-ture, appliances and...cars! (One exception would be a vintage Hermès handbag that defies my wildest dreams of appreciation, but I digress.) A cardinal sin of finance is borrowing for a depre-ciating asset.

Let's say you borrow at 10% interest (more than the average, but I am rounding for easy math) to buy a $25,000 car. That means your monthly payment is more than 500 bucks. In five years, you've spent more than $30,000 for a car that's probably worth $7,500 by the time you sell it or trade it in. Can you tell me why this make sense? Rather, can you tell yourself? Because I already know it doesn't. (And this only gets *worse* if you don't have a stellar credit rating—see Step 3—because your interest rate will be higher, so more of your hard-earned cash will be blowing out your, ahem, exhaust pipe.)

If you *must* take out a car loan, please have at least 20% to put down in cash to shorten the length of your loan term to at most three years, which can save you from some of the rapid depreciation after that. Plus, you want to pay your car off as quickly as possible to avoid what could happen in the event of a bad accident: how much would it suck to keep making loan payments for a totaled car that you don't actually *own*?

However, even if you do have that down payment, let me offer you a suggestion: take that $5,000, or whatever the amount is, and buy a used car. Save the $500 you would be spending on payments for ten months, and presto: that's $5,000 *more*. At that point, you could upgrade to an even better used car (or have more cash to put down on a new car so the loan will be a lot smaller).

SO HOW DO I BUY A USED CAR?

You should ideally buy a car that's four years old, if you can, because it's already depreciated by the highest percentage it will go down. That means you will lose less by the time you sell it or trade it in. You will always lose *something*, but it will be substantially less than what you would lose if you leased or borrowed.

Here's the first step: be super prepared. Look up car values on sites like carmax.com and kbb.com (Kelley Blue Book). When you find a car you like, check out its history on carfax.com, which can tell you if the car's been in a major accident. Be armed with this info and you won't be suckered. *Always* negotiate for cars. Unless you are looking at some crazy exotic one-of-a-kind ride (which you shouldn't be), cars are commodities. There are a ton of the kind you want or similar ones out there.

So where are the best used cars?

1. **Car lots swollen with inventory.** You can get your ballsy negotiating hat on and haggle to get a good deal because the dealer needs to move that inventory off the lot.

2. **Individuals.** People selling used cars are usually more eager than lots to unload theirs.

3. **Repos.** It sounds sketchy, but it's not. Call your bank to find repossession auctions in your area.

4. **Police or government auctions.** These are confiscated cars, so it's a bit of a crapshoot, but the prices are often below book value. If you don't know a lot about engines and whatnot, bring a friend or mechanic who does.

BITCH TIP

Buy at the end of the month. Most car dealerships work on a quota system, meaning that they have to sell a certain number of cars every month. In the last days of the month, the dealership will have greater incentive to knock down the price in order to move vehicles off the lot and meet their quota.

YOU: 1; SALESPERSON: 0

So you're gonna buy a car. You've done some research into what kind you'd like to have. Seriously, don't walk into the dealership if you haven't done your homework, and I don't mean knowing which car is best looking, but knowing which one has the best features, gas mileage, dependability, price—all that good, sometimes boring, stuff. Then, and only then, are you ready to face…cue ominous music…a car salesperson! Here's how your convo should go down:

Salesperson, walking quickly toward you the minute you step over the threshold at the dealership: How can I help you today?

You: I'm interested in buying a 2015 blah blah.

Salesperson: We have several models that might appeal to you.

You, having done your research and knowing full well the models he's suggesting are more expensive: Thanks, but that's not really what I was looking for. I know what I want.

You tell him the model(s) you've chosen ahead of time.

Salesperson: Okay, then, let's get you behind the wheel for a test drive. (Speaks into walkie-talkie:) Bring the blue 2015 blah blah around front for a customer. (To you:) Shall we?

You and salesman take the car for a spin.

You: Great. This is the car I want. It goes for about $17,500, yes?

Salesperson: What color would you like?

You: I like this blue.

Salesperson: This model has Bluetooth and GPS and a bunch of other features you didn't ask for. It's $24,500.

You: No, I don't need all that. I want the $17,500 model.

Salesperson: This is the only one we have in blue.

You: Silver is fine.

Salesperson: Okay, have a seat. Let me talk to my manager.

Manager comes over: I can let you have this car for $19,500.

You: This car is $17,500. That's what I'm going to pay.

Manager: I'm losing money if I sell it for less than $18,500.

You: Sticker price is $17,500.

Manager: I'll throw in the 10-year warranty. $22,500.

You: $17,500.

You get the idea. It can go on this way for a while. It's just a thing car sales folks do. They work on commission, so the more car they sell you, the better they do for themselves. There's almost always a manager called in. Expect to haggle back and forth, but stick to your guns. They'd like nothing more than to sell you a car that's more expensive than the one you had in mind. But don't get angry, either. Stay chill. Repeat yourself as often as you have to. Remind yourself that they'd rather sell you a car than sell no car at all. And if you're really getting nowhere, WALK AWAY. There are plenty more cars out there, and, hey, chances are they will try to stop you and give you the price you asked for.

Let me sum up my feelings on cars: buy good used cars cheap. You might only be able to afford a jalopy, but that's okay. Use it to death, putting aside the payments you would have been forking out for a loan or a lease. Get your financial house in order by tackling debt and saving (hang tight for Steps 6 and 7). Work toward only paying cash for depreciating assets, like your next (used) car.

FYI

Marissa Mayer, CEO of Yahoo, is worth an estimated $300 million...and she shuttles herself back and forth from work in an eighteen-year-old BMW.

BITCH TIP

The benefits you get from your employer aren't limited to health insurance and retirement packages. They might also offer "pre-tax" or discounted passes for those employees who regularly use public transportation. If they do, you can get $125 a month to pay for trains, ferries, buses, subways, etc. If you drive to work, parking costs can be paid for by your employer tax-free up to $240 a month. For those of you who get to work by bike, you can get the costs of bike maintenance and storage paid for by your employer tax-free, up to $20 a month. (FYI: your employers get these tax breaks, too; they're not just offering 'em for your health!) Ask your HR rep pronto if your company offers any of these benefits.

A GIRL'S GOTTA EAT

Yes she does. Food is part of Essentials, but only basics—not your tapas excursions, Thai takeout or triple mocha Frappuccinos. That's all in the Extras section. And if you are a foodie, be a foodie and put that in the Extras category. But if you're not interested in anything more extravagant than frozen meals, then you're not putting food in any category but the Essentials.

A starting point for what is basic is roughly 5% to 10% of your Spending Plan. That's what you could live off nicely from weekly trips to the grocery store. Sure, it depends on how many people you are feeding. But it's a misconception to think that it's cheaper to feed a single person. For starters, if it's just you, it's easier to go out or grab some takeout, right? Temptation is much stronger if it's just you. Also, most grocery stores don't sell single servings of stuff like pasta or hamburgers. If you buy a pound of meat and eat only one portion, that's not saving anything—it's just a waste of money.

I'm not the girl who's going to tell you to clip coupons or buy the on-sale, almost expired stuff. Rather, just for one week, really pay attention to how much money you spend on food and other groceries, like laundry detergent, and see if what you're spending is reasonable. Are you actually using what you buy? If not, quit buying it.

Obsessing over pennies will make you sick. The mere awareness of what you are doing will help more than any coupon will. Once you start organizing and visualizing your Spending Plan in categories, you will start recognizing that if you don't spend your money in one category, you can use it in another. It will start to feel like free money, but it's really just *your money.*

FYI

Americans throw away around $165 billion worth of perfectly good food every year. In fact, 40% of all the food in the United States today goes uneaten.

EAT YOUR VEGGIES

You've probably heard advice that you should grocery shop on the cheap to save money. "The farmers' market and organic foods are soooo expensive." Seriously? Out of all areas in your life to save money? This is not a place to pinch a few cents here and there. Why? Because your health is worth it.

Yes, packaged foods and snacks with a million ingredients you can't pronounce might be perpetually on sale and seemingly cheap and easy, but fresh produce and whole grains give your body the nutrients it needs to stave off colds, obesity and disease—not to mention the time and money it takes you to get better. Shift your focus to getting your groceries fresh. Hit your local farmers' market for great deals on produce, grains, dairy and meat. These healthy foods are as easy to prepare for one person as a nasty frozen dinner, and can protect you against costly medical bills by keeping you healthy and fit. And you'll likely end up spending *less* money once you get the hang of shopping and meal planning this way...yep, last time I checked, an apple was less expensive than a bag of Cheetos.

In fact, studies have shown that buying healthy food and cooking at home (as opposed to "cheap" fast food and prepared meals) are actually less expensive in the long run: a typical family of four will spend nearly $30 for a meal at the drive-through window, while a basic and nutritious meal of rice, beans and fresh vegetables makes enough for a few days' worth of leftovers for less than $10. Winner, winner, tofu dinner!

GET YOUR HEALTH ON

And speaking of those expensive medical bills: yes, health insurance is in the Essentials category. (Where'dya think it would go?) I mean, I don't even need to get philosophical on you about how if you don't have your health you don't have anything because as of writing this, it's basically illegal not to have health insurance.

If you're employed by a company that offers health insurance as a benefit, your costs will probably be less than if you buy your own. Usually an employer will cover at least a portion of the monthly premium (or premiums if you opt for a dental and/or vision plan, too).

If you buy your own health insurance because you're self-employed or your employer doesn't offer it, you need to be up on the latest with healthcare.gov (which as of this writing is a cluster-you-know-what) and health care laws as well as what the individual health insurance policies offer since they are different in every state. Once you identify which insurance companies are offering coverage in your area, you should compare the individual policies that are available.

I know it's a drag, but research your options and make your decision carefully. Health insurance is expensive, no doubt. But there are a ton of different kinds; it's not one-size-fits-all. In general, the lower your monthly premiums, the higher the *deductible** (the amount you have to spend that year on medical expenses) you'll have to meet before coverage kicks in. If you have doctors that you already like, make sure your doctor accepts the insurance policy you choose. The insurers' websites generally let you search for doctors and hospitals that participate in the various plans.

If you're young and healthy and not likely to see a lot of doctors during the year, perhaps a Bronze- or Silver-level policy is for you; the premiums are lower in exchange for a higher deductible if and when you have to go to a doctor. There's even a Catastrophic option if you're under 30, which has an even lower premium in exchange for covering you only in case of major illness or emergency. If you're older or have a medical condition that requires you to make more frequent doctor visits or fill prescriptions, you might look toward a Gold or Platinum policy, which have higher monthly premiums but lower deductibles. (Keep in mind, every state is different depending on how many insurance companies and how many types of policies are available.)

Just don't think you can skip it if you're generally in good health and are the kind of person (like yours truly) who would rather tough it out than set foot in a doctor's office. There are penalties if you don't get coverage, and you don't want a nasty surprise when you find your tax refund is a lot smaller than you thought it would be.

BITCH TIP

Are you in between health insurance plans? Even if you are not, make friends with walk-in clinics. They are not sketchy at all. I go to the Duane Reade or CVS minute clinic facilities for small stuff like a cold or strep throat. They're cheap, quick and easy. You don't need an appointment. You just show up—so you don't have to deal with those middle-of-the-day times when you have to drop everything because your doctor can squeeze you in. Obviously, if you have a real emergency, go to the emergency room, like I did when I slipped and fell on some black ice in NYC (yep, that happened). But if not, stay out of emergency rooms unless you have a real emergency—and walk in the walk-ins instead.

CONFESSIONS
OF A RICH BITCH

A health insurance cautionary tale

Health insurance is expensive. But do you know what's even *more* expensive? Losing your policy and having to sign on with a different provider. Trust me, I know what I'm talking about... I made this boneheaded mistake myself.

When I set out to start my own business, I filed for COBRA, which allowed me to continue the health insurance I had with my last employer as long as I paid the full premium, which was around $600/month. But then—doh!—I made a late payment. I got no mercy, people. The next thing I knew, I was terminated.

I had to find another, individual health plan...for $1,100/

month, nearly double what I'd been shelling out before. As if the universe hadn't paid me back enough for losing track of my bill, before my new plan kicked in, I came down with a nasty stomach virus that sent me to the ER. Guess what? Not covered. It was a $2,000 nightmare.

I panicked, naturally. Then I negotiated my butt off. People think that when they get a bill from a hospital, it's set in stone. It's not (no bill really is, BTW—see the next section for proof). Even if you have all the money in the world, get an itemized hospital bill so you can see exactly where the charges come from. As it turns out, I was on the hook for an $800 X-ray that I never even had (I mean, come on, an X-ray for a stomach virus?? There wasn't much they could say about that argument). But $1,200 was still way too much, so I kept haggling until the bill came down to about $600.

That's right: *I negotiated my medical bill*. Here's the secret: the hospital knows from the outset that there is a small chance they'll never recover the full (and typically outrageous) amount from you, so with a little pushback (okay, sometimes a lot) they'll take what they can get. Look around online to find the fair market price for a procedure or treatment before you pay a cent; average costs vary based on region or even city, so you should know what you're getting into. Then call your healthcare provider and plead your case openly and honestly, offering to work within a payment plan or pay a reduced rate in cash, if possible. If they think they have a better chance collecting 75% of the total cost than 0% of the total cost, they'll likely work with you to make that reduced rate happen. And this should go without saying, but get your negotiation on *before* the bill is due; the provider will be much more accommodating if the bill is still active, not *late*. After all, siccing the bill collectors on you is not only annoying for you but costly for them, too.

> Your health is priceless, of course, but that doesn't mean you should be stupid about your spending.
>
> Oh, and pay your premium…or you'll pay a premium!

SKILLS WITH YOUR BILLS

The rest of what you are going to spend on the Essentials will be on your bills: utility, phone and cable. I'm not going to tell you to cut down your premium channels or limit the texts you are sending to save money, so chill. But I am going to tell you not to take your bills at face value.

As for your utility bills, negotiating them isn't exactly the same as it is with your phone and cable bills. It's not like the electric company is going to give you a lower rate. But, like most things in life, it's not that simple. Some utility companies might offer discounts if you agree to participate in energy conservation programs, such as allowing the company to cycle your air conditioning off for brief periods during high-demand times, or allowing them to install a more efficient thermostat in your home. If you live in a house and pay for heating oil, you might be able to lower, or at least normalize, your monthly bill by asking for even billing. So instead of forking over huge amounts of dough during the winter, and never knowing how much until the oil guy makes a delivery, you can pay a fixed amount every month throughout the year (yes, it sucks to pay for heating oil in July, but it's a good trade-off for not getting a heart attack–inducing bill in January). You might not be able to shave any money off the bill, but you can *always* negotiate a better deal for yourself.

If you haven't picked up on this already: I'm a BIG advocate of negotiating. All it takes is a little chutzpah. Can you negotiate your cable bills down? Um, yeah. You should *always* ask for a better rate. You have nothing to lose but a little time. The worst thing they can say is no. And they usually won't. I speak from experience. Providers will often throw you a bone instead of losing you as a customer. Maybe you can get a discount if you agree to automatic billing—all you have to do is ask, and they might do it.

CONFESSIONS
OF A RICH BITCH

The dark side of bill autopay

I signed up for automatic payments for my satellite TV service in exchange for a $20 discount off my bill each month. When the paper bill arrived in the mail, I just filed it, knowing it was taken care of.

Mistake.

About a year into the service, the provider offered a special football package, free for the first few weeks. After that, an additional 35 bucks would be added to the bill for the duration of football season. When I noticed the extra dough being sucked out of my account, I called the company. I couldn't have cared less about football, and I sure wasn't going to pay for it. But I'd missed the opt-out deadline by a week and was stuck with the extra charge until the Super Bowl.

Just because you choose the autopay option with your regular monthly expenses doesn't mean you should stop *reading the bills*. Ever.

Still not into the whole negotiating thing? Palms sweaty just reading about it? Let's do some more role-playing:

You: Hi, I think my cable bill is a little high.

Cable company rep: Is there a mistake?

You: No, I just think it's a little high for the service I'm receiving.

Cable company rep: Well, you have blah blah and blah blah and you are getting those features at a great deal right now. Do you want to cancel one of the blah blahs to lower the bill? Because you're getting the latest, lowest price for what you have now.

You: No, I want to keep blah blah and blah blah. I'm sure you can see from your records on your computer that I have been a great customer. I heard from a friend who uses your biggest competitor that they are having a much better consumer experience. I don't want to go with the competitor today. Is there something you can do?

Cable company rep: Hold on, let me talk to my supervisor.

It is usually at this point where they hook you up. The key to any bill negotiation is to talk about leaving the provider and going to their competitor. I've done this with all of my major bills at some point and have been successful more often than not. Try to haggle with your bill collectors at least twice a year. First, I promise it will become fun and addictive. Second, if you aren't successful in negotiating, you want to make sure you're in the right plan for you. Are you still bundling with a landline and not using one? Ditch it. Still have that international phone plan tacked on when you haven't traveled in months? Whoops. Always good to get on the latest or most correct/appropriate plan for you. You might not get a big W every time you try this, but even a little win every once in a while is better than nada.

Can you ask your employer to cover a TV bill because it's a work expense? I did. I am in TV news, so it made sense. Does your employer require you to be available on your cell during off hours? That's a good reason to ask them to help pay for your phone bill. Do you bring your personal laptop into the office for work? Ask about that too. It never hurts to ask. Just come up with your most creative rationale. If your employer won't help you pay for it, you might be able to write whatever item you're using for work off your taxes. Those who are self-employed do this all the time. So do actors, writers, YouTube aficionados and…maybe you, too.

I hate clichés, but this one just works: you never know if you don't try. These things can make a difference in your Spending Plan and give you a little boost of self-confidence when your game works. So don't be a bashful bitch.

- You should always, always negotiate the interest rate you get on your credit cards and any late fees you might incur. More on this in the next step, but never take the APR or interest rate offered as being set in stone. It's not.
- In the market for new furniture? I've haggled up to 40% off by purchasing the floor model. If it's not immediately available, ask the

> salesperson if you can wait until it is. Try this with floor sample linens, throw pillows and other decor as well.
> - Clothes shopping? Keep your eyes peeled for any random snag in the fabric or faulty zippers. Most department stores and boutiques will give you a 10% to 15% discount on the spot— but only if you ask.

So, bam! We are 70% done-zo with our Spending Plan. See, blocking, tackling and organizing the bigger percentages first has hopefully put the whole game plan in perspective for you: we all have this big chunk of the Essentials. The sooner you get the bigger parts in check, the better. That way you can make the last 30% count for you; it's the smaller, but more meaningful, part.

BOTTOM LINE

Conventional wisdom: Lease a car; it's simple and cheap.

As we've discussed, leasing is not cheap. In fact, by leasing a car, you are essentially paying for a lot of car that you're either going to have to give back or buy at a price predetermined by the dealership. Leasing doesn't make a whole lot of sense if you think about what you're getting into.

Conventional wisdom: Some expenses just have to be sucked up.

False. Sure, some bills will remain constant from month to month, but a lot of companies, from your cable to even utility providers, may offer ways to reduce costs. *Almost everything is negotiable—even your medical bills.*

Conventional wisdom: Package deals always offer the best rates.

That might be true if you use all the services, but are you paying for a landline or premium channels you don't use? The à la carte menu is the way you want to go.

6

GET THAT MONKEY OFF YOUR BACK
Paying Down Debt

Urrrghhhh...I know. Debt, the only four-letter word I don't like. My motivation for paying off the debt I racked up was simple. It's what was standing in the way of me having my own back. Instead it was the monkey on my back that was weighing me down and not letting me protect myself as a working girl if I lost my job or had something else bad happen to me.

What also scared me about debt was that it was eating into my Spending Plan for other stuff. So before I get to the Spending Plan for other stuff besides the Essentials, we have to tackle this head on.

CONFESSIONS
OF A RICH BITCH

When I met my debt monkey

I couldn't believe it, but there it was staring back at me from the gloom of my bank statement: $5,000 worth of credit card debt. As I mentioned in Step 1, this wasn't just a personal setback; it stood against everything I believed in and the way I had been raised. Simply put: I knew better. And I felt like the definition of a dumb bitch.

But I was also a motivated one, and I knew that the only way to get rid of the icky feeling of having 5,000 big ones hanging over my head was to rid myself of it once and for all. "There's no time like the present," I thought. It was a Wednesday, in the middle of the month. Rather than wait until the first day of the next month, as some people might have done, I jumped right in. *No excuses.*

So how'd I do it?

1. **I acknowledged it.** I wrote it down on a sticky note and stuck it to the top of my computer screen: $5,000. I was already obsessing over it anyway. Having a physical reminder of the hole I had dug for myself gave me some clear head space and kept me motivated to pay it down. I would cross out the number every time it got smaller, which was extremely gratifying. It felt the same way it does to cross something off your to-do list.

2. **I set a deadline.** Being in the news business, I was all about deadlines. I knew that if I was going to stick to a repayment plan—any repayment plan—I had to set parameters around it. Otherwise it would be too easy to dip back into the pool for "needs" like new work clothes or nonwork-related airfare. I gave myself two years, which worked out to $2,500 per year, about $208 per month, or about $7 per day. $7 per day?? That's one glass of wine with dinner (less than one glass if you live in Manhattan!). I could do that, no problem. It seemed way more manageable in little chunks.

3. **I put myself on autopilot.** Through my online banking portal, I set up an automatic payment of exactly $208. This meant that every single month, the money came out of my checking account and went right toward paying down that credit card debt. Because I didn't ever see that money, I found that I didn't really miss it (and I didn't even have the option to spend it on something else).

4. **I reminded myself why I was doing this.** Every time I was tempted to skip a month's payment so I could buy myself something or have a night out, I reminded myself what I wanted to be doing with that money in the long term—my Endgame. Like a production company, a two-bedroom apartment and, yes, a family. That kept me focused, and at the end of two years, I was monkey-free. In fact, by the end of about a year and a half, I was so pumped to just be done with it (the end was in sight!) that I upped my monthly installments to $308 per month (I kept the 8 bucks because it felt easier to stomach than a round number—in the same way you feel like 99¢ is way less than $1) and ended up debt-free a few months ahead of schedule.

THE PYRAMIDS WEREN'T BUILT IN A DAY

Think of your overall financial plan as a pyramid. Visualize the base as your protection and security, which includes savings and insurance of various kinds, like health, life, car and home-owners/renters. If you're wondering why all that insurance is so important, it's because no matter how much you invest or grow your money, if you have an unexpected circumstance or get sued and don't have savings or insurance, then everything you worked for crumbles. You won't be able to invest in your future—the Endgame—for things like retirement, starting your own business or a fabulous round-the-world trip.

If you do get the base set up, however, it won't matter even if there's an earthquake, because you'll be ready. But as long as you've got debt in your way, you'll never be able to build that base.

PRIORITIZE TO PULVERIZE

Chances are that you are going to have more than one type of debt load to carry. We will talk in detail about the four major kinds of debt: credit cards, car loans, student loans and mortgages. But before we get to that, make sure this is ingrained in your head: debt needs to be prioritized by rate. If all the rates feel jumbled, go back and check what the current rates are or the range for "revolving" debt (the kind for which payments vary from month to month) and put them in a list from highest to lowest to prioritize your plan of attack. Typically, debt ranks in this order:

1. **Credit cards**: because they have the highest interest rates, this form of debt will add up the fastest.

2. **Car loans**: because a car is already a depreciating asset; no sense paying more interest on it as it decreases in value.

3. **Student loans**: because they are long-term debt and thus will eat into your Endgame.

4. **Mortgages**: because your home is a solid asset only if you actually own it.

This doesn't mean you should ignore paying off the lower-priority debt completely. Just put more oomph into paying off the highest-ranking ones first.

JUST HOW MUCH IS YOUR DEBT COSTING YOU?

Here's a general snapshot as of writing this book. Of course, these rates can change over time—and often do. But this should still give you an idea of just how quickly your dollars add up:

TYPE OF DEBT	ANNUAL PERCENTAGE RATE (APR)
Credit Card Debt	13–15%
Student Loans	4–7%
Car Loans	4–5%
Mortgage	3–4%

The naïve way to read this is to say, "Yikes! This means that for every $100 spent on a credit card with an APR of 15%, I'll be paying $15 extra dollars in interest."

But you're a pro, so you recognize the scary power of compounding interest—or the idea that you pay interest on your interest. So you would be paying 15% of $100 the first payment cycle and then 15% of $115 the end of the second one, or $17, for a total balance of $132. And this vicious cycle goes on and on. (Einstein once said, "The most powerful force in the universe is compound interest," and he even called it the "eighth wonder of the world," no joke.)

We are going to love compounding interest when we get to Step 9 on retirement and Step 10 on investing because the exponential increases will work in our favor. But for debt, we want to kill it before it kills us.

AN EASY-PEASY DEBT-SLAYING PLAN

There are a ton of diet books that tell you to "think thin to be thin." You might think that's a load of crap, and it obviously will be if you keep pigging out and hating on the gym. But there is something to be said about positive energy yielding positive results. In this case, "think debt-free to be debt-free."

Give yourself some motivation: tally up all the debt you have, then think of something you could be doing with that amount of money if it wasn't being the stupid monkey on your back. If it's $5,000, for example, then imagine what you could be spending that on. A trip? A new couch? Equipment for your own business? Write it down, print out a picture for inspiration and put it in a place where you can see it every day. I put mine in my letter holder, where I put my bills every month. If I had an extra $5,000 then, instead of that amount in debt, I would have purchased a broadcast-quality camera, Anderson Cooper–style. I printed out a picture of one as my motivation. I liked seeing what I was working toward every day and hated the days of wanting it so badly. Remind yourself of your goal every time you get cranky that you're paying off debt.

Then follow a plan to make that picture a reality:

1. **Look up interest rates.** Based on history and my experiences, the order, considering tax benefits, goes 1) credit cards, 2) car loans, 3) student debt, and finally,

4) mortgages. Identify which loan carries the highest interest rate, and pay that off first, whatever that is. When that's done, move on to the next highest; save the lowest rate for last. (If you've got only one source of debt, lucky you, you'll be done paying it off a lot faster.)

2. **Set a schedule.** Give yourself a realistic timetable to pay it off, but don't set comfy deadlines. Paying debt off isn't a comfy thing. Don't forget: the longer you drag it out, the more money you'll be shelling out for interest. And again, just like a regular diet, you're cheating yourself if you slack.

3. **Try to get your rates down.** Before you start on your payback attack, call your lenders and try to see what they can do for you; that way, you aren't paying more for the debt than you have to. They have an incentive for you to pay the debt back even at a lower rate, especially if it is "unsecured debt," like credit card debt, since they don't have any collateral to take if you don't pay them back, unlike with "secured debt," such as a mortgage, which is backed by something the lender can take away if you don't pay them back, à la a house in the case of a mortgage. So try and try again. You might also qualify for a hardship plan, which could lower your rates or payments or both.

4. **Put it all together.** If you are really serious about paying your debt off soon, you might want to look into a "balance transfer," which is basically putting all of the credit card debt you have from different cards onto just one card at a lower rate. Usually this rate is good only for about a year until it skyrockets, so do this only if you plan to pay it off quickly.

5. **Get methodical.** Whether it's autodeposit, which is my method of choice, or writing a check to yourself, create

a realistic payment plan, one that you can stick to. If you can put $200 a month toward your debt, I prefer to break it down to the day, which just feels more palatable. So $200 is about $6.70 a day. $150 is just 5 bucks a day. If you want to deposit daily, weekly or monthly—go to town.

6. **Give extra love.** If you find you're making more money or receive a bonus or other windfall, give some love to your repayment plan. Try to increase your monthly contribution a little. Even a little bit of an increase to your payments will get rid of the debt that much faster.

7. **Don't be rash.** If your major debt is on a credit card, don't cut it up and close the account. That's just going to hurt you when you want to take out another line of credit.

8. **Ask for help.** If you are finding it difficult to make your minimum payments, then get help. Seriously. There is no shame. You might want to meet with a credit counselor who can help you come up with a plan you can stick to. Just be sure to find a reputable one or you could end up in even more financial trouble than you were in before. The website for the National Foundation for Credit Counseling is a good one to start with.

9. **Don't forget the pain.** Once you're done with the previous steps, don't forget the painful process you went through—or you're bound to repeat it all over again. Once your debt is paid off, you're going to have a lot of temptation, too. Your mailbox will fill up with new credit card or other loan offers. That's because your credit score just went up, and financial institutions are attracted to how responsible you are. To keep the temptation in check, don't even open the envelopes.

10. **Keep up the routine.** Now that you're used to paying a small amount of your paycheck every day, every month

or whatever, try to keep that autodeposit up. Instead of going to debt repayment, make it go to beefing up your Endgame goals, which we will focus on in Step 7.

CREDIT CARD DEBT

Don't pay off your balances every month? You're *definitely* not alone. I've been there, and I'll bet you've been there or will dip into and/or flirt with being in the proverbial hole in the future. Accept that for whatever reason, you may need your credit card to get you through, and that's okay—for a hot minute. It's *not* okay for an extended period of time for a bunch of reasons we will get to, but mostly because you are sacrificing the Extras and the Endgame, which is really what we live for. By getting caught up in a life you can't afford, you are really just making it impossible to ever get to the life you *want* to lead in the future.

WHY ARE CREDIT CARD INTEREST RATES SO COMPLICATED?

There are hundreds of credit cards, each carefully (and often sneakily) designed to appeal to you and make lots of money for the credit card companies. Remember, Visa, Amex, etc., are all publicly traded companies with hundreds of billions of dollars in earnings to their names—yes, nine figures! They aren't in it for *your* financial health—they are in it for *theirs*. They are thrilled that you are giving them as much money as possible and will try anything to try and entice you to do so, namely making the APR look attractive.

Supposedly, APR is the annual percentage rate you are going to pay on your credit card purchases, but you will end up paying more than the figure listed on your credit card statement by the time the year is over. Why? Because the "annual" in "APR" may not actually be, well, *annual*. Most interest compounds monthly or even daily. So, let's say you have a $10,000 balance on a card with a 15% APR. That breaks down to about 0.04% per day. So you pay day one on $10,000, which gives you $10,004—and means that on day two you are paying interest on *$10,004*, not $10,000.

Those numbers might have been too much, but I wanted to demonstrate how compounding interest is a wicked snowball effect. The higher the rate, too, the more quickly it snowballs out of control.

THE CASE OF THE ARGYLE SOCKS

It's a silly example but likely one you can relate to (after all, we've all swiped the plastic for some pretty out-there things). It's the holidays, and you impulse-buy a pair of festive socks to wear to work (under your grown-up work clothes, of course). They cost about $10 now, but how much will they cost you down the road in interest?

After six months…	$10.72
After one year…	$11.50
After three years…	$15.21
After five years…	$20.11
After ten years…	$40.46

*Based on an initial cost of $10 and the national APR average of around 14%.

$40.46 for a $10 pair of socks!! You could have purchased an entire holiday outfit for that amount! Scary.

WHAT'S THE BEST WAY TO MAKE PAYMENTS?

The answer should be to pay them off in full, every month. That way it doesn't matter if your interest rate is 10% or 15% or 8,000%; it's 0% if you don't carry a balance.

Yes, the credit card companies offer you a "minimum payment" option. You may think the line on your bill is like a present from the credit gods. You're wrong. It's a joke. On you. If you pay only the minimum, it will take you *twenty to thirty years* to pay off the card. With the interest that accrues over that time frame, you'll likely end up shelling out more than double what you originally spent. Uh, on what planet does this sound like a good deal?

I know that every credit card offers a "grace period" of about three weeks for making a payment. But that is not a gift, either. If you miss that window, it's easy to fall into the "I already messed up so what's a little more?" cycle, like when you eat a piece of chocolate cake during a diet and then think, "Why not eat the whole cake since I already screwed up?" DON'T. The average credit card debt is *$15,480* per US household as of 2014. That adds up to more than $2.5 million over forty years. Yes, MILLION. Being a statistic is not cute.

BITCH TIP

If you still want to be able to make purchases if you don't have money in your bank account, you need to opt into "overdraft protection," which means that the bank will cover you (for a fee, of course). If you don't opt for the overdraft protection, then your transaction will be denied. The name is confusing, because who wouldn't want "protection"?? The terminology makes you think you *won't* be charged. But don't be fooled. Studies have shown that people who signed up for the "protection" paid four times the fees compared with those who didn't. Make no mistake, this is a type of short-term debt in disguise. And with fees averaging $35 if you overspend by even a dollar, overdraft fees are some of the highest-charging debts around!

SHOULD I JUST BE A DEBIT DEVOTEE?

Remember, our Rich Bitch diet is a lifestyle, not a quick fix. It might seem like the logical move simply to cut up those credit cards and walk away. DON'T for the following reasons:

1. **If the card still has a balance on it, the credit bureaus won't find anything for your "available credit" and the "credit limit."** That's good, right? WRONG. Since you still have a balance on that credit card, and with no credit limit (because you have closed it), it actually looks like you maxed it out. And that can—and likely will—wreak havoc on your credit score.

2. **If you have paid off your balance, but cut up your card anyway, you're missing out on a valuable steady payment history.** Remember, you're going to need that credit down the road to take out a loan, buy a house or negotiate better deals on existing payments. Cutting your card is essentially taking you out of the game before you have a chance to play.

And even if you *do* have a good reason to close a card (it charges exorbitant annual fees or stops offering the perks that made you sign on in the first place), cutting it up isn't all you have to do:

- **You have to tell someone!** If you cancel over the phone or online, follow up with a signed letter to your credit card company's customer service department stating that you wish the card to be canceled and a brief explanation of why you are canceling.

- **Ask for a written confirmation in response from them, stating that the account has been closed.** Monitor your credit reports (you are obviously already doing that) to make sure the account is no longer active.

Like I suggested in Step 3, keep the card alive by leaving one recurring payment on it, like a utility bill, and using autopay. That way, you don't have to think much about it, and it's still active. In the meantime, you can start switching a majority of your daily spending to a debit card, where you are spending money that's actually in your account, which makes it far more difficult to overspend. Studies show that people using credit cards spend 12% to 18% more when using credit rather than debit cards. So if you are having trouble sticking to your Spending Plan or anticipate doing so, you're better off resisting temptation by becoming a debit devotee.

BITCH TIP

Debit cards make bookkeeping easier because you can see exactly what you are spending on a cash basis every month. This will go straight into the outflow section of your *balance sheet*/ *cash flow* statement (which we talked about in Step 3) since it is coming from money you have. A credit card bill, on the other hand, will have two steps accounting for the interest. That is, the things you pay

> for with credit cards are listed out as expenditures *and* then retotaled with interest factored in.

BUT I WANT TO BUILD CREDIT, LAPIN

Yes, please do. But to boost your credit score, you need to use credit cards strategically. That means paying them off strategically, too, as in paying the balances off every month.

I always get the question, "How many cards should I have to keep up a good credit record?" There's really no right answer, but there are a few considerations. I'd say at least two cards just for practical purposes: if a card or its number is compromised, you should have a backup until the replacement card arrives. Likewise, having a couple of cards—but not running balances—can improve your credit score because you have access to credit you're not using. I carry an American Express and a Visa (because not all places take Amex), and this seems to work for me.

If you have bad credit or no credit, it might be difficult for you to get a credit card even if you want one. In that case, you should apply for a *secured credit card** or one that is backed by collateral since you are a risky person to lend to. Normally you put up $300 or $500 and you can "charge" up to that amount. The average time it takes to graduate to a normal credit card (an "unsecured" one) is usually about a year.

CONFESSIONS
OF A RICH BITCH

Chill, you little grasshopper you

A woman who came to me for advice had used only an ATM or debit card to make purchases, but she knew that she had to start building credit if she had hopes of buying/financing a house someday. So she took a baby step and signed up for her first card at...Gap. She knew that getting a Gap card would allow her to combine building credit with her favorite store—a fun, practical combination for her. She paid off her card in full every month and was never late to make a payment. She got an extra discount for using it, too, which kept her incentivized (but in dangerous shop-a-holic territory, too).

About a year down the road, she decided to open another card, this time at Ann Taylor. She figured that she had successfully handled her first card, so it was time to keep the good credit karma going. Plus she needed some new clothes for work and saved a ton of money with the discounts they offered.

A few months after opening her Ann Taylor card, she opened a Best Buy card to finance a nice camera that she wanted. The camera cost around $500, and it was the first purchase on credit that she would have to repay over several months instead of right away. That was okay, though, because she knew she would be able to make the payments every month.

Another two months passed and she was introduced to the Kohl's charge card. She figured she didn't use her other cards extensively, and she shopped at Kohl's a lot, so she thought a Kohl's card made sense. However, after filling out the electronic information in the store, she was presented with a small receipt and an unhappy look from the cashier.

"You didn't get approved, I'm sorry."

"Say WHAT?" she thought. She had been a good credit card payer-backer. "Why in the world would I *not* be approved??"

Well, she got her answer a week later. She got a letter with her credit score and notification that she had opened too many credit lines within a short period.

Here's the moral of my girl's story: too much of a good thing, no matter how responsible you're being, can be a *bad* thing. Pace yourself when building your credit. While it's great to start building your credit history with a store card, don't go overboard. Each time you open a credit card, even if it's at a store, your credit score gets dinged a little. A handful of little dings can lead to a huge dent. So pick one that has perks or discounts on things you purchase frequently. You can bet that if you don't slow yourself down, the credit card companies *will*. Yup: sometimes the road to hell is paved with good intentions.

CREDIT CARD PERKS

Who can deny the joy that can be had from credit card reward benefits? I, for one, am obsessed.

The only thing the credit card companies are obsessed with is playing psychological games with you so you think you're better off spending more. After all, those cash-back, frequent-flier mile rewards can end up costing you more than if you just bought your own plane ticket. However, if you pay the balance every month as if it *were* a debit card, you can get some good stuff. Look into the lesser-known perks of your card, too, like rental or trip-cancelation insurance.

Quick PS: figure out if an annual fee makes sense. Some cards charge one in exchange for certain services or privileges. For instance, say your airline card charges $95 per year, for which you earn miles for every purchase. But how many miles are you *really* getting? If you're collecting only a fifth of a ticket, you might be better off with a no-annual-fee, lower/no-perks card. On the other hand, if you're racking up a couple of free tickets per year, 95 bucks seems like a pretty good deal. Just take a second and analyze if the perks make sense before you go ga-ga over them.

> ## BITCH TIP
>
> The ability to dispute a charge is one of the greatest powers you have by using a credit card over a debit card or cash (tied with fraud protection). If there's a problem with something you bought or you didn't get it, your credit card company has your back. You have to initiate a "chargeback." Usually you can do this online, or you can call or write a letter, and your credit card company goes to war for you. In my experience, these disputes are usually resolved in *your* favor.

Paying off credit card debt isn't a game of chess. It's not that complicated. You can win, easily. If you pay attention and stay disciplined, you can take advantage of the convenience and other benefits that debit and credit cards offer (and there are many…hello, points!). But ignore the downside or overspend, and you could end up in plastic purgatory.

CHOICES, CHOICES

You have both credit card debt and student loan debt: which to pay off first?

Short answer: whichever has the highest interest rate. This is almost always your credit card, so focus on making extra principal repayments on the credit card debt first. Student loans usually have lower interest rates. However, if you find this is not the case and your student loan, in fact, has a far higher rate than your credit card, then try to pay the student loan principal back first. If they are all blurring together, take a deep breath and look them up. The higher rate is the one that takes precedence.

FYI

The average student debt load in this country is $30,000. I hate stats that aren't put into perspective, so let's decode that number:

- If you have that much debt and are on a ten-year repayment plan at 7%, you will be paying around $11,000 in interest.

- If you are on a twenty-year plan at 7%, you're paying around $25,000 in interest—and on the hook for about $55,000 when all is said and done.

STUDENT LOANS

You likely have them; consider yourself extremely lucky if you don't. Here's the good thing: you are paying them off because you are a smarty-pants in the area of study you took loans out for. Student loans are also technically considered "good debt" because in taking them out, you're investing in yourself, which, in theory, will give you the tools to pay the debt off many times over. (It's like with avocados being "good fat"—but it's still fat, so don't gorge on them.) Business loans are typically in that bucket for the same reason. The bad news is, you probably didn't get the smarts in paying them off.

We were always told that the sky's the limit when it came to what we could do for our careers as long as we got a good education. But what's never said is that those dreams of infinite possibility will cost you. There's no buzz-kill like hearing you can't afford your dreams, right?

Also, I can't totally wrap my head around why this is the case, but being burdened by student debt affects women disproportionately. More of us are attending college, which is awesome in theory. But in practice, the awesomeness is anything but. Where college was once the ticket to ride, it's also become a major way to crash and burn.

It's the great and crappy equalizer. Yes, I've been there, but so have really famous, smart people. Hopefully that puts debt in perspective and makes you feel less alone. I mean, even President Obama and First Lady Michelle Obama finished paying off their student loan debt just before he entered the Oval Office. "And that wasn't easy," he has said. "Especially because when we had Malia and Sasha, we're supposed to be saving up for their college educations, and we're still paying off our college educations." He wasn't alone, either: 12% of all members of the US Congress currently carry student debt. High-powered (and, as is the case for many, affluent) members of society are still burdened by student loans, too.

DID I "MARRY" MY STUDENT LOANS WITHOUT REALIZING IT?

Well, it's a good way of looking at it. A lot of people tell me that's how they feel. Your student loans will be with you in sickness and in health, in most cases for the long haul.

What's most annoying about paying off student loans, along with other debt, is that the payment amounts are structured so that in the beginning, you are paying off mostly *interest*. Unless you're lucky enough to land a job with a big fat salary right out of the gate, it'll probably be a few years before you can afford to increase your payments to knock down some of the principal, too. So, when you're making diddly-squat, you're working your tush off without paying back what you *actually borrowed* in the first place.

All in all, you ultimately pay *two to three times* the principal you started with to finish off the loan. It's criminal, but that's a whole other book. For now, keep calm and outsmart the repayment process. And it's not always by throwing extra money you might have come into at your loans haphazardly. If you got a raise at work or inherited some money, congrats. So maybe you're thinking, "Time to get this student debt monkey off my back." (I like the way you're thinking.) But sometimes, this can bite you in the backside instead. Ramp up payments *only* if you're prepared to sustain that amount for a while, not just one beefy hit-and-run check. If you drastically increase payment from what you've paid in the past only to lower it again, this can look bad to the credit agencies. Not totally sure you *can* keep up with the higher payment? Go for a more manageable payment amount, one that you can stick to in the long-term. It might not feel as gratifying as taking a big bite out of your painful student debt loan, but in this case, slow and steady wins the race.

> **BITCH TIP** Student loans can't be eliminated if you file for bankruptcy (which you won't by the end of this book, but just sayin'). No matter what happens in your financial life, student loan debt will follow you around until the day you either pay it off or…die. The only other loans that fall into this special federal "no escape" category are debts from criminal acts and fraud. Including student debt in that category…now *that's* criminal.

SHOULD I CONSOLIDATE?

The idea of consolidating is simple: smoosh all your student loans into one single loan and one monthly payment. You may be tempted to consolidate your student loans all together in one payment, which makes life easier, but beware: loan consolidation isn't a magic cure-all. There are *a lot* of traps out there. A few words of caution if you *do* decide to go this route:

1. **Timing is everything.** If you can, wait until you've graduated before consolidating your student loans, but don't wait too long. Typically, you get a six-month grace period when you graduate before you have to start repaying your student loans. And that's where the sweet spot is: you can often get a lower interest rate for repayment if you consolidate during the grace period. Quick PS: if overall interest rates are high during your grace period sweet spot, it might be better to jump into paying (or trying your best to pay) right off the bat and then wait for rates to come down before considering consolidation.

2. **Lock in a fixed rate.** Regardless, once you decide to consolidate, you want to choose a plan that lets you have a fixed rate. That way, your budget doesn't hate you for having a different payment amount every single month. This can save you a ton of money in the future, especially if rates climb higher, and will make your monthly payments more predictable.

3. **Don't assume the advice you got from your college financial aid office was right.** Financial aid offices exist to make sure students find a way to pay for college, which is not the same as making sure you're doing what's best for you. They're really about doing what's best for the school. That's their obligation first and foremost.

4. **Don't get scammed.** Some "consolidation experts" (a.k.a. scammers) claim to be able to lower that monthly payment, so you're somehow paying less each month than before. This would be awesome...if it were true. What is true is that the "standard" consolidation fee that you're supposed to pay to cover processing and administrative costs can range from a few "low" payments of $29.99 up to several hundreds of dollars. Student loans are expensive enough. The last thing you want to do is pay even more than you need to.

If you *do* want to consolidate, DIY! After all, loan consolidation companies are charging you a fee for something you could just as easily do for free. The government's student loan portal, studentloans.gov (notice the .gov stamp of approval), allows you to consolidate your loans yourself for no charge. It takes about twenty minutes to apply, and this keeps *you* in the driver's seat. Stop saying you know nothing about this, because I promise people at these companies are not smarter than you are. In fact, if you assume they are and trust them, you could get caught up in even more of a mess. Their version of "consolidating" typically consists of moving one or all of your loans over to a private student loan with rates that might be worse than those you started out with. If you did your research ahead of time like a good Rich Bitch and hand-picked the loans with the best rates, there is simply no reason for putting those rates in jeopardy.

Moral of the story: with student loan consolidation, as with most things in life, you've got this. If you want it done right, do it *yourself.*

FORGIVE ME, FEDERAL GOVERNMENT, FOR I HAVE SINNED

If you are on the brink of not paying and going into default, don't give up so easily. Going into default means that money to pay for the loans can be taken out of your salary or taxes, and it becomes a black mark on your credit report. Check to see if you qualify for "forbearance," which gets you off the hook for paying the loans for a year without going into default. BUT, remember that interest will still be accruing during your payment hiatus, so do this only if you really need it due to an extreme financial hardship, like a serious illness.

If you've already missed payments and are in default, hope is not lost. You can qualify for "loan rehabilitation," in which the lender sets up a program for you based on your financial situation. If you stick to it for nine months, you get another chance. A clean slate: no *wage garnishments,** and defaulted status goes off your credit history. If you are getting grief from your lenders, ask to talk to their special assistance units.

If you are really in trouble, stop ignoring it and spring into action. I know you hate your lender's guts (I do, too), but you have to talk to them if you are in a really bad place. Feeling like David against a big, mean Student Loan Goliath is normal, but inaction because you lose one battle will make it harder for you to win the war.

BITCH TIP

Your job can pay in more ways than one. For instance, if you want to teach and end up at a low-income elementary school for five years or more, the government might pay off your loans. The program is called Teacher Loan Forgiveness, and you may be eligible to have up to $17,500 worth of loans paid back for you.

PRIVATE LENDERS DON'T HAVE MERCY

The payment options you could qualify for with federal loans don't translate to private loans. They have virtually no flexible repayment plans. And they are far more aggressive in getting their money back from you.

Private lenders will sic rabid debt collectors on you if you aren't paying. And your only option: take them on. You can't pretend like they don't exist, or they will sue you or take money out of your paycheck. Sure, they can be mean, and they can be scary, but all they want is to make a deal with you.

So while there is no official hardship plan, there is always an unofficial way to negotiate for yourself. It may make you sick to your stomach to haggle with these guys, but it's the only way to get yourself out of what could be credit score mud-dragging. And as much as you want to scream and yell at them—don't.

You'll get more from being calm, professional and armed with a potential solution. If you can swing a lump sum, they will usually take what they can get. Just remember that once you settle on a plan that includes paying your debt off as a lump sum, that's due right away, even within a few hours.

CONFESSIONS
OF A RICH BITCH

Paying with a broken heart

While you might be the one faced with a monthly headache when you write your student loan checks, the stress that comes along with debt can lead to heartache, too. More and more young people are drawing a hard line on getting married to someone who has a boatload of debt. After all, if it's nasty debt in your name before you're married, it's joint nasty debt after you're married.

I recently counseled a brilliant young woman who had been having a tough time in the dating world (for all of the reasons why it can be tough to date). But then she had encountered two different guys who had potential—who then bailed on her when she told them about the $100,000 in student debt she had after finishing her PhD.

You might be thinking: "What jerks!" And, yes, that's probably true. But, to their credit, they split early on because they didn't want the burden of the loan baggage she was carrying. They knew what they wanted and what they didn't want. Some guys draw the line at having a child from another marriage or belonging to a particular political party. For these guys, it was debt. It might be sad to hear about, but I don't actually fault them. What would you do if the tables were turned and you worked so hard at getting your own financial you-know-what together, only to meet a guy who would put you back in the hole? There's no right answer...but think about whether you would continue dating, or if it would be a deal-breaker.

THE CAR OR THE HOUSE?

You probably know by now that my preference is, if you can't pay cash for a car, buy a used one dirt cheap instead of leasing one, and to rent your home instead of buying. But let's say it works for you to buy both. Fine, so that means the monthly payments for them will go into the Essentials part of your Spending Plan (and just a warning: you will have a debt load monkey hovering over you, constantly nagging you to be fed).

While you should be prioritizing your debt by interest rate, and car loan rates tend to be higher than student loans, they should also move up the list because cars are a "depreciating asset"—the longer you wait, the more their value goes down, and the more ridiculous it is to be spending more interest paying it off. Because a car depreciates faster than a home, most people choose to tackle their car loans first. Also, these days, car loans have taken precedence because people know they have plenty of options to rent if they get kicked out of their house but in many places don't have the option of *not* having a car.

Another reason mortgage debt is usually last on the list is that the interest you pay on it is tax deductible. This isn't always a truism (what in finance *is*?) but IF you have, say, 20% equity in your home and are meeting your bills adequately, you probably want to make sure you're saving for the Endgame, à la retirement, which we will get to in Step 9, before you pay down mortgage debt. That's because the interest you're *saving* by getting the mortgage monkey off your back is likely not as much as what you can *earn* in a retirement account over a long period. Now, if you have plenty of cash at the ready, by all means go to town with paying down mortgage debt, but if you don't, you should accumulate an emergency fund (Step 7) first. After all, you can't pay for your groceries with equity in your house.

Also, keep in mind: while the extra you pay toward the debt load will lessen the *total* interest you pay and the time 'til repayment is complete, it won't lessen the monthly payment.

BITCH TIP

Refinancing is just a fancy word for negotiating a lower rate on your mortgage. The idea is to go to your bank and figure out a good give-and-take to make your mortgage repayment plan advantageous for you *and* for them. You might consider refinancing your mortgage if interest rates drop significantly below what you're currently paying. It's the same kind of feeling you get when you just bought something at full price and then the item goes on sale.

If you've got good credit and make your mortgage payments on time, you should be able to lock in a lower rate for the rest of your mortgage duration. Ideally, going through a good refinancing—or "refi" for short—will reduce your monthly payments and possibly save you money if you do it at the right time. However, keep these two things in mind:

1. **It can be as big a pain in the butt** paperwork-wise as getting the mortgage in the first place.

2. **There may also be substantial closing costs,** just as there were when you first got the

mortgage (see Step 4). Be sure to ask about all the costs involved, because it may turn out that the money you save by getting a lower interest rate will be reduced, or even wiped out, by those costs. For example, if you reduce your monthly payments by $100, but closing costs are $3,000, it's going to take thirty months to break even. Only then will you start saving money. So you want to be sure the interest you're saving is enough to make the refi money you are spending worthwhile.

And although it might seem counterproductive, in some cases it may still be worth refinancing even if your monthly payment goes up, if you are cutting down your total payoff period.

WHY DO YOU HAVE SO MUCH DEBT, ANYWAY?

You can come up with the most badass plan to pulverize your debt, but what good is it if you don't break the cycle?

This brings us to another serious question: *are you a debt addict? or a debtaholic?* (This is a serious thing, by the way.) If you're having a hard time sticking to your Spending Plan and continually revert to bad habits, the answer may be yes. Beyond not being able to live without plastic, here are some of the telltale signs:

1. **You spend money when you're emotional.** This doesn't just mean when you're upset or angry (although who hasn't engaged in a little retail therapy?) but also when you're happy. No matter your mood, buying new things makes you feel better, just like emotional eating is a nasty

cycle. Much like people who eat to suppress or celebrate their feelings, those who spend when they're emotional are at risk for larger issues. Small indulgences like your morning latte are one thing; stick to those harmless pick-me-ups so you don't blow your money on something more expensive in the heat of the moment. Those same feelings that you might be trying to suppress by spending often lead to additional feelings of stress and anxiety. Chances are that when you go on a spending binge, the results are more costly than you expected—which will only lead to more of an emotional roller coaster ride.

2. **You don't know when to stop.** There's a big difference between going to the store and buying one DVD and going to the store and buying ten. If you're the kind of person who can't walk down a five-for-one aisle without stocking up, this one's for you. Compulsive spenders do not know how to set limits or differentiate between necessity and desire. These kinds of spenders buy on impulse instead of reason. Remember: if something is offered at a discount for buying in bulk, the price per item is usually the same, and just because it's on sale doesn't mean it's cheap. At the end of the shopping trip, you're not actually getting more of a deal by purchasing five jars of jam when you need only one. Ask yourself if you really need that item, or if it's just a want. Better yet, try walking away without buying it, and if in a week you still want it, then go back. I can guarantee that most of those impulse items will be forgotten soon after you leave the store.

3. **You are a subscription junkie.** Come clean: how many monthly memberships do you have? You have a gym membership? Tea of the Month Club? Really? The *New York Times* subscription? A tanning membership? Netflix? BarkBox? Birchbox? Think hard. If you're using

and loving it, fine. But if not, get rid of it. Monthly sign-ups are the biggest culprit of budget shortfalls. "Oh, yeah," people say to me, "I totally forgot that Fast Pass or the Harry & David thing I signed my grandma up for." Duh, that's why your balance sheet doesn't add up. Think long and hard before you take on a recurring financial responsibility, even if it's a small amount per month. Chances are, you'll forget that you even have the subscription. It is indeed easy to forget about these $10/$20/$30 monthly obligations, especially if they are random and you're not actively using them! Or, if you're like me, you'll get lazy and annoyed by the process of canceling them later on. Companies make it difficult to opt out for a reason.

BITCH TIP

You know how it goes: you're shopping around online and find, say, a super cute pair of shoes. You might click "add to cart," but you don't buy them right away, because you're a smart bitch who knows to avoid impulse spending. But then that same pair of shoes follows you all around the internet, thanks to targeted advertising. No, it's not a sixth sense that advertisers have: when you shop around online, you leave a trail of "cookies" behind you everywhere you go. Advertisers pick up on this cookie trail so they can suggest items to you that they already know you love and hope you'll buy. Resist the temptation by cleaning up your cyber-crumbs, and *delete those cookies*! It will be a lot easier to avoid splurging if you aren't faced with that super cute pair of shoes at every online turn.

How you spend depends in large part on the way you are raised and the mores you've grown accustomed to along the way. And like with many personal habits, you often don't think about what you're doing—it's just what you do. Well, wake up. You're not a kid anymore. Your parents aren't your examples. There's no dumb peer pressure from friends. It's just you. So put on your big-girl undies and break the cycle. Start thinking for yourself and your best interests. It's time to realize that there's no one else to blame or answer to but *you*.

DON'T GET *TOO* CREATIVE WITH DEBT REPAYMENT

Life can feel chaotic when you are struggling with debt. And who do you normally turn to in times of chaos? Your friends. They're always supposed to be there for you, right? Well, emotionally, yes. But financially? Proceed at your own risk. There are few things that can strain a relationship as much as money. It's one thing to piss off your creditor, but quite another to put out someone you care about.

"Before borrowing money from a friend, decide what you need most." I'm obsessed with that proverb because it reflects the reality of what ends up happening most of the time when you borrow from family and friends. It is tempting, since after all, they're the ones who've got your back no matter what, right? Chances are, for that reason, they'll give it to you. You think, "I'd do it for them." But if you can avoid it on both ends, the giving and the taking, do.

CONFESSIONS
OF A RICH BITCH

Pay me back, bitch!

When I was a green reporter making below minimum wage, I borrowed $400 from a close friend to buy a dining table. I didn't have one and sitting on the floor with questionably sanitary Thai takeout and a bottle of Two Buck Chuck ($2 wine from Trader Joe's) became depressing. I promised to pay it back in two months, but it took four months (I wasn't willing to give up my cheap wine for my own sanity). Well, I did pay it back, but it was beyond awkward until I did. Ten years later my friend still gives me a hard time about it. I mean, please. Who wants to be the butt-end of that joke forever? Not me. And not you.

"Needing money" from anyone can put a knot in your stomach, for sure. It's uncomfortable and makes you feel beyond vulnerable if you're asking someone you know. But, beyond feeling awkward, you could get doubly screwed by hurting your relationships in addition to your money. However, I understand that there are some instances in which you really want to help someone you care about; after all, you *are* the Good Bitch. Or maybe you've already gotten yourself into a bind with lending money, and now need to get out of it. So: how do you get your loved ones to cough it up without compromising your relationship? Try this:

1. **Talk in person.** Don't text, email, or call; it's all too easy for faceless communication to be taken the wrong way. And she will have a harder time avoiding you face-to-face.

2. **Be specific.** Chances are, she doesn't even remember that she owes you money, or the specific amount. Regardless, don't leave room for doubt by asking: "When do you think you'll be able to pay back the $100 that I lent you?" You've named the specific amount, so you're on the same page with what she owes, and you've asked for a specific timeline so you can hold her to it.

3. **Set a deadline.** Some people need multiple reminders. That's life. If she doesn't pay you back right away, set a firm deadline for paying you back. Soften the ultimatum by referring to an upcoming event, such as, "You know, with my vacation coming up, I could really use that money I lent you. Could you please pay me back by Friday?"

4. **Offer flexibility.** If your friend is having a hard time paying you back, or if the amount she owes you is more substantial, offer to break the repayment into smaller chunks.

5. **Pick your battles.** Sometimes you have to decide what's more important: getting your money back or remaining on good terms with your friend. If it's a small amount, say $10 for cab fare, and you're in the financial position to do so, let it go. It's annoying, but pestering her over and over again could cause a rift in the relationship.

You've probably seen the neon signs on those sketchy-looking places offering payday loans and tax refund loans, also known as "cash advances." The signs flash things like "LOWEST RATES," "NO CREDIT CHECK," and, of course, "CASH." Don't be blinded by the lights; these are absolutely scams.

> The idea of these sketchy places is that they give you a small loan ahead of your next paycheck…but between now and then they charge you *absurdly* high interest rates. And if you defer (which many people do: they have a 10% to 20% default rate, much higher than most other types of debt), those rates only jump even higher. Don't use these. Ever. Period. End of story.

Yes, paying off debt is the worst. I know. I did it, and trust me, I hated it. Putting aside a couple hundred bucks every month isn't easy, especially when it feels like you've got nothing to show for it. I hear you. But carrying debt will mess up your situation a lot longer, and a lot more painfully, than sucking it up and taking care of it now. Even as you're sitting there reading this, your debt, if you have it, is quietly growing…and growing… and growing.

Seriously, if you're going to do something crazy like spend $40 on a pair of friggin' socks, then they better be worth $40. Don't spend $40 over time, though, on something that's supposed to cost you $10! That's for naïve bitches or dummies, and you are neither—you're a Rich Bitch.

BOTTOM LINE

Conventional wisdom: Debt is good to build credit.

Nope. Building up your credit history, so that you can get the lowest rate on a mortgage or other loan *if you absolutely have to take one*—yep, that's good. But owing someone money just for the sake of it? That may be the American way, but it's just throwing away your money…to a bank, of all places. Wouldn't you rather throw your money at something you can actually use?

Conventional wisdom: You can't negotiate your credit card rate.

Total BS. This is another instance of my favorite saying: "It can't hurt to ask." If your interest rate is higher than average, or even just higher than you think it should be, call the credit card company. Many will lower your rate if it means keeping a (good) customer.

STEP

7

LOCK IT UP

Saving Sucks but So Does Being Broke

THE ENDGAME

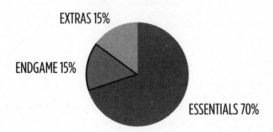

EXTRAS 15%

ENDGAME 15%

ESSENTIALS 70%

S hit happens. One of the following will more than likely happen to you during your lifetime: you lose a job, you change a job, you have to quit a job, you have an illness, someone in your family has an illness. Not to be the grim reaper, but you would be totally delusional if you thought everything in your life was going to go as planned. It's not. And you would be even more delusional if you didn't plan for the doomsday scenario by saving for what's likely the *inevitable*—which you should start thinking of as the *evitable*.

You wanna be a Rich Bitch for life? You gotta protect yourself.

HOW MUCH CASH SHOULD I STASH?

By cash, I don't mean the physical paper like I thought in my naïve years; I mean money that's available to you if you aren't making money but still have to pay for stuff like rent, food and transportation. Think about it: if you lose your job, you can't pay for your groceries with an asset like a boat. Although that boat would be valuable if you sold it for cash, it's not cash now and would likely take too long to turn into cash if you were in desperate need. (Plus, it's never a good idea to sell stuff when you are desperate.)

So you need some cash squirreled away. A doomsday fund, a treasure chest, an "oh, crap" fund, a "break in case of emergency" fund. Whatever you want to call it, you need one. Do it now. You need one before you do *anything* else with your money. Before the fancy stuff, like investing (which we will get to in Step 10). Yes, even before putting money in a 401(k) (we will get to that in Step 9). Again, can you pay for groceries with those things? No.

You're probably wondering, "How much we talkin' here, Lapin?"

Well, a good rule of thumb is have three to six months of living expenses readily accessible, which you can easily figure out now that you've worked out your Spending Plan in Steps 3 and 4. When I say three months, that's only if you have a steady job with a steady paystub, say in an office or in a trade or service industry, and feel confident that you can always get work if, God forbid, shit happens. Otherwise I'm going to suggest strongly that you tuck away six months of whatever money you need to live on. This is especially true if you have less secure employment or less steady pay, à la bartenders, waitresses and freelancers.

Then you really should build up more cash, ideally nine months. If you work mostly on commission, like real estate brokers or salespeople, you're probably going to need more reserves—a year is probably a better number for you.

Again, we are talking about just the basics here: enough to cover bills to live, eat and transport yourself from A to B. My hope is that you don't need a new dress when you are dealing with bigger, more important stuff. So just the basics, dah-ling.

WHEN IT RAINS, IT POURS

As you are building your rainy day fund, you also have to take into consideration the fact that lightning could strike twice. Let's face it, bad things always seem like they happen all at once, so should you find yourself in this situation, I don't want to hear you say, "Urgh, Lapin, my finances are screwed. How could I ever have imagined [insert terrible thing here] would happen! Oh, well, I tried." Okay…no. You *can* prepare for [insert terrible thing here] if you just look at your spending habits over time. Never imagined you would get your car towed? Oh, it happened last year, too? It was $120? Well that's $10/month for you to wrap your mind around.

Here are a few things to think about tucking aside in addition to your super basic housing, food and transportation needs:

- **Medical expenses.** The leading cause of personal bankruptcy is medical bills—even if you have insurance! If you're generally healthy, you still might want to account for health expenses that might come up. Got a $2,500 deductible on your health insurance policy? Try to set that aside, too, plus whatever your total annual out-of-pocket expenses might be. Let's say you get an annual physical and two dental cleanings. You can check your policy to figure out how much the co-pays per visit are, which can be anywhere from zero to $50 or more, depending on the kind of policy you have. Some policies require you to meet a deductible before coverage starts, which means you could be responsible for the entire bill until you hit that number. And know whether your health insurance deductible makes you eligible for a high-deductible *health savings account*,* which allows you to put money away tax-free to cover health expenses that aren't covered by insurance. If you don't use the money in any given year, yippee, you don't lose it. You can keep adding to it, and it keeps accruing interest—yes, tax-free.

- **Car issues.** Sure, you're already accounting for upkeep and insurance and gas, ideally, in your Spending Plan, so that should be factored into the amount you are stashing. BUT, what if BOOM! someone T-bones you at an intersection and now you've got to come up with your thousand-dollar deductible. Maybe you bust a rim or two in a pothole. Whatever happened to your ride, car issues are beyond costly. (Like the time I busted the side mirror off my car backing out of the garage...not once but twice. In the same week. Sad but true. Like I said, bad things seem to occur at the same time.) It's wise to think about a special "I busted my ride" fund in addition to the normal car upkeep in case you aren't making regular money.

- **Family.** Say (God forbid) your mom breaks her leg and she needs help around the house for a few days (or weeks). Even if your company allows family leave, chances are you're not getting paid for it. Do you have enough cash to cover you while you're not at work? Sorry, but you have got to think about that kind of stuff—and even if you don't want to think about it, you still need to plan for it.

- **Home expenses.** If you own your own home, you'll need to keep maintenance expenses on hand—annual chimney cleaning, mucking out the gutters, paying the neighbor's kid to mow your lawn, all the fun stuff that's probably not in your Spending Plan. Water heaters, roofs, furnaces, windows—things always need replacing. (A friend of mine describes it like this: when you buy a house, you might as well lie down by the front door with your wallet open on your chest and a sign that reads "Help Yourself.") This can be a double-edged sword, though. If you dumped everything into your house without focusing on saving for other areas, are you going to have to sell it or risk losing the house and everything you invested to *foreclosure** (when the bank takes your house away because you can't make payments) if you need cash in case of a nonhousing-related emergency?

- **Freak of nature occurrences.** A parking ticket, stolen bike, computer died... Life sucks sometimes. But weird stuff happens. I usually estimate about $250 per year for that stuff that makes me go, "Seriously? Why me?"

CONFESSIONS
OF A RICH BITCH

The $300 rule

My friend recently bought his first house, and he and his wife told me that they've got a running joke they dubbed "The $300 rule": everything that the house requires costs $300. Broken tile? $300. Plumbing problem? That will be $300, too. Hose replacement? You guessed it. They are now convinced there is a secret $300 society that homeowners are forced to join when they buy.

BITCH TIP

Once you figure out the categories of extra savings you might need, open up "subsavings" accounts within your savings account. That way, when you log in to your online banking you can read the label of what you're covering yourself for, so you don't have to stress about where that money went later.

For example, I happen to drop my phone...a lot. I hope you aren't the same klutz I am, because it's an expensive habit. Yep, I have a subsavings account in my bank account called "Nicole's iPhone Screen Fund." I wanted to have $240 in that account for if (when) I crack my screen again. So I set up an automated system that takes $20 from my account every month and puts it in my "Nicole's iPhone Screen Fund" account. Who cares what the online bank techies think if they see that account name? I like knowing that it's there for me to get my butterfingers on the next time I need it.

I know all this saving for a rainy day stuff is a drag. But let's say you look outside, see the sun shining, and decide, "To heck with being safe. I'm leaving my umbrella at home!" Instead, you think, "I'm gonna go buy a new laptop!" Then, whammo: the shit storm! You lose your job, can't find another one that pays the same, or another one at all, and then what? Is that laptop going to pay your subway fare? Is it going to pay your rent or your mortgage? I. Don't. Think. So.

CONFESSIONS
OF A RICH BITCH

When it's time to break up (with your bank)

When I first started saving, I did it automatically. I took $500 out of my salary and told my bank to stick it into my savings account automatically. If you don't see it coming out, it doesn't feel as bad, right? For me, that was a huge step in becoming a responsible adult. But it was a *first* step.

On the plus side: my money was safe from me spending it on a whim, which would have happened were it still in my checking account. So I felt good about that.

On the flipside: I was accepting a crappy 0.1% interest rate and thought it was awesome because it was better than nada. In hindsight, I'm pissed at myself because I missed out on my favorite money tool of them all: *compound interest*.* At 0.1%, it would take over a thousand years to double my money. A MILLENNIUM. Seriously.

Then I talked to the lady at my bank. By the way, it was a community bank down the street from where I lived. I loved the fact that I had a "lady"; her name was Ruth, and it made me feel better that I could talk to her in person. It was comforting. I talked to Ruth about "graduating" to a better investment than my savings account. So I bought a 1-year certificate of deposit (CD). The rate was a whopping 0.25%. Hey, it was way more than my 0.1%. Now I would double my money in almost 300 years. Better than a millennium! (Oh, the lies we tell ourselves, but I digress.)

In order to make better savings choices today, my first step was not a shameful one; it was just my first one. I love Ruth. She's always gonna be my girl—but we needed to break up, and I needed to trade up.

POP QUIZ!

Let's say you're bringing in $5,000 clean each month (for easy math). You've made a commitment that you are going to save 15% of that, which is 750 bucks a month. But where do you put this savings?

A. Under the mattress/somewhere in your house in actual green cash

B. In a savings account

C. In a CD

D. In a retirement account (get ready for this in Step 9)

E. Educational/health accounts

F. All of the above

If you guessed F, you are correct-a-mundo! It's a combination. A mix-and-match of all of them—yes, even the cash one (I'm still a fan of having a little emergency cash). I'll tell you how I've done it—the successes *and* the failures. The failures are always more fun to read about anyway.

WHERE TO PARK IT

I'm going to be honest with you. This part isn't sexy. There hasn't been a lot of innovation in the finance world for saving money. But sometimes, the tried and true works.

Cash: Famous economists might revolt in the streets when I say this, but I am still a fan of having *some* green cash in your house. Why? Because at the end of the day, you can't get more liquid than cold hard cash. No matter what happens to the banks, the stock market, or your own credit/debit cards, you can always rely on a little cash on hand. I'd say a couple hundred bucks is a good amount to keep on hand; it's not so much that it's a major liability to be stolen, but it just feels like enough to cover many emergency situations (like having your car towed before work, or getting by for a week after losing your debit card).

Savings accounts: You're not going to get rich by putting your money in a savings account—but it will be there and be accessible. I find that the physical separation from your checking account is often enough to keep your savings in…savings.

The rates are insanely low at the time of this writing, around 0.25% (although if you dig hard enough, there are still some 1% high-yield accounts out there), so don't expect to make bank (pun intended) here. The rates are calculated in a way similar to the way APR rates for credit cards that we talked about in Step 6 are calculated, but in reverse. When you are making money from the glorious force that is compounding interest, it is called *APY*.*

Let's say you put $10,000 in the bank at 2% APY. After year one, you will make $200 in interest, for a new total of $10,000 + $200 = $10,200. After year two, you will make 2% off $10,200, which is $204 (for a new total of $10,200 + $204 = $10,404) and the next year, you will make 2% off $10,404. And so on.

Again, this is the concept of your interest making interest. When it comes to borrowing money, we hate this concept. When it comes to making money, we love it.

Where do you start when you are looking to open an account? Here are some steps you should take:

1. **Look at the three different places you can get savings accounts and see which one you feel comfortable with: credit unions, regular banks and online banks.** If you need a "Ruth" like I had, then online banks probably aren't right

for you. But if you don't crave one-on-one interaction, I would strongly suggest an online bank. They don't have the overhead of brick-and-mortar banks and can thus pass those savings on to you in the form of better rates. I for one care much more about a higher APY than free peppermint patties in the bank lobby. You should try to get a savings account at a totally different bank from the one where you have your regular checking account so that you'll be less tempted to transfer money from your savings to your checking just because it's easy.

2. **The top two perks you should look for are free transfers between checking and savings (for the times you legitimately *need* to transfer) and the ability to make subaccounts like I talked about previously.**

3. **Hunt down the highest APY.** Online banks tend to have the highest rate because, as I mentioned, they have lower overhead costs than traditional banks. The most popular ones are Capital One 360 and Ally.

4. **Look into special promotions.** Some banks offer bonuses for new customers, like $100 cash back if you deposit a certain amount. I've seen other wacky ones like concert tickets or an entry to win a new car.

5. **Find out how tech-tastic they are.** Do they offer online banking or mobile options like a check depositing app? Most big banks have the basics, but if you are a gadget girl, you might be into a bank that has the latest and greatest.

6. **Think ahead and know the process for shutting down an account.** You never know why you might need to close an account, so you should know what to expect. Some banks make you pay an early termination fee if you close the account between 90 and 180 days of opening it.

7. **I'd bet that the options you are looking at are insured, but just double-check.** In case something happens to the bank, you want to make sure your money is safe. The *Federal Deposit Insurance Corporation (FDIC)** insures banks, and the National Credit Union Share Insurance Fund (NCUSIF) insures credit unions

8. **Open the account!**

9. **Don't sign up for overdraft protection.** I talked briefly about this in Step 6. By law, you now have to opt in if you want to have the bank cover an overdraft charge when you don't have money in your account to pay for your purchase—and then, of course, they charge you a fee. Don't do this. If you don't have the money, you'll likely not have enough to pay the fee. Even if you do, the principle of overdraft protection doesn't sit well with me. It's basically a quickie loan to you in exchange for an exorbitant fee. It might be embarrassing in the line for coffee when your card doesn't go through, but a $35 fee for that $2 Danish just ain't right. If you're spending $37 for a Danish, it had better be for several dozen of them.

BITCH TIP

The FDIC guarantees all deposits up to $250,000 per account, and twice that for joint accounts. (Note: this applies only to checking, savings, CDs and money market accounts.) If you're lucky enough to have to worry about that limit, keep your balances under it, which is easily accomplished by spreading money around to different banks.

Bonus Bitch Tip: If you have the high-class problem of having even more money, like $750,000, instead of spreading your own money around willy-nilly to try to keep your FDIC protection in check, sign up for a program called the Certificate of Deposit Account Registry Service (CDARS), which is comprised of a network of banks and spreads the wealth around for you. Literally.

Money market account: A money market account, or MMA, is like a savings account on steroids. Because this type of account requires a higher minimum balance (typically from $1,000 to $10,000 or more) than a savings account, MMAs tend to offer better interest rates, usually double that of a traditional savings account (although with interest rates being so low right now, there isn't much of a difference). However, they are less liquid (a.k.a. available to you) than a standard savings account because they limit the number of withdrawals you can make (typically monthly or yearly). I happen to like the lockup period aspect of MMAs because it keeps your temptation to withdraw in check. You'll find these accounts at traditional banks. Online banks usually offer high-yield savings accounts in place of the MMA, which is basically the same thing without the lockup or minimum balance.

Certificates of deposit: The difference between a CD and a regular ol' savings account is that a CD comes with a fixed term (the length of time you can't touch the thing; one, three and five years are common) and a fixed interest rate (the amount you earn gets higher with the longer CDs). Typically, they give you a *little bit* of a better interest rate than a regular savings account. If you must, you *can* withdraw sooner, but of course, you gotta kiss the extra interest buh-bye. So don't get a CD if you think you are going to withdraw early, because the penalty fee will likely just cancel out the smidge of extra interest you were getting anyway.

College savings: Got kids? Got sweaty palms thinking about paying for them to go to college? Well, yeah, because it's estimated that college costs eighteen years from now (for those who just had a baby or are thinking about it) will be $361,000 for private schools and $100,000 for public. With that amount of money, a traditional savings account, MMA or CD definitely won't cut it (at 1% interest, you won't even keep up with inflation, which is around 3% a year on average, not to mention college costs are rising about 7% on top of that!). Say what you want about the college conversation—I don't think it's for everyone, but that's a whole other book—chances are your kids are going to *want* to go to college. If you don't want them to procrastinate with their schoolwork, then don't procrastinate paying for their school. What you need is a savings account for education. The big one is a 529 plan. Here's how it works:

1. **Get on the horn with one of the investment companies** (Fidelity, Vanguard, and T. Rowe Price are all well-known companies that offer 529 savings plans), perhaps one you've worked with in the past. Although, remember, brand loyalty does not always save you money so compare several for the best rate.

2. **529 plans are based by states and often have benefits for in-state residents.** Look into what your state's specific plan is. Once you've narrowed it down to a few plans that work for you, you can compare plans at savingforcollege.com.

3. **Do some comparison shopping; online is obviously fastest.** Then find your best deal.

4. **If you can, put money in up to the "gift tax amount" (currently $14,000 anually), which is the amount the IRS allows you to give to somebody without it being taxed as income for the recipient.** In this case, it's your kid. (Note, you can give up to five years' worth of contributions in one year, but then you have to sit on your hands until the five years are up before you can contribute again.)

5. **Name an owner of the account** (well, you), a beneficiary (the future student, a.k.a. your child) and a successor (in case something happens to you; typically this would be your kid's other parent or relative).

6. **Then your money grows tax-free until your munchkin goes to school.** As long as kids use the money for eligible college expenses, they pay no federal tax and usually no state tax.

You might be thinking, "Okay, Lapin, but I seriously don't know if my kid will even want to go to college." Well, guess what? If one of your kids doesn't need the money, you can use it for another or even for grandkids. Technically, you can name anyone a beneficiary—even a friend's kid or other non-relative—just keep in mind that any change of beneficiary must be made within the original beneficiary's family. So if your friend's kid doesn't use the plan, either, it would have to be reassigned to someone else in that friend's family. And, if this isn't your stage of life right now, I hear you, too: "Okay, Lapin, but I'm not a mom—let alone a GRAND-mom." Sure, but when and if you are, you'd be the coolest granny ever. All kidding aside, the benefits of seriously considering a 529 savings plan likely outweigh the incidence of your child opting out of higher education altogether. AND: if none of your offspring uses it, you can use the money to go back to school yourself.

Healthy savings: Paying an arm and a leg for your medical bills? (Bad pun absolutely intended.) You might want to take matters into your own hands before your financial health affects your mental health. The health savings account, or HSA, is a tax-advantaged health-care spending account that you might be into if you have an insurance policy with a high deductible.

Why do you care that it's tax-advantaged? Well, if you have a $100 out-of-pocket medical expense and you are in the 25% tax bracket, then you actually have to make $133.33 and pay $33.33 in taxes before you make $100. If this money comes out of your salary pretax, then you are keeping that $33.33 in your pocket. If you happen to have a lot of medical expenses and a high deductible, the tax love should really help.

Here's how to get one:

1. **Call the same place you got your savings account or your 529 plan.** Chances are they will also offer an HSA.

2. **Make sure your health insurance plan qualifies you.**

3. **Try to put money into the account up to the maximum allowed per year** (currently a little over $3,000) and pick a plan.

P.S. Don't confuse HSAs with flexible spending accounts, or FSAs. FSAs are run by your employer, and you can use the dough for co-pays, deductibles, and both prescription and over-the-counter drugs. It used to be, whatever you didn't spend in an FSA in the calendar year stayed with the company (annoying), but now employers can offer a grace period or rollover of up to $500 into the next year. If you have more than that you still lose it. All of the HSA money, however, rolls over from year to year for you (woo-hoo) even if you switch jobs. Even though HSAs and FSAs sound similar, they are not. I personally vote against

FSAs because I'm not down with giving my employer money if I don't spend it all.

GAH, TAXES!

Well, now you are saving money and ideally *making* money in interest. Hooray! It's not that much, with the measly interest rates offered by most banks, but it's something. And that means that that "something" is going to be taxed.

"Wait," you say, "savings are taxed? You mean I work, pay to live and pay tax and somehow am able to save some money, and some of what I make there is going to get taxed, too? WTF?!" Yeah...don't shoot the messenger.

Your savings, MMAs and CDs are "nonqualified" accounts or ones that get no tax love. So that means the little bit of extra money you are making in these accounts is taxed just like it would be if it were tacked onto your paycheck (which makes the minuscule interest rate you got in the first place even smaller).

The 529 plan and HSA are known as "qualified accounts" or those that *do* get tax love. So you aren't taxed on what you make on those, unless you withdraw for something other than what it was intended for. (There are more of these kinds of tax-loved accounts like IRAs coming up in Step 9, so get excited.)

TAXES, SHMAXES

Face it, taxes are complicated. Like, *really* complicated. The current federal tax code is more than 70,000 pages long! And each state has different tax rules as well. Then there are exceptions to the rules and rules to the exceptions. It's truly enough to make you want to poke your pretty eyes out.

So does that mean you need to hire an accountant? Well, that depends on how complicated your financial life is.

If you're single or married but don't own a home or have kids, and your only income is the salary from your job and maybe some interest from savings, you can probably prepare your own taxes. Even if your life is a little more complicated—say, you're married, have a newborn, own a home, have investments, or run your own business—you can likely do it yourself with a program like TurboTax or TaxACT (which you can download right from their website and you'll only be out the cost of the software). The price to prep your taxes with these programs varies depending on how complicated your taxes are, ranging from simple individual to small business owner; and remember, you'll need to file federal taxes *and* taxes for whichever state you live in. (If you live in one state and work in another, you many need to file returns in both states; it's an extra paperwork hassle, but you do get credit in your home state for anything you pay to your "work state," so you're not paying double taxes.)

I suggest spending the money for the software. That way you won't have to deal with delays on your tax return because something was filed incorrectly. Plus, the "free interactive tax assistant" on the IRS website will probably make you want to break your computer...and that will be more costly.

If you're not into the DIY idea for your taxes, or stuff gets complicated, sure, you can go to a pro. But think of it as going to a personal fitness trainer. Like working out with a trainer, you have a few options. You can do the following:

- **Turn yourself over completely and have your trainer/ accountant tell you exactly what to do.** This option will cost you some coin (albeit tax-deductible coin): according to the National Society of Accountants (I'll bet they have the best parties over there), the average cost in 2013 to prepare a Form 1040 plus state return was about $150 and with itemized deductions about $260. Also, you don't really learn anything by going this route...and you know how I feel about giving up your financial autonomy.

OR

- **Meet with your trainer/accountant once or twice and have her walk you through the basics of filing so you can do it yourself.** This option is a lot cheaper *and* you get the benefit of understanding how your taxes work, so you can make the most of them. You can always check back in with your accountant down the road if your situation has changed, or just to make sure you're doing things right—just like you would with your personal trainer.

- **Storefront accountants** like H&R Block (they have a software, too), Jackson Hewitt and Liberty Tax Service have offices all over the country. These guys get the job done for super basic stuff. The name-brand locations are also less likely to hit you with document fees or application fees (which you shouldn't have to pay) than the independent, no-name brand storefronts.
- **I bet you've heard of a CPA, certified public accountant.** These folks are tax wizards, but they do all things accounting, not just income tax. If you want to explore this option, I honestly think the best way is to ask someone you trust—a friend, business colleague, your

> boss—for a recommendation for a good CPA, preferably one they've used before and have been happy with.
>
> - **I like the option of trying to find an EA, or an enrolled agent.** They focus only on tax prep and resolutions, unlike CPAs, who cover a broader spectrum of tax matters. So if you have more complicated taxes but don't run a business that needs payroll, etc., this could be a perfect fit. If you don't know anyone with EA recommendations, just type "find an enrolled agent" and your location into your browser and start there.

I love the Endgame because of the Samuel Beckett play of the same name, *Endgame*. I am a nerd, as you know, and it's not only limited to finance. The play is in the theater of the absurd style, which always seems fitting for virtually anything in my life. In the play, there is a line that says, "Old endgame lost of old, play and lose and have done with losing."

I love this line because it embodies what I wanted to share with you in this section. Be done losing. Whether it's losing out on savings plans or an opportunity to invest in your kids' education or your health...stop. I lost out on years of investment opportunities by thinking CDs were the investment world's Shangri-la. I played that *old endgame*, like in the quote. I'm happy I played, but I lost. Now I'm done losing. You should be, too.

BOTTOM LINE

Conventional wisdom: There's no safe place for your money, so keep it in cash.

Half true. True, because there are no guarantees in this world. False, because cash is a lousy place for your long-term money. As of this writing, had you put money in the stock market 10 years ago, you'd have doubled your money today (we will talk about investing your brains out in Step 10), even given the horrendous years we lived through during that time. Over the same period, savings accounts have grown about 18%, which is not quite at the rate of inflation over the period. That means if you put your money in savings accounts over that scary period, you would have lost *purchasing power*,* or in other words, your money 10 years ago wouldn't have gotten you as much today.

Conventional wisdom: Your local bank will offer you the best rate simply because, obviously, you're their favorite customer.

Nope, sorry. Loyalty in this case doesn't necessarily pay off. As with everything else we've talked about so far, shop around for the best rates. You can always go back to your personal banker and tell her you can do better elsewhere and see if she'll step up to match or better that other offer. Otherwise, bounce. It's business, bitches.

STEP

8

WORK IT, BITCHES

Put Your Career in Overdrive

At this point, we've come up with a pretty solid financial plan, right down to an "oh, crap" fund that's there if the unthinkable happens. But the Endgame is also about the *thinkable*: namely, the career goals you've outlined for yourself in Step 2. Until now, you've dealt with your income as if it is what it is and always will be. And that might be good enough for some folks, but certainly not for a Rich Bitch.

What your Endgame is going to cost you:

- 15% of your monthly paycheck
- Six to nine months of expenses
  (more if you plan to start a business!)

Now we are going to shift our focus to *making more money*, because if you up the money you make, you don't have to stress as much about saving every last penny because you will, um, have more money. Before we zero in on investments, which we will talk about in Steps 9 and 10, we are going to focus on investing in *yourself*. I always say that investing in yourself will pay the most dividends later on. After all, true optimists don't see the glass as half full. They see it as *completely* full. In this step, we'll look at how you can up your career game to reach your fullest potential. This can translate into more income or just more satisfaction or both. Hopefully both.

BITCH TIP

Those other "financial experts" will tell you to give up your daily coffee shop run and save more than $1,500 per year. But I say: Think of yourself as having billable hours, like a lawyer. Whatever it is—$20/hour or $500 like a lawyer— your time is extremely valuable. So go ahead, buy your $5 morning latte. You can even buy it every morning, if you want to. Let's go on the low end and say that you value your time at $20/hour; that's one-quarter of an hour, or 15 minutes. To save that $5, you could waste more time and aggravation by making your coffee yourself at home. Whereas, if you just stop on your way to work, you'll get into the office earlier, plus you'll have more energy which gives you a leg up on productivity, so you'll work harder and then bam! You might just get a bonus at the end of the year that is even bigger than the $1,500 you could have saved, not to mention benefiting from the less tangible opportunities at work that are worth even more than that.

I hear it all the time: $5 a day for 40 years will earn you close to $1 million if you manage to get a return of

10%. But remember: not drinking coffee doesn't mean you will become a millionaire automatically. Cutting it out doesn't mean you won't spend that money elsewhere.

Keep in mind, in the end, money is there to enjoy. It's not worth your valuable time to get overly bogged down in the small expenses. A financial diet is like a regular diet: crash-dieting rarely works, and only leads to binging. Allow yourself the small indulgences—lattes, lipstick, a Netflix subscription—while keeping an eye on the bigger picture.

BE THE CEO OF YOU, INC.

Let's start with your vision. You've already made a list of your goals, but when it comes to career, you've got to get specific about what you really want. I promise, that's the hardest part. You want to move up in the company you're working for? Run it? Move to a different firm? Which type? Try a different career? Like what? Start your own business? And what does that business do?

Whatever it is, figure it out and write it down with as many details as possible, because "success" isn't a specific enough goal. You need a specific destination so you can get there. It's like saying "I'm going to a party in Los Angeles." Okay...but where? What's the exact street? What's the exact address? Once you have that, you can break your journey down into smaller steps.

Once you have your specific goal in mind, you need to ask yourself a simple question: do I *know enough* to get there? Chances are, you don't—and now is the time to admit it. You're likely going to start there. I did. It's okay to not know something only if you *know* you don't know it—and cop to that honestly. The only thing worse than being dumb is being dumb and delusional. It's endearing to stay idealistic and foolish; it's not cute to be totally out of touch with reality. Realize that this is a learning and growing process. You're not the first to go through it and certainly won't be the last.

BE A BOSS

Lots of people are dissatisfied with their careers and feel they'd be better off braving it on their own. We live in a new normal, and the new normal is not so pretty: job uncertainty, financial uncertainty, pay cuts, furloughs. With the jobs picture so bleak, I hear from many people that they would rather get paid in happiness. The recession made us realize that we can follow our passions and make money without putting much initial money into it. Maybe it's a conscious choice, or maybe it's the result of a layoff or other job loss that's given you the itch. Whatever the impetus, I think we have all seen that the traditional American dream—2.5 kids, a white picket fence and a pension fund—is dead. But yours isn't. Now it's Your Dream, your destiny. At the end of the day, the only life worth living is the one you're proud of. And, of course it sounds cliché, but life's too short not to dream about the "what if" if the "what if" can make sense for you.

Entrepreneurship has become part of our culture, our zeitgeist. It seems like *everyone's* starting their own thing. People look at the new billionaire tech founders and say, "I can do that." Small business resources online have democratized entrepreneurship.

Everyone can have their own business card, everyone can have their own domain, everyone can have their own virtual assistant. And those things are great! It's easier now than ever to go into business for yourself, at a time when job frustration is at a fever pitch.

Still, that doesn't mean you're cut out for the task. So let's figure out whether it's right for you and set you on the right path.

BOSS QUIZ

Do you:

A. Hate your job?

B. Not have a job?

C. Have this great idea for a business?

D. Feel like you're just not the type who works well for someone else?

It's likely that at least one of these has applied to you at some point, and if they haven't yet—I bet they will. I have claimed all of these things to be true at one point or another in my career. So maybe you're feeling like I once did, like you want to be the next [insert your passion here] mogul. You look at companies like Facebook and Instagram and you think, "I can do *that*!" Or you look at less tech-y companies like Spanx or Drybar and think, "I can do *that*!" Or you might just say to yourself, "I want to have a little jewelry business on the side of my day job, or as a stay-at-home mom." Or, "I want to be more of a boss in my current business." Deep down, I think we all have a little itch to be our own boss, in different ways. And I'm here to tell you that you can be one…maybe. I want to encourage you. But I'm gonna keep it real: it's not for everyone.

Starting your own business might be something you've always wanted to try and, I'll tell you, you should *think* super hard about it…but not necessarily *do it*. And if you have a different kind of boss-dream, you should think about the right way to go about fulfilling that desire, too. I tell you to think about it only because the fancy headlines and glossy magazine covers of superstar entrepreneurs might seem sexy, but what you don't see are the warts, the struggles, the failures. For every Sara Blakely, who started Spanx, there are thousands of women who tried something similar but failed. There are thousands more who have thought, "What if?" Doing something entrepreneurial is not all rah-rah magazine shoots and billion-dollar buyouts; it's tough and scary most of the time. I tell you this from experience: the awesome days are slim in comparison to the "I want to rip my hair out" days. But for me, the awesome days are so awesome that the hair-ripping days are worth it. Are they that way for you?

FLIRT FIRST WITH BEING FUNEMPLOYED

Being funemployed is not making the most of an unexpected "vacation" from work (thank you for the layoffs, Mr. Recession). Instead, it's when you say, "I love my job. I love my life"—and you're totally in control of both things. Funemployed people can have seemingly oddball jobs that they love, like being an alpaca farmer or owning an artisanal chocolate shop, and that's all that matters. For others, it's running a computer fix-it company, being a travel writer, being a YouTube songstress, or working as a manager for a touring metal band. It's about choosing your own adventure (as you know from the intro to this book, I *loved* those books as a kid). Sure, with all of that fun comes uncertainty, but there is a ton of opportunity, too.

If you already have a job, try your passion as a part-time job first. Dip your toes in the entrepreneurial water. Going all in too early is like being a firework that is fantastically extravagant but quickly burns out—and is soon forgotten. You don't want to go so big that you quickly go home. Take your time. Does alpaca farming sound awesome in theory but, in practice, you hate raking poop? Know that now, before you burn your corporate bra, so to speak, and dive in. Knowing what you *don't* want to do is just as important as, or even *more* important than, knowing what you *do* want to do. Do you start an artisanal chocolate business while you are still working at a boutique? Do you spend your nights and weekends figuring out sourcing and packaging? Do you love it? Is it one hundred times more fun than you ever could have imagined in your wildest chocolate-tasting dreams? You can't knock it 'til you try it and get it out of your system. But, I would strongly advise you, don't go all in 'til you get your tootsies wet.

IS YOUR HOBBY A CAREER? OR JUST A HOBBY?

Let's take a look at a few funemployment ideas to see which could turn into a career…and which are better left as hobbies.

- **You LOVE kickball.** You can't get it off your mind. You know you are destined to make it in the major leagues, despite being slightly past your prime. Sorry, sweetheart: it's not a wise career move.

- **Cupcakes are your thing.** You are constantly coming up with crazy concoctions that sound terrible but are actually shockingly brilliant, like Swiss chocolate with cayenne pepper frosting or gingerbread with salted buttercream. You could be on to something. There are dozens of at-home bakers who are killing it with their own cupcake shops. And the crazy concoctions concept? Well, Voodoo Doughnut in Portland is legendary for their bizarre flavors. Still, do you really want to bake in bulk? Do you understand the business and marketing behind building a brand that attracts the masses? Know that making your hobby into a day-to-day business opens the door to losing some of the enjoyment factor that drew you to it in the first place.

- **You "have a book" in you.** Since you were young, you have always known that you're destined to be a writer. But your day job doesn't leave enough time or energy for creative thought. You're positive that if you could just write it, your book would be a bestseller. I've heard that too many times to count. On occasion they're right. More often they're not. Sorry, just keeping it real. Most writers, even successful ones, have day jobs. The ones who can write *for a living* are few and far between. If you think you can beat the odds, actually write it. Selling a concept only works for people like Angelina Jolie. For the rest of us, showing that the work is already done increases our chances exponentially. After all, if someone, in this case a publisher or editor, takes a chance on you, I promise you, he or she isn't going to want to put in a boatload of work or time.

Just because your hobby isn't a good fit for full-time employment doesn't mean you can't still make some extra money doing it. There are tons of ways you can bring in some cash on the side to supplement your income if you just get creative:

1. **Become a virtual assistant.** Gone are the days when everyone had a personal assistant, *Mad Men*-style. These days, even big bankers and major celebrities have someone helping them out remotely. And that someone could be *you*. Expect to screen your boss's emails, arrange travel, make appointments and phone calls on behalf of your boss, manage the calendar, and take care of any other random administrative tasks that might come up. *(How much you can make: $20–$100/hour.)*

2. **Make the most of e-commerce.** Etsy is the world's most vibrant handmade marketplace, with a community of millions of buyers and small businesses. Think artisanal anything, from homemade soap to needlepoint belts. If you're the creative, right-side-of-your-brain type, turn your fun DIY project into some extra cash. *(How much you can make: $10–$1,000; price varies by item.)*

3. **Get focused (grouped).** Get on your computer and search for companies that conduct paid focus groups. I'm not talking about weird science experiment stuff. Focus groups can be for stuff like watching movies. Yes, please. In most cases, all you need to get involved is to place your name on a list and wait to be called. You can make a quick $50 to $100 just for answering an hour's worth of questions about a product or service—and potentially more if the gig calls for hitting the stores in person as a mystery shopper or the

restaurants as a secret taster (yum!). *(How much you can make: $50-$200/hour.)*

4. **Ref sporting events.** You have to take a quick certification session (but it's no biggie, usually just a weekend of training) and then you are assigned by your local recreational association to games. If you're a new sporty spice, you might be assigned to youth basketball, soccer, lacrosse games and the like. If you played sports in college or have a degree in athletics, you might be eligible to ref high school, college, or even semipro games, which are more lucrative and typically offer better schedules. *(How much you can make: $20-$1,500 per game.)*

5. **Be a writer.** Many websites need part-time writers. This doesn't mean you need to be a professional novelist. Write reviews for restaurants, shops, parks and concerts in your area. Blogging job boards like BloggingPro, ProBlogger, and Freelance Writing Jobs (FWJ), which consolidates all Craigslist and other posts from around the country, are good places to start. Organize your clips if you have them, or come up with a few writing samples ahead of time. *(How much you can make: $0.01-$0.10 per word.)*

ARE YOU A BOSS TYPE?

If you try it out and decide that your passion isn't just a hobby or a fad, it's a business, then do you have what it takes to be your own boss?

Here are a few dos and don'ts to consider:

- **You DO have to be a self-starter who is completely dedicated to your craft.**

- **You DO have to be passionate about your business.** Talent can be taught. Passion comes from within. Either you are or you aren't.

- **You DO need to understand every role within your company (once you are able to hire that team).** You might not be the best at each position (which is why you hired someone who is the best at it), but you do need to know the basics.

- **You DON'T have to be loud to be heard.** A soft-spoken demeanor can be a deadly weapon in business.

- **You DON'T have to be a barracuda.** In fact, if you're not, you can create a positive work environment that will pay dividends later on with strong customer and employee relationships.

- **You DON'T have to micromanage every element of the business.** Once you are able to hire a team you trust, allow them to take ownership of what they do. Still, that doesn't mean that you should be totally hands-off. You always need to be in the know—but not necessarily a know-it-all.

CAN ANYONE BE THE NEXT MARK ZUCKERBERG OR SARA BLAKELY?

Yes and no. But probably no. However, if Mark or Sara are motivating and inspiring you to work your ass off because, yes, there is a *chance* that you could make that kind of impact in the industry that you're in, then dream big. But don't let your huge aspirations get dangerous. Don't fly the G5 until you can afford to buy it... or at the very least until you can afford to fly first-class.

That's where so many entrepreneurs with big dreams end up falling on their faces. It's so easy to get carried away by the intrigue, allure and hoopla around being rich and living the jet-set lifestyle. Turn on your TV to pretty much any channel and you'll be bombarded by shows that show off the wealth of celebrities, most of whom are famous just for being famous. Chances are that's not you, and ideally you don't want to be known for doing nothing of substance. No shame in admitting that every once in a while you might feel envious; we all do. But that "presto, you're an insta-millionaire!" moment only happens on reality TV, and I'm not going to let you be a Real Housewife.

The women you should aspire to be have not achieved the dream overnight. Instead, let's look at women like Sara as an inspiration. She not only created Spanx but also is the world's youngest self-made female billionaire (yeah, *billionaire*, with a *B*). She was selling fax machines door-to-door when she came up with the idea for Spanx and developed it into a product she could sell. But she needed to sell the sizzle, not just the product. She had no money for advertising, so she pounded the pavement instead. She became notorious for lifting up her pant leg to every woman walking by. She was creative, to say the least, in getting her message out. She hit the phones, begged friends to help get the word out, and called print outlets and TV stations.

Her tenacity worked. She did $4 million in sales the first year, $10 million the next, and never looked back.

Strive for greatness, and use others' success to drive you. But first, let's pick the right others: the Saras of the world, not some reality phony.

CONFESSIONS
OF A RICH BITCH
The (sweet) smell of a side gig

When I was at CNN, I made extra money on the side by selling all my old clothes on eBay. Being thrifty by nature, I saw dollar signs in things other people might have given or thrown away. So to realize that value, I opened up an eBay store. No, I wasn't going to leave my job to become an eBay seller (although plenty of women do and make a killing). It was just a hobby, albeit a lucrative one. And if I ever had thoughts to the contrary, the one time a man asked me for a photo of my feet in the old shoes I was selling made it remain forever…just a hobby.

ARE YOU *REALLY* READY?!

To determine if you truly are ready to start your own business, or at least if you're the ideal candidate to become an entrepreneur, ask yourself these eight questions:

1. Do you have six to nine months of expenses saved up?

2. Have you done a ton of research into the profession? Have you studied the competition and talked to others who are already in the business?

3. Have you come up with a *business plan**?

4. Are you already established in the industry, with a good résumé, complete with experience and references?

5. If your grand plan fails, can you quickly get another job?

6. Do you need extensive health coverage for yourself or your family?

7. Have you recently become frustrated with work and want to pursue what seems like a cool idea?

8. Do you have a new idea for a business...almost every day?

If you answered yes to 1 through 5, it seems like you just might be the ideal candidate to pursue your grand scheme. If you answered no...well, you need to do more homework.

If you answered yes to 6 through 8, you might need to give your idea a reality check. That doesn't mean that it's destined to fail; it just means that you may want to give it a bit more thought.

ARE YOU MENTALLY, PHYSICALLY AND EMOTIONALLY PREPARED?

Just because you passed the eight-question quiz doesn't mean you're ready to jump in feetfirst. You've got to be mentally, physically, emotionally and realistically prepared to make it work.

Mentally: You have to be okay with failure. You are going to fall on your face. You are going to screw up from time to time. You may have a business card that says "CEO," but you'll feel like you're at the bottom of the totem pole—and you've got to be okay with that.

Physically: You'll be tempted to work your butt off to the point of exhaustion—passion does that to a bitch—but don't run yourself into the ground. Twenty-hour days are impressive, but they're counterproductive if they make you sick. I speak from personal bouts of stress-induced illnesses and ailments. Ask yourself if you have the energy to do what it takes, and do everything you can to take care of yourself and stay healthy. (Besides, you may not have the same robust health insurance you had before undertaking your own business, so you're going to foot way more of your medical bills than before.)

Emotionally: You need to be a self-starter, ready to earn a precarious income, and prepared with an "in case of emergency break glass" personal fund to finance those inevitable bad months. The truth is that when you are first starting out, you will likely find it tough to budget for the day-to-day, save for the future, and plan for big purchases. When your income is unstable, it can cause more anxiety than a frustrating job does. The best way to get over this obstacle is to have enough money saved so that you can make it work and forecast how long it will take to get cash flow–positive. This way you can get back to your normal Spending Plan and ideally make more than you did at your previous job.

HAVE I SCARED YOU?

I don't mean to scare you away, but I want to make sure you are aware of what you're getting into. If you've read all this and said, "Okay, Lapin, this isn't for me," then cool. Better to know now than to always wonder "what if?" But even if you are not into building a full-fledged start-up, strive to "start up" yourself. Be entrepreneurial in the business of *you*.

However, if you're reading this and are excited about the prospect of starting a company, now that you know the risks, you can avoid them more easily. Being scared is natural. Now is the time to find the confidence to push past that fear and (wo)man up.

ASSUME YOU ARE GOING TO SUCK AT STARTING YOUR OWN BUSINESS

No matter how big your dreams are, how much you have researched your field, how many people you have spoken with, how many books you have read, how prepared you think you are—you are probably going to suck at first. In the beginning it's better to have low expectations. Then you can exceed them. Just because you're a small-business owner doesn't mean that you know how to be a boss. A great chef doesn't necessarily know how to run the restaurant. An internet whiz doesn't necessarily know the ins and outs of marketing herself. A celebrity personal trainer isn't necessarily capable of attracting new members to the gym. Know what you don't know. Admit that. You can learn what you *need* to know. Or you can know a little about a lot and get to a point where you can hire people way smarter than you are for the rest. My manager always says, "If you are the smartest person in the room, you are in the wrong room." Think about it.

Delegating is a must, but you still have to get your hands dirty. Don't think that someone else is going to make you successful. This is your business, your career, your vision, your technique, your voice, your style, your flair—and that can't be hired out.

The dirty little secret is that *no one* has it totally figured out. Every day it gets better. Every day you feel more comfortable in your own skin. We all fake it to some extent...'til we make it.

CONFESSIONS
OF A RICH BITCH

My fake assistant

When I was starting out, there was no chance I would have had an assistant. But, sometimes it appeared better if I did, so I could look like "kind of a big deal" (which I wasn't). So, I made one up. "Her" name was Dorothy. I don't know why I picked that name, but it sounded like she was legit (looking back, it had some *Wizard of Oz* symbolism going on). I set up an email account for "Dorothy" and whenever I reached out to pursue an opportunity, I sent it from Dorothy. When I needed to schedule something with someone important, Dorothy (a.k.a. yours truly) handled the calendar. I'm not sure if the perception made much of a difference in the opportunities that came my way, but I know that when I finally got a real assistant, I couldn't have been happier: "Dorothy" was overworked and ready to retire.

HOW TO AVOID COMMON ROOKIE MISTAKES

Have a plan. A business plan is a playbook for what you're trying to create. The subject of business plans could fill a book (and it has, hundreds of them), but basically it's a description of your company, your proposed product or service, the market for that product or service, who you'll be competing against, how you'll find your customers, and a financial analysis of how you expect things to go. Yes, a lot of these details will be an educated guess, but you can run it by your nearest and dearest for a quick market test. Invite family and friends over, load them with yummy eats and good drinks, and ask them about your idea. Be specific but make sure that your questions are open-ended, and listen carefully. Better to learn of your weaknesses and glitches in the comforts of your own home than during a big meeting with an investor, or after you launch.

If you can produce your product easily, make samples, find vendors for it and build from there. Lara Merriken, the creator of LÄRABAR, made her original bars in her own oven after mixing the ingredients in her (sanitized) bathtub. It wasn't until years of bathtub baking later that she acquired a professional bakery operation (and eventually sold to General Mills).

As for financial analysis, you don't need a MBA for this. Just figure out what your costs are and whether you can make money. Jennifer Fleiss, the woman who started Rent The Runway, and her cofounder, Jennifer Hyman, both went to business school, so I asked them, "Do you need a business plan?" They said maybe not—if you have a clear elevator pitch. Theirs was "the Netflix for fashion." Try both: have a paper plan and a pitch plan. They will work for different audiences, but you never want to have to answer "I don't have one" if someone asks.

Know the jargon. Most new business owners don't have a handle on their jargon or their numbers as much as they should. You should know the difference between *revenue,** *profits** and *valuation.** It's easy to beef up your financial jargon; for starters, check the back of this book for some key financial terms that will help you talk the talk. Improperly using the lingo, or avoiding it altogether, is an immediate giveaway that you are out of your league.

Put it in writing. You might be wide-eyed and excited to start a new adventure, but get everything in writing and a clear agreement in place, even if it feels uncomfortable. Contracts are for worst-case scenarios. You might hate them when you are first signing them, but you will be endlessly thankful for them if things don't go as planned.

Dream with your eyes wide open. Yes, dream big. But know that you can't achieve greatness in the first six months—and be at peace with that. Have one-, three-, five- and ten-year goals, like you are already accustomed to creating.

Don't be a dictator. You want people to want to work for you. You also want people to root for you. By being a dictator, or, let's be honest, a *dick*, you might get people to do the work, but they won't like it. And if they don't like it, if they don't believe in you or your purpose, then they won't give you their best. Be respected. Be liked. Don't be feared.

Maintain your relationships. Burning old bridges, or failing to keep up with your contacts from your previous career, can be the end of your next career. If you totally fail in this new endeavor, you want to have a fallback plan. Don't dismiss all of your former colleagues, even if they aren't in your new industry. You never know whom you might need to employ, whom your future clients may be, who might make a career change just like you and end up in a position to hire you or work with you. If you were assistants together, don't dismiss them just because you were elevated to the next rung first. You never know when your past might come back to help you, or to haunt you.

Eat a slice of humble pie. You don't know everything. You have to take the time to understand all aspects of the business. And don't be a douchebag. Period.

CONFESSIONS
OF A RICH BITCH

Get it in writing...
and then take the time to *read* it!

From Alli Webb, Founder/CEO of Drybar (sidenote: a Drybar blowout is one of my favorite small indulgences and frequently appears in the Extras section of my spending plan):

Today, Drybar employs over 2,000 people and operates 37 shops across the country. But four short years ago it was just me, my husband, Cameron, my brother, Michael, and his wife, Sarah, scrambling to juggle thousands of little details every day to get the business going. We were all working around the clock just to get our one little shop in Brentwood open each day. I'll never forget the loads of paperwork and all the confusing government and cosmetology forms and business licenses I had to deal with to get this business off the ground.

At that time, Michael and Cameron were still working at their other "real" jobs, so a lot of the prep work fell on my shoulders. I like to believe that I made a lot of great decisions in those early days, but I also made quite a few mistakes—some small and some big. One was regarding towels. Seems pretty simple, right? I thought so, too, but boy, was I wrong.

After calling a few different local towel services, I found a vendor who gave me what I thought was a fair price. So I signed what appeared to be a basic agreement and voilà, we had towels! Check. Then I went on to the seventy other things on my preopening to-do list.

Well, a few months after we successfully opened our Brentwood shop, we realized the towels were actually costing us a small fortune. My brother, Michael, who at this point had quit his other job to join Drybar full-time, noticed we were paying way too much for our towel service and called up the company to cancel. Err, think again: "We're sorry, Michael," they said. "Your sister signed a contract with us, and in order to break that contact, you will have to pay us $60,000." Doh! I'll never forget the panic and guilt I felt hearing this news. But I learned the valuable (and now super obvious) lesson not to sign *anything* without reading it first—and then to have a lawyer review it, too. The lawyer fee is a small investment to protect you from the risk of throwing in the towel, so to speak.

HAVE SUBSTANCE BEHIND EVERY MOVE YOU MAKE

Have provocative ideas, but don't be provocative for the sake of being provocative. Think outside the box, push the envelope, balance on the edge, shake up your industry…but do this all strategically. All successful businesses fill a need in the marketplace.

Clothing designer Tory Burch started a preppy lifestyle brand because she wanted it. She personally wanted great all-American pieces like cigarette pants and cardigans at a good price point between designer and contemporary. She was convinced that others would want that, too. And, boy, was she right.

So, how are you different? It can be subtle, but you have to be different. That shouldn't overwhelm you because just by being you, you are different. What's your brand? Do you really know who you are, genuinely, to deliver an authentic experience to your customer?

Rock-star businesswoman Angela Ahrendts was the CEO of Burberry who made the trench coat sexy and fashionable again and, in 2014, she moved to Apple to lead retail. She credits her dad for saying he could teach her anything but couldn't teach her how to feel. She turned the Burberry brand around by killing the "sell, sell, sell" mentality when a customer walked into a store; instead, she tried to make the customer "feel" something authentic and unique. She took what was done before and made it different and better.

Be risky but don't be gimmicky. Today's customer is too savvy to have the wool pulled over her eyes. She sees through bullshit. I get it—when you first start your own business, you're really eager to make that announcement that you have arrived, get noticed, gain a fan base quickly, start raking in the cash. But don't fall for your own hype. Be real. And if your version of real is raw, is risky, is sassy—great. Embrace it, like the wildly successful brand Nasty Gal, an edgy fashion brand that now has more than half a million customers in sixty countries. On the surface, Nasty Gal is just an overtly suggestive brand with a catchy name. It gets your attention. But the business itself has to be airtight once it gets the customer's attention. A recipe for success for someone else is not necessarily going to be yours.

When I left my job at CNBC, I had a dream of being a financial expert people didn't need a dictionary to understand and to start a production company to produce financial media that was actually entertaining. I saw a void in the market, and I wanted to—and thought I could—fill it. I had a lot of haters; a lot of people said I was crazy, that it would be the end of my career and the death of the trajectory that I had spent a lifetime building. They were wrong. It was the move I had to make, and it was just the beginning.

GET A CHEERLEADER

Find a mentor, a friend, even a family member, someone who will be your personal cheerleader. Someone who believes in you, supports you, uplifts you, and will catch you if you fall. Especially if you are going off the conventional career track, you will deal with haters, people who are jealous, think you're crazy, or believe you're making a huge mistake. Screw them.

If you have even one person who believes in you, one person you can go to when things are shitty, one person who reminds you why you took the leap in the first place and why you should keep going, you *will* keep going. Because there will be days when you are overcome with doubt, when you listen to the naysayers, and you want to give up, scrap the whole damn thing and go back to your miserable job and your comfortable life. That's when you need someone there for you, your cheerleader, to help keep the dream alive. Your cheerleader is the person you can share your weaknesses with, the one and only person with whom you can bitch and moan and pull the armor off. "Yeah, my business is not doing as well as I expected, I'm completely in debt and I am questioning why the heck I decided to do this in the first place."

A word of caution: say whatever you want to your cheerleader, but don't bitch and moan to anyone else. People don't want to be around an oversharing Debbie Downer. Nor do they need to know about the lows in your business or the flaws in your plan. Diarrhea of the mouth isn't going to make your business better. It's just going to make yet another person a nonbeliever, and at this point you need all the believers you can get.

So where the heck do you find a mentor? And how do you get the most out of that relationship? Both are very good questions. Let's go back to that mentor I told you about in Step 2, the one who told me point-blank that I needed to get my shit together. Sure, she took a pretty tough-love approach, but at the time that was exactly what I needed. As a young, career-driven, have-it-all kind of woman (sound familiar??) she had made her mistakes, career and otherwise, and was determined that I wouldn't make the same ones. That's not to say that I had to take everything she said or suggested as absolute; in fact, one of the strongest relationships you can have with your mentor is that of thoughtful partner, absorbing everything she shares with you and then *deciding for yourself* what your next move is.

As I shared with you in Step 2, I was lucky enough for her to find me. But that doesn't mean you can have only one person in your corner. Keep looking. Look for people who are doing what you want to do, and doing it *well*, and then ask them to get together (for coffee, a drink, lunch, whatever seems appropriate; and remember: *you should pay*, or at least offer to pay). Tell them that you admire what they do and would love to learn everything you can from them. Flattery here is critical, but don't overdo it—be sincere. Be sure to do your homework before the meeting. Be prepared to ask questions. Again, don't be afraid to admit what you don't know; these are people you can't fake out. They've been there and likely have the smarts and experience to smell a fake a mile away. Some aspects of being inexperienced are unavoidable, so don't pretend. Don't be a smarty-pants with people who are smarter than you. It won't curry any favors. Be humble. Show that you've put time and effort into the get-together, and that you care deeply about the field. Don't just spit their bio back at them; ask thoughtful questions about *how* and *why* they have made the career and personal moves that they have, and take suggestions on how you can do the same. If this person has agreed to meet with you, then she's interested in helping; you make her feel good about that choice—and make her want to keep making it—by not asking for everything under the sun.

Always ask her how you can be helpful to *her*. Did she mention that she's had trouble finding a babysitter? See if you can come up with a solution. You don't need to buy anything; a little sweat equity will go a long way in strengthening your relationship. Inevitably, your mentor will help you by making a call or an introduction or doing something for you in your career that you couldn't do yourself. Don't push it. Don't ask. Make it her suggestion and keep asking if *you* can be helpful to her in personal or professional ways. Chances are, you can be. Be an eager beaver to offer help, not to ask for it.

You might need more education to do what you want to do; in fact, you'll *always* need more education. The best way to learn is not at (an expensive) school but from talking to people who have traveled your path or a similar one before you. Pay them with whatever effort you can. It's cheaper and more valuable than tuition (and student loans). Take it seriously and sincerely.

WORK HARD, PLAY HARD

Whether you decide to start your own business or to be more innovative and entrepreneurial in the way you approach what you are doing now, you need people to help you. A mentor to turn to, bounce ideas off, and learn from is invaluable, but a Rich Bitch doesn't stop there. As the old adage goes, "It takes a village." And while you are the mayor of that village, you should populate it with as many helpful and inspiring people as you can.

This may be controversial to say, but in order to build your network, you need to stop drawing such a hard line between work and play. It shouldn't exist. People work harder for people they know. People pull for people they know. We like doing business with friends. It's the way the world works, and I would be lying and doing a disservice to you if I sugarcoated it.

People often ask me, "Guys are doing business on the golf course. Is that an unfair advantage?" First of all, "Fair?" Seriously? In business?? Um, don't they say all's fair in love and business? I say, if you can't do business where business is being done, then do business somewhere else. Great, guys are doing business on the golf course; you can do business in the yoga studio. Move the course. Or learn how to play golf.

CONFESSIONS
OF A RICH BITCH

Your course, your rules

When I moved to Atlanta, I signed up for golf lessons and tennis lessons. Both were short-lived, to say the least. I was terrible at both sports and could only think about doing them as a utility to get "there"—a.k.a. the court or the green…wherever the business action was happening. If I could talk to my former self (that girl who picked up soccer cleats by accident for her first golf lesson…yep, that *actually* happened), I would say, "Fun doesn't need to be work—but work can be fun."

If I had enjoyed the golf lesson, then maybe I would have gotten so great that I would have taken on Annika Sörenstam and done major deals on the eighteenth hole. But I didn't. I suffered through a class for an end that didn't justify the means. I needed to move the course.

The coolest thing about moving the course is that you can move it wherever you want to move it. I moved mine to restaurants. I love eating…and I assume I'm not alone on this one. I said to myself, "I'm going to eat out anyway. Shouldn't I be getting the most I can out of these meals?" Why, yes, don't mind if I do.

I was going to try all the new restaurants in Atlanta (on my own, admittedly), so I signed up for Taste of Atlanta, which is a festival of the best food and restaurants in the city. But instead of just going, I asked if I could volunteer. I thought, "Who *doesn't* want a volunteer? So, they obviously want moi!" Honestly, it wasn't much sweat off my back to help them with the event, and it gave me the opportunity to talk to people within the organization, restaurateurs and other foodies like me with a sense of purpose. It offered me structure and a conversation starter, and that's all I needed to get me going to network on "my course."

Because I was volunteering with other CNN colleagues, I met a ton of people from work in different departments I wouldn't have had the chance to meet otherwise, folks I still keep in touch with to this day. Still, here's the thing about business relationships: they don't happen at one event (they are called "relationships" for a reason), and they don't always happen with the person you met in the first place. I can't say for sure, but some of the business I do now could very well have stemmed from long roots that go all the way back to Taste of Atlanta. Social ties can and often do lead to "doing business," but that can happen on any turf. So, it should be on *your* turf.

Networking usually goes like this: so-and-so introduces you to this person, and she introduces you to another person; you don't know exactly where you know someone from or who introduced you. It's the networking gift that keeps on giving. You just have to give yourself the chance to turn your passions into opportunities. Who knows if "something comes of" a specific event? I would assume it won't. Just focus on whatever you love to do. It can be basket weaving, pottery painting, kickball or even something as basic as eating, as it was for me. You were going to weave baskets anyway, right? What about finding a basket-weaving group? Or going to a pottery-painting class or joining a kickball league? Find a place that gives your passion structure, where you can talk about your dreams and ideas in a socially active environment like the guys on the golf course do! And to think: I could have tortured myself trying to walk in cleats on the green for the chance of some nebulous business opportunity. If nothing came of it, I would have felt let down, not to mention ridiculously sore. Instead, I helped with the Taste of Atlanta event and left with a full, happy belly—whether some business deal would eventually come of it or not. After all, a girl's gotta eat anyway.

BITCH TIP

No matter what business you're in, whether you work for someone else or for yourself, you've probably had a friend or acquaintance (or even a relative!) who you suspect is really only interested in how the friendship can benefit *her*. Don't be that girl. Err on the side of sincerity. You'll make connections that are real if you just put yourself out there.

ALL WORK AND NO PLAY MAKES JILL A DULL BITCH

Now that you've found a mentor and started building your network, it's safe to say you're well on your way to a solid support system, both at work and after-hours. But how do you fit in "you" time?

The first step to playing smart is to play. "Hey, Lapin," you say, "I don't really need your help having a good time." Maybe not. But that doesn't mean that your playtime is unimportant, or that you don't need to give it thought. And you need it. As we get busier and busier, our free time slips away, even though it's a key ingredient to our success.

Listen, there is nothing I love more than vegging out on the couch with some ice cream and watching mindless reality TV after a long day at work. The idea of going out after putting my heart and soul into work exhausts me just thinking about it. So whenever I have an event after work, I don't even change my clothes, because the possibility of putting on PJs instead of a dress increases too much. But nearly 100% of the time, I am happy that I actually got my butt up and met people.

CONFESSIONS
OF A RICH BITCH

[Insert your name here] time

I know you might find this hard to believe, but I am shy. I saw a shrink for a while and she told me that I'm an "outgoing introvert." You may ask (like I did), "What the heck does that mean?" Well, it means that if I go to a party, it's almost scary for me introduce myself to others. But when I *do* meet someone, I'm "on," and I can talk and talk and talk like I'm the most animated, social person in the room. But actually doing it terrifies me. The only way to get over this, for me, was to plan ahead. It sounds beyond nerdy, but it's true. Yes, I planned my fun. As I built a career, work was fun to me and, I quickly realized, fun could be work. They were so blurred that they were one and the same.

I know you might (not) find this hard to believe, but I am also a workaholic. I'm not advocating being so work obsessed, but that's who I am. So I carve out a little bit of Nicole Time every day to remind myself to have fun. You might find this habit to be ridiculous, but I'm not the one who came up with it; my friend Mindy did. Mindy Grossman is one of the most brilliant, well-respected, kindest (female!) CEOs there is. She had a huge job at Nike as one of the few ladies in the boardroom, then went on to run HSN. What I love most about her is that she ALWAYS keeps it real.

One day when we were grabbing coffee, she told me that she had figured out a perfect formula for work and play. She said that she'd actually started putting "Mindy Time" into her Outlook calendar. Sometimes it's just five minutes in the middle of the day, but it's *her* five minutes. And with her Mindy Time, she does what she loves: she talks to people. She walks over to the HSN TV studio and catches up with staff on camera and off. The fact that it's given her a great reputation as someone people want to work with and for is an unintended benefit. Sure, this has made her better at her job, but her goal of having Mindy Time is to feel replenished herself. She accomplishes this by being religious about putting it on her calendar. I told Mindy that I borrowed her term, and she said, "I want more people to borrow it!" So, Mindy, here goes—Bitches, it's all yours.

Since I am a naturally reclusive person, I have to take steps to optimize "Nicole Time." Usually, I am able to wing it and don't have to plan too hard. But for times when I can't do that, and putting myself out there feels scary, being strategic about it helps. Here are ways I make the most of Nicole Time. It might sound cheesy, but this is a Networking 101 class I would have loved to take in college:

1. **Find *two* passions: something you already love and something new you'd love to try.** I told you about trying to turn my love of food into a more meaningful experience. I have also tried to be social around new things I've wanted to try, like golf, albeit unsuccessfully. Don't even think about saying, "I don't want to/I'm too old to/I have some random excuse not to learn something new." Trying something new for the sake of trying something new is something I'd never argue with, but I'd strongly argue for learning something to help you be better at work. Learn from the greats; those "ah-ha!" moments can be pushed along by doing things out of your actual job or focus. It's at those times that you allow yourself to get outside your comfort zone, like Steve Jobs did by taking a calligraphy class in college. You know all the awesome fonts we now have the option of using? That stemmed from a class Jobs audited. It led him to think differently (no pun intended) about how typefaces were created. So at the risk of sounding cheesy and like a total Apple fangirl, think differently about things that may expand your skill set to improve what you are already doing in unexpected ways.

2. **Schedule up!** Industry events are important for getting to know more people within your world, and I can guarantee that the more events you go to, the smaller

that world will become. So how do you get invited to industry events? Make it known that you're ready and eager. Talk about your passions to friends, colleagues, mentors and acquaintances. It sounds so simple, but just talking about your passions is a great way to move them along. People you talk to might have recon on an event, recommendations for people who might have event connections in that space, or just interesting intros to help you out with. So aside from the obvious research you should be doing yourself, ask around. All it costs you is breath.

3. **Do your homework: who's going to be at your event?**
    Do you have a mutual friend? Is there a piece of work or accomplishment the person achieved that you admire? Have genuine conversation starters at the ready. "Oh, do you know so-and-so?" or "Hey, I saw your blahdy-blah. It was incredible!" You want to get a sense of who is going to be there and try to prep a little in advance. I'm not talking about putting together a document or getting crazy with your research; you can just do a quick check on your phone on the way over. And by the way, getting there "on time" means getting there ten to fifteen minutes early. Why? Because just like you, every party host is afraid that no one is going to show up. If you're one of the first to arrive, you will have the opportunity for the host's undivided attention without him or her being bombarded by all of the fashionably late guests.

4. **Have some "chutzpah": it's one of my favorite words.**
    Chutzpah is Yiddish but applies to everyone with a can-do attitude. *Supreme self-confidence, gall, nerve, guts* and *balls* are all close synonyms. Having chutzpah is having a headstrong, self-assured knowledge that you can

and will succeed. So put on your chutzpah pants before you head out the door.

5. **Let friends be your social lubricant, not alcohol.** You might have had a long day, you might be nervous, but stay in control of yourself. Do you need to bring a friend to be your wingman or -woman? Bring one. He or she can help you socialize. Repeat after me: Don't. Get. Shit-faced. If you get out of hand, you will forever be that girl who can't handle her alcohol and you won't need to worry about making an impression because you'll be remembered for all the wrong reasons. I know what you're thinking: "Thaaaaanks, Mom." But, seriously, I've seen it happen. It's not cute or cool. And there's no greater blow to the next day's productivity than taking too many shots and wasting it nursing a hangover.

6. **Be smart, not a smarty-pants: be ready to be "on."** You are presenting a valuable product: yourself. Don't make your first meeting your last meeting. Make it a lasting impression in a charming, savvy way. Show your strengths as a cool conversationalist, not a show-off. The trick to being strategic is not to come across as strategic at all.

7. **Be a player: Nothing is worse than starting a conversation about the weather: "Wow, I'm glad it's cooling down." "Urgh, this rain sucks."** No, those statements suck. I hear them all the time, and they are a major turn-off. Rich Bitches are too smart for fluff (unless it's the kind you eat, which is ah-mazing)! If you are not a meteorologist, think of something more clever. Live in Chicago? Have some idea about the Bears, Cubs, Sox, Bulls and Blackhawks. You may be a rabid fan or truly not care about sports, but I'm here

to tell you that knowing something about sports is probably going to be important to your career. So get in the game. Sports is the great equalizer.

CONFESSIONS
OF A RICH BITCH

Don't be a wimp

I'm the first one to admit that I did all the networking things and I still chickened out when it really mattered. I've been ready to go in swinging and then totally choked. Once I was caught off guard by seeing a powerful woman in my field. So, naturally, like the total wimp I was that day, I hightailed it to the bathroom. Needless to say, I didn't really have to go. I got into the stall. Phew, made it. Just gonna hang out for a while, then head back in the opposite direction of where she was. Good plan, right? Wrong. Someone came into the restroom, but whatever…I was in my stall now, trying to pee anyway (not to get too graphic). Then, suddenly, my stall door flies open! Yep, genius wimp here didn't lock the door. And, naturally, there SHE was! The very woman I was trying to avoid. And there I was with my pants down, literally. Busted. I *wish* I were joking about this story. It was one of the most embarrassing encounters I've ever had. In hindsight, I should have just gone over to her with my chutzpah pants on and said hello (we both knew of each other, just never really talked). Instead, I looked like an idiot.

8. **Listen: it sounds so, so obvious, but listen when people talk.** I often say to the kids in my family, "You have two ears and one mouth, so listen more than you talk." Sure,

talk about work if it comes up, but never, ever hard-pitch yourself. Instead, ask questions and pay attention to the answers. You know why people think Bill Clinton is so charismatic? Because he makes every person he talks to, from a head of state to a busboy, feel like the most important person in the room. Do the same (minus the flirty business).

9. **Follow up: I know sometimes it feels awkward, but always get contact information at the end of a good chat.** Bring business cards (if you have them from work, great, but you can/should make your own, too) and also get her number or email. If she doesn't have a card? Casually suggest having her type it into your phone. You can make a self-deprecating joke about it, like, "You can probably type better on it than I can. I'm a serial spell-check violator." At the end of the night (or when she walks away, if you think you'll forget), type some of the details you gathered while you were chatting into the notes section of your phone: a child's name, where the person will be vacationing, or other identifying yet personal pieces of information. That way, when you follow up, you can say something like, "Hey, hope your son, Charlie, is feeling better," or "Hey, still jealous of the tan you got from going to the shore." Or, if it's her birthday, send a thoughtful present. Make it specific, inexpensive and special for her. It doesn't even need to be her birthday to send something either funny or creative. I can write an entire book on the presents I've given to people after meeting them. They are tokens of appreciation, nothing lavish. I've sent a USB drive to someone who said she liked the one I had on my keychain. I've sent a bottle of nail polish to someone who said she was thinking about doing a daring yellow manicure. I've sent gluten-free snacks

to someone who said she had a tough time finding gluten-free food at work. The point is that it should be personal, not pricey.

10. **Continue the conversation; don't rush it.** Wait a beat before trying to set something up with someone you hit it off with. When you do ask for a "second date," suggest a specific time and place. The "whatever you want" game puts you in a position of weakness, and no one likes the "which restaurant do you like?" ping-pong match. Even if you are totally wide open, still suggest a couple of times and places; it's helpful, it's assertive, and it gives the impression that you're wildly busy (which, hello, you are). For example, say, "How's Tuesday at ten or three-thirty?" instead of "Got any time next week?"

BITCH TIP

Make BFFs with the assistants. Remember their names (you can write them in the contact notes you already have going) and always ask how they're doing. It sounds like a basic lesson in being a good person, but you'd be surprised how many people are total meanies to assistants. You don't think that gets back to the boss? You don't think that assistant will move up the corporate ladder someday? If you don't, you are plain wrong.

I wrote this book to help you with *every* detail of improving your work and money situation. And this, my friend, surprisingly happens to be one of the biggies. I've seen people totally screw themselves by acting rude to an assistant. I can also write *another* book about gifts I've given to assistants. Some have moved heaven and earth to get me in for a meeting. And why

> do you think they did that? Because people want to work for and with people they like. Don't pretend. Just be your likable self. Be human, be kind, be authentic. Did the assistant say she wasn't feeling well? Send her the link to an article about home remedies. In business, you live and die by the little things.

Remember: nothing happens overnight. Relationships, whether with colleagues or clients, take years to build. So keep building. Building faster will only result in a wobbly house. Build more carefully and you'll get something more solid, and something you actually want to *live* in.

CONFESSIONS
OF A RICH BITCH

A perfect pair

A friend of mine who is a real estate broker is methodical about her "customer service." The first week of the year, she sits down and addresses birthday, anniversary and holiday cards to her clients. Then she sets up a calendar message to send them throughout the year. Now that's a woman after my own organizational heart.

She has another creative idea to try to get more business from the clients she treats with more TLC than her competitors. For each referral she gets from a client, the client gets *one* Tiffany champagne flute. Just one. Why? Well, what do you think of when you have one champagne flute? Clinking glasses with someone else, right? In order to get another glass to complete the pair, the client subconsciously wants to refer

> *another* client—which is exactly what my girlfriend wants them to think. Genius. Cheers, lady!

Your "customer" doesn't need to be one in the traditional sense of the word. You might be trying to build a "brand" as an expert in a particular area of the business you're in. Do you think you are the best conflict manager at your call center? Do you want to be the best latte barista at the coffee shop where you work? Market yourself that way. *You are your own business*—even as an employee.

Try free services like HARO (Help a Reporter Out) to let journalists know that if they are ever doing a story about the best [insert what you're good at here] in your area, you are their go-to source (or anything else you might be the best at). Try. Push. You've got to be your own publicist with new ideas. If your ideas are different, most customers (bosses and journalists are included) are going to be naturally apprehensive, or *risk-averse.** Most would rather say no than rock the boat. But for us, "no" means "yes." For you. For me. All we need is one taker to start changing the tide of success. Momentum begets momentum. So keep at it; it's a numbers game, and eventually you'll get a yes.

When I was a young reporter, I sent my sample tape around to two hundred TV stations…two hundred! All I needed was *one* bite. And I got one in Palm Springs, California. I was hired as a reporter for the CBS station there. At that point, it didn't matter where else I applied. What mattered is that I got *one*. All I needed was one offer to get noticed by CNN. Likely, all you need is one press hit or one big buyer to get the ball rolling toward big opportunities.

BLURRED LINES

Obviously not *every* fun thing you do needs a ten-step list in order to get every last possible business opportunity drop out of it. But some of the activities you already do might be helpful to your work, and you don't even realize it. Here are a few examples of how my love for *shopping, Twitter* and *charity* helped me in my business in addition to just being a few of my favorite pastimes.

Shopping, window or otherwise, is something you're probably well versed in. (Me? Guilty as charged.) Still, until now you've probably been shopping for yourself or someone you know. But when I go to the mall, I pay attention to what the *other* shoppers are doing. I'm not doing it as a creepster. I'm doing it for work. This has helped give me good clues as to what people are buying and thus what businesses are doing well (north of 70% of the American economy is comprised of consumption—that is, shopping). This information helps me spot business trends and ultimately which investments might be good ones. Major business leaders I've met have all the financial data and best modeling on the planet to predict stocks. But the best indicator sometimes? Taking their kids and their friends to the mall so they can see which stores are crowded. This can work for you, too, as you start investing. You're in the lululemon store and like the new displays and lines? Hate the customer service experience at Toys"R"Us? Well, trust yourself. You're probably not alone. As of writing this book, a "layman's" view of those companies are reflected in their stock prices. Yes, lululemon (ticker symbol LULU) is killing it, and Toys"R"Us (ticker symbol TOY) is in the pooper. My work is around finance and buying trends, and I don't know what your work is, but I'll bet if you tried hard enough, you could find a reason to justify going to the mall as being helpful to your line of work.

And then there's *Twitter*. I know I just rattled off those stock ticker symbols like a champ, but it wasn't always that way. I've learned a lot about stocks on...yep, you guessed it, Twitter! I was an early adopter of social media. Facebook launched when I was in college, and I was at CNN when Twitter was founded. I remember getting phone calls from the bosses at CNN when I would mention Twitter on the air. "WHAT is she doing?" It was still a new platform, and big media hadn't caught on yet to how useful it could be for finding and promoting stories. Now, of course, people on TV use their Twitter feeds all the time. But no one really knew how Twitter worked; I was still learning, too. Back then, the community created things like hashtags; that wasn't something the founders thought of. In the same way, the more financially savvy Twitter community started tweeting about companies using the dollar sign plus a ticker symbol. So lululemon would be $LULU or Toys"R"Us would be $TOY. The more I followed companies on Twitter, the more the tickers became ingrained in my head. And the more people within the investment community I followed, the more people I felt I knew. Of course, they were "Twitter friends," and I didn't actually *know* them, but by @replying to them, it started a dialogue—and when they started following me back after that, I had direct access.

Almost anyone I wanted to interview at work or wanted to meet, I tracked down on Twitter (if they were using it) before I tried to email or call. I made quite a few real friends that started as virtual ones. In fact, I needed to interview a major *venture capitalist (VC)** for a segment I was doing and tracked him down on Twitter to see if he would be interested. He was, and when we met, he said one of his biggest pet peeves about entrepreneurs pitching him is that they call or (honestly) write him real, physical letters. He was like, "C'mon, just find me on Twitter if you really badly want to talk to me. I'll get back to you the fastest that way." Alrighty then. Twitter for venting about the songs that are in my head, sharing quotes I love, mindlessly scrolling headlines AND meeting people. Score, score, score and score!

All those were scores for me and my industry, but I'll bet you have similar ways you can look at Twitter and other social media platforms as a creative way to multitask your work/play.

And, finally—*charity*. I'll admit it, I hide behind my computer a lot. I actually find myself not going to the mall much, if at all these days, and ordering everything online. And, like I said before, I find myself reaching out to people on Twitter instead of calling. So charity has become my must-do offline passion. The main reason to do charity work is that it's the right thing to do. Yes, "thank you, Captain Obvious." For as long as I can remember, I've been involved with charities that speak to me. There isn't any charity work that I don't support, but organizations that I've offered most of my time to involve sick children. It's a personal decision, but it stems from my father, who was a doctor, taking me to the hospital to talk to and play with kids in the ICU. So over the last decade or so, I've proudly served as an ambassador for Starlight Starbright, an organization that brings "fun centers" to kids in hospitals; and Operation Smile, an organization that helps children with cleft lips and palates get the care they need. If you haven't already, I'd suggest you pick a charity that's doing things you care about and get involved. As an offshoot of that, you will network with other volunteers and event sponsors, who are all people likely to swim in your social or professional pool (maybe both).

CONFESSIONS
OF A RICH BITCH

Doing good can be great

I've had some of the best experiences of my life on mission trips for some incredible organizations. I'll never forget traveling with the stellar Operation Smile crew to Alexandria, Egypt, to help offer hope to kids getting much-needed surgeries who wouldn't have had either if it weren't for the organization. The more I got involved, the more I wanted to get involved. And I'd venture a guess the more you get involved, the more you'll love it, too.

So I decided to take my volunteerism to the next level and join a board. I am on the only all-female charity board in NYC for an organization called Women in Need. I get to help homeless children and their families get much-needed care and support. I also get to meet some pretty amazing women who inspire me through their outreach and career prowess—and you, too, will be amazed at how much the relationships you build around charity will enrich your personal *and* professional lives.

Some of the most accomplished, brilliant women I know are on my board. I recently got my nails done with one who is a major force in the fashion world and had dinner with another who is the CEO of a huge clothing brand. Those great friendships started on the board; if those women ever need anything from me personally or professionally, I'll be right there. I know they would be for me, too. But these aren't my go-to girlfriends to whom I whine about my love life. They are work girlfriends. You know, the ones you go on a girl date with every few months and talk about work a good chunk of

> the time. They are mentors in some ways, colleagues in others and job seekers all in one. We all need each other from a work perspective at some point, whether it's at this job or the next one.

Don't stress over it, but with a little thought, the stuff you love to do anyway can add some professional value, too. We've all got limited waking hours; you might as well make the most of them and multitask in any way possible. Whenever I feel like there just isn't enough time in the day to do everything I want on a personal and professional level, I think, "Well, Lapin, you've got the same number of hours in the day as Beyoncé!" And that should be plenty to rock your job, your career and your would-be empire.

BOTTOM LINE

Conventional wisdom: Good things come to those who wait.

Oh, please. You want something, you have to go get it—you cannot just keep your head down and expect to be rewarded. A particularly astute manager *might* notice you, but don't rely on that or anyone else, for that matter. Chances are you're really going to move ahead only when you identify your dream destination and *you* do everything you can to get there.

Conventional wisdom: Your education is your fate.

A good education is important, but many have succeeded without one. If you didn't go to a good school, or go to school at all, you can still study what you need to know on your own and make yourself as valuable as anyone else. Once you're on the job, what really matters is your performance—and that you *do* control.

Conventional wisdom: The way not to have a boss is to run your own business.

Don't kid yourself. Running your own business can be grueling, and no matter what, you're going to have a boss. In fact, if you're running your own business, you have two bosses: your customers and yourself. Oh, and do you have investors in your company? Then make that three bosses, because you're beholden to your investors as well. Although the rewards are often far greater, working for yourself is as much or more work as toiling for someone else.

Conventional wisdom: Shut off "work mode" to have fun.

Fun can have elements of work in it, too. And you might find that if you think differently about your passions, things you like to do anyway can add work value, too, without much more effort.

9

AGING GRACEFULLY
You Will Get Older—Do It in Style

T alking about retirement is no fun at all. It's hard enough making plans for next weekend; how am I supposed to plan for retirement? Or, even death??
What your Endgame is going to cost you:

- 15% of your monthly paycheck

Research has shown that when we think about our future selves, our brains recognize that self as *another person*. Yep, our brains don't think of the Future You as the same person as the Present You. We are detached from the old people we will become—and certainly detached from the old people we will become who will need money to live on.

Don't think of planning your retirement as a drag on Present You; think of it as setting Future You up for living out her days in style. It's all you, baby. So it's time to merge both of those Yous together and plan on aging gracefully.

WE ALL DESIRE TO RETIRE

What are your favorite things to do: sunbathing? yoga? pottery? travel? Think of doing those things all day long once you retire. You can be a fun old lady, a chill old lady, an adventurous old lady—you can be whoever you want and do whatever you want. As long as you have the money to do it.

When you retire, typically around age sixty-seven based on the national average, you likely won't be getting a paycheck anymore, so you'll be living off the money you saved up during your working life. So by then, you should have enough saved up to be able take care of all your Essentials *plus* all the Extras you've dreamed about.

"I'LL START SOON"

You know you should get going on saving for retirement, but you think "there's time." Well, maybe. But that depends on what kind of life you want to live when you retire. Want to take that trip to Fiji? Or are you good just doing crossword puzzles and living at your grown kid's house?

I'm not going to go on and on about why it's never too early to start saving for retirement. I'll just give you a little example. A twenty-year-old woman who puts a one-time $5,000 investment into a retirement account will have $160,000 by the time she retires. However, if she had waited until she was forty years old to invest the same amount, she would have only $40,000 by the time she retires. Let's say, however, that this woman puts in $5,000 *per year* starting at age twenty. By the time she retires she will have...almost $2 million!

The magic ingredient to making yourself an amazing retirement feast isn't money. It's time. The more time, the more your interest compounds, the more your balance rises and the more money you have to enjoy when you retire. Remember that quote from Einstein, marveling at the power of "compound interest"? Embrace the genius of it.

PAYING FOR RETIREMENT OR PAYING DOWN DEBT: HOW DO YOU CHOOSE?

You choose debt first, then retirement. While you might have the best intentions by investing for retirement and paying down debt at the same time, those good intentions could come back to bite you on your old bum. It's like ordering a Diet Coke with your cheeseburger and fries; you feel like you're making a healthy choice by ordering the slightly less sugary soda, but who are you kidding? You're only lying to yourself by ignoring your bigger problem. The same goes when saving for retirement. There is no point in maxing out your retirement contributions if your credit cards are maxed out. Tackle those high interest rate loan payments first and then invest for retirement. If you are carrying debt at a lower interest rate, say student loans, you can likely pick away at both—shrinking your debt and growing your money at the same time—but remember that, in doing this, you take one step back for every two steps forward.

To see how this works in real life, let's say you are a 35-year-old with $20,000 in debt. You have the following options:

A. Just pay off your debt and deal with retirement... someday.

B. Chip away at the debt while also squirreling (a little) money away for retirement.

C. Pay down the debt as quickly as possible and then move full steam ahead on investing for retirement.

Here's how that plays out:

A. By making minimum payments on a standard credit card, you will pay off your $20,000 debt by the time you turn 65 (and you'll end up spending $78,000 with interest).

B. Making minimum payments on your debt and putting 5% of your monthly salary toward retirement (say you make $100,000, at 7%), you will make $490,000.

C. Paying off your $20,000 debt in total and then contributing 10% of your salary (assuming $100,000 at 7%), you would have almost a million bucks.

So which path do you choose? A, B or C? Definitely C. If you went for A, you wasted $78,000 to pay off $20,000 of debt over thirty years, and you missed out on a million bucks. A MILLION DOLLARS. Don't be stupid. Get that debt monkey off your back *first*.

I know bad habits die hard. But Rich Bitches do hard shit. Don't be like my friend who smokes and is freaked out about wrinkles so she's religious about sleeping on her back. I'm sorry to say that she can sleep whatever way she wants, but if she keeps smoking, she's ignoring and lying to herself about the bigger issue that will make her become a wrinkly mess. You will be, too, if you don't choose to deal with debt before making big retirement plans.

HOW MUCH WILL I NEED TO RETIRE IN STYLE??

There's no number crunching involved here, so don't worry. There are plenty of calculators that do all the heavy lifting for you out there. My favorite retirement ones? Check out AARP and FINRA or nicolelapin.com (duh). Let's go over what you'll type into the calculator, though, because sometimes it can be a little confusing:

1. **How do you want to live in retirement?** This is a biggie. Conventional wisdom has long held that you need less money in retirement than you do in your working life, the idea being that some expenses (work clothes, for example, or commuting, or maybe mortgage payments) go away. But...if you're not working, are you just sitting around the house? You probably want to get out and do stuff. Better to assume you'll spend at least as much in retirement as you do during your working years. Heck, maybe you want to assume you'll spend more—go for it!

   - **Frugalista:** You should aim to have nothing less than 60% of what you currently make but mentally prepare for taking advantage of senior discounts. In all seriousness, stressing that you will live longer than you can afford to is not exactly ideal or relaxing.

   - **Comfy and Cozy:** Aim for 80% of what you are currently making if you want stress-free flexibility. You'll likely have paid off your debts by the time you retire, so the money you used to allocate to those bills can give you some wiggle room in case of an emergency or the urgent need to splurge.

   - **Betty White Status:** Aim for 100% of what you are making now so that you can live large, whether it's by covering health-care costs or tackling your bucket-list dream of shopping on the Champs-Élysées.

2. **What do you expect back from your retirement investment?** This is a delicate little dance. If you assume too low a return, you are forced to save more, maybe a lot more. That lowers your standard of living in your nonretirement years…a.k.a. now. If, however, you assume too high a return, the calculator might say you don't need to save as much now, but you might end up eating cat food when you're ninety.

    So what's not too crazy and not too conservative? What's your sweet spot? I'd say no more than 7% to 8%. "Lapin, that's a 1% difference…is that really a difference at all?" Over thirty or forty years, you betcha it is. For example, invest $10,000 today, just once, at 7% for forty years you end up with roughly $150,000. Nice. But at 8% you end up with roughly $220,000, or 45% more money. See, you gotta shake your moneymaker just right.

3. **How much do you need to account for inflation?** Throughout this book, I've been assuming a 3% rate of inflation, so I would use that for your retirement calculator, too. We need to account for inflation because what you really care about is the *value* your money will have in retirement. What will our money buy us when we need it? After all, we can't assume movie tickets will be the, er, $15 they are now (remember when they were $5? *That's* inflation). On a bigger scale, one million bucks today will likely buy half as much in twenty-five years. You need to account for that when planning for your golden years so you don't show up to the retirement party shortchanged.

4. **When will you retire?** The calculator will ask you to input the age at which you'd like to retire. Like I said, the average age is sixty-seven, but different strokes for different folks. Obviously, the longer you work, the more you can save and the less time you have in retirement. You can play around with this number to see what's feasible. A lot of us would like to retire ASAP, and if you win the lotto or strike it big, that can happen. But for now, don't be unrealistic about the age at which you can realistically retire.

5. **What's your life expectancy?** I know, I know—morbid. Sorry, but this is another question your calculator might ask you. Don't use anything less than ninety-five. One hundred is better. We're not going to live forever, but we *are* living longer and longer. Women do, on average, live longer than men. (Our health-care costs also tend to be higher than those of men, which is another reason we need to get our retirement situation in check.)

6. **Get anything from Social Security?** The calculator might also put in a "*Social Security** assumption." The Social Security Administration likely sends you a report every year of what you can expect to get if and when you retire, based on your earnings year to year. Type in what you see on your report—but with Social Security always in danger of being eliminated, don't take it as gospel. You might want to put in a lower number or skip it altogether in your calculations.

Once you've put in figures for 1 through 6, the calculator will spit out a number you will need to save to make all your retirement dreams a reality.

BITCH TIP

What if you can't fund both your retirement and your child's college fund? Choose retirement. Hands down. First of all, who pays the sticker price for college anyway?! As a Rich Bitch, you negotiate *everything*. The college or university probably won't change the actual price of room and board, but they often will offer scholarships and grants to meet you halfway. So, just like you aren't going to pay the sticker price for a car, you're not going to pay it for your kid's college tuition. Students can get loans and scholarships; they can work; they can work off their loans. But if you wait 'til your child is out of college to start saving for your retirement, it's gonna be too late, and you are going to miss out on all the compounding interest fun. The money you need for retirement doesn't have much negotiating wiggle room like other things. Yes, of course, any good mother puts her kids first. I get that. But this is a case where you have to be realistic. Also, consider the burden you're going to be on your kid if you're a bag lady in old age. One of the best things you can do for your kid is to take care of yourself first.

WHERE DO I SAVE FOR RETIREMENT?

Studies have shown that we will spend more time researching buying a car (four hours) or a vacation (three hours) than we will looking into retirement (two hours). You might be thinking, "Yeah, but there aren't that many options for retirement, so what is there to research?" False. There are dozens of options that you can either access through your employer or get on your own to help save toward the goal number your retirement calculator spat out. Let's talk about the three biggies that you've probably heard about: 401(k), IRA, and Roth IRA.

WHAT THE HECK IS A 401(K), ANYWAY?

A *401(k)** is just a retirement plan established by employers. If you're at a company that has one, you can make contributions before the money hits your paycheck, and it's invested in an account with your name on it. People get really excited by a 401(k) because sometimes an employer can make a matching contribution to your account, which is like getting free money. One of the most awesome parts of 401(k)s is that any money you contribute goes in before taxes and grows until you need it. You *do* pay tax when you take the money out. Don't think it's tax-free. (If you take it out before you're 59½—the number that the IRS came up with—you have to pay penalty fees as well.) So while you might be bummed to be taking home less dough, you're giving that money to Future You instead of Uncle Sam.

BUT I want to say up front that *it is not gospel that you should invest in a 401(k)*. To clarify, that doesn't mean it's *not* for you; just know that you don't have to participate just because a 401(k) is offered to you. A 401(k) can be good. It can even be great—but it all depends on you, your debt situation, your goals, and your company plan. If your employer doesn't match contributions, or if there are high fees involved, or if the plan doesn't come with the right investment choices for you, you might want to rethink it. In this scenario, you can and should take control and plan for

234 | RICH BITCH

retirement yourself—and choose another option or options for retirement that I'll tell you about in a second in addition to or instead of a 401(k).

Most people don't realize that 401(k)s *aren't* actually meant to be retirement accounts. They are technically "profit sharing" accounts because they allow you to have 100% of your money in the company's stock (which you should never do—hello Worldcom, Tyco, Enron). Maybe it's just me, but the basic idea of having your retirement and your job being so closely linked seems wrong. After all, familiarity might breed contempt in family, but it breads blindness in business. If you put all your money into your company's stock and the company goes out of business, your livelihood is doubly screwed: *now*, with losing your job, and *later*, with losing your retirement savings.

Just remember that 401(k)s aren't and were never intended to replace your income when you retire. It's just how we started using them once traditional pensions (which *are* meant to replace your income when you retire) started becoming less common. Pensions would guarantee you money when you retired, but that put the burden on your *employer* to make sure that money was there when you did. Nowadays, 401(k)s are cheaper for employers to run because they put the burden on *you*.

I remember when I was at CNN, my fabulous would-be hedge fund manager boyfriend said I was stupid if I didn't invest in a 401(k), so I marched up to HR and told them I wanted a plan. It took all of fifteen minutes, I was enrolled and I got a big fat packet of information. I didn't study it like I should have, which was kind of boneheaded of me. I regret that I didn't take charge and think for myself. It was just dumb luck that investing in the 401(k) at the time and investing in the default plan was actually the right call for me then, but I never stopped even to consider my options. And that makes me mad at my former self. Live and learn from me. Remember, trusting your employer with your money is…trusting your employer with your money. Why not trust yourself instead?!

A 401(k) is right for you if:

1. **Your employer matches your contributions.**

2. **You need something easy or you won't save at all.**

3. **You want to go craaa-zy with your contributions.** The limits in 2014 for IRA/Roth IRA (which we will get to next) are $5,500 per year if you're under fifty; for a 401(k) it's $17,500 for your personal contributions. These numbers do tend to go up year to year, so check with your plan or the IRS website to see current max contributions.

4. **You want to get the benefits from your employer match and *rollover** whatever you earned into an IRA/Roth IRA when you leave.** It's all yours to move over without penalty. (Just a quick FYI: always choose a "direct rollover" so you avoid taxes. It basically means that you are transferring the money straight into the IRA of your choosing so you aren't taking possession of it, ever. That way it doesn't look like you are withdrawing early, which will mean the tax bill that goes along with doing that.)

5. **You might need to borrow from yourself.** You can take out up to $50,000 (or 50% of your balance, whichever is less) if you need it for an emergency and have no penalty if you pay it back within five years. But if you don't put it back on your set timetable, I'll smack you. No, seriously, try your hardest not to exercise this option (especially if you have a precarious work situation, because if you lose

your job, you have to pay it back within sixty days or it will be considered a default and hurt your credit score), but know that a loan option is there if you absolutely have no other choice.

If you find that a 401(k) is right for you, here are some DOs/DON'Ts:

- **DO sign up for automatic contribution options so everything is on autopilot.** If your company has "automatic escalation" or "rebalancing options," sign up for those, too.

- **DO pick your own "asset allocation," not just the default setting,** and keep the investment in your own company's stock to no more than 10% (you could have the best employer ever, but sorry, that's what the Enron folks thought, too).

- **DO beware of 401(k) fees.** "Expense ratios" can range from 0.25% to 2%, and if you let them get out of control, they will eat into your nest egg.

- **DON'T cash out your 401(k).** Yes, it's *your* money, but you can't take it out before 59½ without a nasty penalty. The penalty, along with missing out on the joy of compounding interest (yes, my most favorite joy, but I'm a nerd), can really undermine your retirement power if you decide on cashing out early.

- **DON'T be tempted to contribute less to your 401(k) in favor of shiny short-term objects.** You want to build a deck or remodel the bathroom? Start a savings subaccount that I told you about in Step 7. Don't sacrifice 401(k) contributions. Putting short-term gain first will bite you in the butt because you're not benefiting from the growth you would have seen from your investments. The longer you're out, the harder the bite.

- **DON'T borrow from your 401(k) unless you really need to, because when you pay it back, you will be using money that was already taxed.** Then, when you take it out to use for retirement, you will be taxed *again*. No one wants to be double-taxed.

> **BITCH TIP** Many 401(k)s allow you to contribute up to 15% of your salary until you reach the cap, but there's nothing that says you have to contribute that much. It's ideal to put in at least as much as your employer will match, typically 5% or 6%, so you reap the benefit of that "free money." But if you're worried about overextending yourself, contributing just 1% or 2% to start until you get comfortable with it or start earning more money is okay. After all, 1% is better than 0%. Just don't think for a second that you are maxing out if you reach the amount your employer matches; that's *their* max, not yours.

*A 401(k) is **not** right for you if:*

1. **You don't have six to nine months of emergency reserves in the bank.** Yes, you need to save for retirement, but you need liquidity first. You can't pay for stuff with a 401(k).

2. **Your employer doesn't match your contributions.** Many, but not all, do. So check. (During the Great Recession, many employers stopped making matching payments.

Even big corporations like Amex and Coca-Cola suspended matching payments during the worst of it in 2008 and 2009. Today, matching isn't as much of a given as it once was.)

3. **You have a significant amount of credit card debt.** Paying down debt is a form of long-term savings (because if you don't pay it down now, you'll pay more and save less later) and risk reduction (ack! credit penalties). Avoid the potential avalanche of debt and tackle the mountain of interest-accumulating bills first.

4. **You want freedom of choice on fees and investment options.** Since this is your employer's show, they pick the plan and the fees. You get a few options, but that's it. Even if the fees seem small at the time, they add up, and you may be able to do better if you feel adventurous and studious enough to tackle it on your own.

BITCH TIP

If you don't have employees, you can look at a "solo 401(k)," which is really just a one-woman 401(k), one that you control. If you work for yourself and you're killing it, you should look at this as a great retirement vehicle for yourself. You control the costs and the investment options. But they are more advantageous than a regular 401(k) because there is a far higher contribution limit. In addition to the $17,500 you can invest annually as an employee—the same limit you'd have in a regular 401(k)—as an employer you can add matching funds up to 25% of your compensation for a total of $52,000 in 2015. So you're reaping *both* the employee and employer benefits for yourself.

By the way, only 32% of small business owners have benefits plans. This is nuts to me. On the surface, you might think of it as yet another expense you can't afford while you are working for yourself. But it actually saves you money by acting as more of a tax shelter (a legal one, that is), shielding your hard-earned money from getting taxed up the wazoo, thereby not leaving you as much to save for yourself.

There's a big trend right now in offering you more choices for retirement. Back in the day, it was Social Security, Medicare and pensions, and that was it. (Say what you want about those programs, but they were massively successful. The expenses of running them made them cost-prohibitive, so they were run into the ground.) Today, employers don't want to be on the hook for as much money and liability, so they push the choice onto you. That's a huge responsibility. There are eight different kinds of "qualified" benefits plans (ones that give tax love) that your employer can offer. There might be one that's a better fit for you than just the ones you hear a lot about, like a 401(k). Don't be a follower.

BITCH TIP

401(k)s might be the most popular of retirement plans through your employer, but they aren't the only kid on the block. Here are some of the other retirement accounts your work might offer:

- **401(a):** This is like a 401(k), but you can't choose the amount you contribute. Your employer takes the same amount out of everyone's paycheck as a set contribution.

- **403(b)**: This is like a 401(k) but for people at nonprofits or in public education fields.
- **457**: This is a plan for government workers.
- **Roth 401(k)**: This is the same as a 401(k) except that it is taxed now so that you don't have to pay tax in the future.
- **Pensions**: They are less common, with only around 10% of employers still offering them, but if you are at a job that has one, lucky you, because they guarantee payments for life.

Another word about pensions: Yes, old-fashioned corporate-sponsored pensions are quickly going the way of the BlackBerry, but they haven't completely disappeared yet. These days, it's mostly public employees who still get them, and if you've read the papers lately, a lot of cities—and even the US Postal Service—are struggling under the weight of pensions promised to employees in years past. That's why today, you're more likely going to be offered a 401(k) instead. Another way to get a pension is if your trade requires you to belong to a union—whether it's the Teamsters or the Screen Actors Guild. You'll have to make contributions while you're working. Then retirement benefits come from a communal pot of all members. But like all pensions, these are threatened too, and benefits are likely to be reduced in the coming years.

But if you are a small business owner, even if you are your only employee, another retirement savings option is a pension for *yourself*. You'll probably need an accountant or financial advisor to help you set it up, but it has the advantage of giving you control over where the money is invested, and you (as the employer) can put in an amount equal to up to 25% of your annual salary in a pension for you (as the employee). Any money you (the employer) contribute now (to you, the employee) is deducted from your business taxes. The returns can be a lot better than the solo 401(k). Win, win and win.

WHAT THE HECK IS AN IRA, ANYWAY?

IRA stands for individual retirement account. They've been all the rage lately when it comes to retirement savings because you can open one with money you don't pay taxes on until you use the money when you retire (59½ is the earliest you take it out without a penalty), the same as with a 401(k). But unlike a 401(k), an IRA is not offered through an employer; you set it up yourself, and you keep that account no matter where you work throughout your career.

But how do these darlings of the retirement savings world work? I found out by opening one. I put $5,000 (the max total for people under 50 is $5,500 in 2014) into an IRA to learn the ropes. When I started working for myself, I didn't really know where to start with setting up an IRA. So here are the steps I took:

Step 1: Call companies that offer IRAs, like Vanguard or Fidelity (you could also go online).

Step 2: Talk through the account set-up process (also easily done online).

Step 3: Decide what to invest money in (which we'll talk about in detail in Step 10).

Step 4: Fund the account (that is, put money in)…and voilà! You'll have an IRA!!

Step 5: Claim the amount you put in as a deduction on your tax return.

A word on funding: you can do this all at once, or at any time up to April 15 *after* the year for which you're making the contribution. For example, you have until April 15, 2016, to make a contribution for 2015. Still, if you can, fund your IRA on a regular basis—ideally, monthly. To max out an IRA in a given year, this would be a monthly contribution of $458.33 ($5,500 divided by 12). If this is too much, pick a smaller number; when the end of the year rolls around, you can still add to the account to get to the maximum $5,500 contribution, if you have the money.

Here were the *pros* of an IRA for me:

1. My $5,000 would be growing without me paying taxes on the amount I invested or on the interest I would have had to pay with a savings account.

2. The money I put in actually reduced my taxes today. I'm in the 25% tax bracket. When I put $5,000 into the IRA, my taxable salary or income was reduced by that amount. That meant my tax bill was reduced by a cool $1,250 (25% of $5,000). Which is nice. It's not that I "saved" that money per se (since tax refunds are really just your money coming back to you), but I didn't have to pay more for it.

3. I could still have a 401(k), and if I had enough money to max them both out, I could.

4. The IRA rules for withdrawal aren't super stringent. If you are using the money for medical expenses, to buy a house, or for educational expenses, you can skirt around the 10% penalty fee.

> If you're still hesitant to invest in your own benefits plan as a business owner, and you have employees, remember these IRA names because they are cheap and get the job done: Simplified Employee Pension (SEP) and Savings Incentive Match Plan for Employees (SIMPLE). Unlike a solo 401(k), these plans can apply to your employees, too. Think of this as an awesome benefit to being self-employed. You have two more IRA options than everyone else.

The one *con* to starting an IRA:

1. **You are limited by the amount you can contribute each year.** Once you max it out—as you should try to do annually—the show's over until next year. So having an IRA alone isn't going to catapult you into retirement rock-stardom.

> There is clear power to the *pre-tax* retirement savings game à la 401(k)s and IRAs, as you see.

	PRE-TAX INVESTMENT	POST-TAX INVESTMENT
Initial investment	$5,000	$5,000
- Taxes paid on investment	$0	$1,250
= Investment after taxes	$5,000	$3,750
+ 5% interest incurred	$250	$187.50

continued on next page

	PRE-TAX INVESTMENT	POST-TAX INVESTMENT
- Taxes paid on interest incurred	$0	$46.86
= TOTAL saved	$5,250	$3,890.64

This example would make anyone's panties bunch. EXCEPT you are not considering the tax you are paying when you take your 401(k) money out or the possibility of the non-401(k) investment yielding more than 5%, like finding your own awesome fund to invest in [or if the 401(k) tanked below 5% like during the Great Recession]. Or, better yet, investing in yourself, which I always say could pay most to you later on.

Another way to think of it would be if you invested $5,000 *post-tax* in starting a business or getting a certification that will advance your career, who's to say that you couldn't yield an extra $100,000, trumping the $5,250 that was touted in the 401(k) example? That's not to say that you couldn't lose that $5,000 investing in yourself, but what other business investment do you know the ins and outs of like yourself? I've seen a lot of crappy investments via 401(k)s or otherwise out there. Don't sell yourself short by thinking you aren't the best stock around. Test your idea and any other career advancement you are thinking of (going to bum around in Europe to get "cultured" is not on the list of career advancements, obviously), and ask more than just family and friends who will usually tell you what you want to hear. Review Step 8, although you could be your own safest bet and surest investment.

WHAT THE HECK IS A ROTH IRA, ANYWAY?

Roth IRAs, or just Roths for short, are a lot like traditional IRAs except you put the money in after you pay tax. Unlike a 401(k) or traditional IRA, though, you don't have to pay tax on the money you take out (because you already paid it). This makes your nest egg easier to account for over time. You don't know what tax rates are going to do in the future, but they will likely go up, so those investing in a 401(k) or IRA have an unknown tax bill looming, while those with a Roth IRA will have no surprises.

You are eligible for a Roth IRA if you make less than $129,000 (as a single person), but you are *not* eligible if you make more than that. So if you are given the option, you should a billion percent put money into a Roth. Don't hesitate. Yes, you are paying tax now, but you're paying it before your money has even grown. When you pay tax later [deferred tax like with a 401(k) or traditional IRA], you will be paying taxes based upon the amount that it has grown, too.

It really comes down to a tax thing: now or later? Assume you have $80,000 in the account when you want to take it out decades from now. With a traditional IRA, that $80,000 is all taxable as *ordinary income,** at the same tax rate you pay for the salary you make. Assume a 25% tax rate and the amount of money you really have, after tax, is $60,000. Put another way, you'll have to give $20,000 to the government before you can use it for all the fun things you planned for.

With the Roth, you keep the full $80,000. That's right, you don't have to give the $20,000 to the tax man when you turn 59½—because you already paid taxes on the money when you put it in the account in the first place. The only thing you gave up to get this awesome deal was the tax deduction when you made the original contribution (you can't deduct contributions to Roth IRAs like you can if you qualify for a traditional IRA). Sticking with our assumed 25% tax rate, you paid an extra $1,250 of tax when you started (25% of $5,000) for the privilege *not* to pay $20,000 later. That's a very, very good deal. So don't pass up making Roth contributions if you can.

On top of a good tax deal, one of the most brilliant things about a Roth IRA is the ability to use it as your "secondary emergency fund." You can take out whatever you put in scot-free. You know when you hear about all of that "penalty" business? It doesn't apply to the amount you contributed, just the amount you made on that money. This was intended to be a huge incentive for young people to start a Roth IRA. Whatever you put in, you can take out and it doesn't matter what you use it for (you could get a boob job with it, not that you should, but no one would bat an eye if you did). However, above and beyond that you'll get penalized unless you show some hardship or special circumstances (in which case, you'll avoid penalties but not taxes):

- You can withdraw $10,000 to buy your first home.
- You can use the money for educational expenses.
- You can use the money to pay for medical expenses or health insurance if you're unemployed.

As you can probably tell, I *really* like Roths. You should sign up for a Roth anytime it's available; it's one of the best deals going. But if you don't qualify for a Roth, you're not totally out of luck. A common but sneaky (legal) trick is to fund a nondeductible IRA (so you don't get the tax write-off), then immediately roll-over to a Roth IRA that very day. The best time to do this is when you are in a low tax bracket, because you'll pay less now and still nada later.

BITCH TIP

You can (and should) name a beneficiary for your various retirement plans, just in case shit, you know, *happens*. With an IRA, you can name any beneficiaries you want, including friends, family members, even a trust or charity. For a 401(k) or other plans offered by an employer, you have to get your spouse's written permission to leave it to anyone else. In the event that something happened to your spouse, you would then file an amended form to change the beneficiary to your name. And like a good Girl Scout, "Be prepared": Make sure to name both primary and alternate beneficiaries.

TAX LOVIN'

Remember from Step 7 that "qualified accounts" are ones that get a little tax love. They include the typical retirement accounts we just talked about: 401(k)s, IRAs, and Roth IRAs. I know all this tax stuff is ridiculously confusing, so let's recap.

For 401(k)s, your money grows either "tax-deferred" or "tax-free" (which isn't actually free) since you don't pay tax until the end of the retirement savings rainbow. You don't get the write-off when you contribute, but do get tax-deferred growth. Once you reach the age of 59½, there are no penalties for taking money out of either plan, though you will owe tax then. (Note: company matches are pre-tax, like your own contributions.)

Let's recap:

- Present-day tax deduction ✗
- Tax-deferred ✓
- Pay taxes on withdrawal after 59½ ✓

For IRAs, you get a deduction on your taxes today if your income qualifies for it AND you get to put money in a tax-deferred account. If you make too much to qualify for the deduction, then you get a nondeductible IRA, which doesn't give you the current tax write-off, but your money still grows tax-deferred. So, essentially, whatever you are making on your money doesn't get taxed until you take it out, with the caveat that you can't withdraw more than you put in until you are 59½ (to be exact) without paying taxes on that plus a 10% penalty.

- Present-day tax deduction ✓ ✗
- Tax-deferred ✓
- Pay taxes on withdrawal after 59½ ✓

For Roth IRAs, you don't get a tax deduction when you put the money in, BUT when you pull the money out after the age of 59½, you don't owe any tax at all. *None.*

- Present-day tax deduction ✗
- Tax-deferred ✗
- Pay taxes on withdrawal at 59½ ✗

No matter which plan you decide to go with, make it a *real* plan. Ideally it's a combination of all of these options since you're going to need around $1 million on average, accounting for inflation (so aim to max them out), to live out your life gracefully. One measly 401(k) contribution isn't going to get you there. You don't need to be exclusive to one retirement option, and while you might want to grow old with one person (aww), you don't want to get there and have to live off only one source of income. As much as you love each other, love shacks are for young, broke folk.

FYI

Helen Gurley Brown was the original Rich Bitch. The *Sex and the Single Girl* author spent 31 years at the head of *Cosmo* before retiring—but she wouldn't call her step down from the editor-in-chief position at the popular women's magazine retirement, per se. "When you retire, you die," she once said. Instead, she was still hitting the town, exercising religiously, and, yep, having sex up until her death at age ninety.

Her secret? "Self-discipline!" she said in a 1996 interview. "Self-discipline means making simple little decisions. You have a cheese omelet instead of a hot fudge sundae. You exercise every day: it's tough, it's ugly, but it brings results. You keep your temper—you don't go around reaming out everybody although you'd like to—you just shut up. You do the thing that's good for you. And it reaps such incredible rewards." A successful career, rockin' bod, and an amazing sex life until age ninety?? Our girl Helen had her retirement you-know-what in order so she could focus on aging gracefully (and naughtily at the same time). If that's not motivation enough for you to confront a retirement vehicle right for you, I don't know what is.

LIVE LIKE YOU'RE DYING

Let's do some *estate planning*,* which is really just a fancy name for having a will. What, you don't plan on dying anytime soon? Good for you. Do one anyway.

I don't think I'm dying anytime soon. But even in my twenties, I did a little estate planning. Here's what my first will looked like:

ASSET	VALUE	BENEFICIARY
Cash	about $5,000	My BFF Nicole (yes, also Nicole!)
Furniture	about $1,000	Habitat for Humanity
Clothes	about $3,000	Dress for Success

I didn't have much, but at least I could be sure that what I *did* have could make a difference for others after I was gone. If you're young and single like I was at the time, your first will will likely look something like this.

Writing a will can be super simple: list what you have, what it's worth and who you want to give it to. Then put it in a Word document, print it out, and sign and date it (or, better yet, have it notarized—you can go to your local bank and pay a couple of bucks to have someone watch you sign it and put an official stamp on it). Then let someone close to you know about it and where to find it. Finally, a good use for a safe! A safe-deposit box at the bank is also a good option, as long as you tell your spouse, parent, child or the person you designate as the executor of your estate where you keep the key or provide the combination.

If you want to have a more formal will, that's easy, too. Just spend fifty bucks or so for an online form—try LegalZoom or TotalLegal or any one of the dozens of companies out there that offer this service. It won't take much time to fill out if your estate is simple. Then get it notarized, and that's it.

If you have more complicated assets, like if you own your own business, or you want to establish a *trust** for your kids (even ones you don't have yet), then you can use an estate attorney, which will cost a few hundred bucks, but you'll know it's done right.

And since I mentioned kids, let me emphasize: *whether you have a lot to give or not, having children makes a will a must*, even if there's no money to leave. A will gives clear orders as to what happens if, God forbid, something happens to you. The main purpose of a will as a parent is/will be to determine how your kids get your money and other assets (assuming you want them to) and who will look after your children if their other parent is also deceased. Just contemplating this horrible situation can be heartwrenching, but the only thing scarier than thinking about dying is thinking about what will happen to your kids if you do.

While we're on the really morbid stuff, let's talk about making a "living will," also known as an Advance Healthcare Directive. It specifies which medical measures you may want to have performed on your behalf should you become unable to decide for yourself. You also decide who you would trust to make medical decisions for you if you can't. Yes, I get it, this is almost as nice to contemplate as your death. But hey, better a friend, sibling, spouse, or parent making these calls than someone who doesn't know you from the patient next door, right? Each state makes an advance directive form available for free online, although you can also have your attorney draw one up when you do your normal will.

Depressed yet? Bear with me just a little bit longer. While you're getting a will and an advance directive together, you might as well have a power of attorney drawn up. This is where you decide who you trust to make all nonmedical decisions and conduct personal business on your behalf, like paying your bills, selling your house and preparing your taxes. It can be the same person whom you designate to make medical decisions for you, or someone else.

With all of these documents, it's a good idea to review them every few years to make sure there are no changes you want to make. And, hopefully, they won't be executed yet. (Bad joke?)

And one more thing: if you die without a will, your property will be distributed according to state law rather than where you'd like it to go. So don't do that.

INSURE YOUR MOST VALUABLE ASSET

The main purpose of life insurance is to replace your earning potential for those who will need that money if you're not around to earn it, because, you know, you're dead. Typically, this means your young kids, your spouse or partner, or a business associate/partner. If you have none of these, then you really don't need life insurance—unless you want to get all Leona Helmsley about it and leave your dough to your dog, but, bitch, please.

If you're young, single, and don't have any dependents (i.e., people relying on you for their financial well-being), then you don't really need life insurance. Better to start investing in other ways. However, if you are married (or soon-to-be) and/or planning to have children, now is the time to start thinking about taking out a policy. Premiums can cost as little as $25 per month to cover you and your spouse for $250,000 each—an amount that ideally you'll never need, but that will make a big difference should the unthinkable happen.

So before you skip to the next section, let's go on a little shopping trip to see what getting a life insurance policy might look like.

LET'S GO SHOPPING! (FOR LIFE INSURANCE)

Who? A thirty-year-old woman who makes $50,000/year and just had a baby girl.

Why? You're in the market for life insurance because you want your spouse to have that income if something happens to you before your daughter goes to college; plus, you'd like to fund her college education.

When? If you drop dead tomorrow, that's roughly twenty years of your income to support your child through college.

Here's the basic math:

20 years x $50,000 = $1,000,000

What? Sign up for *term life insurance*,* which is a policy for a set amount ($1,000,000) for a fixed amount of time (twenty years). If you die within those twenty years, your heirs get the money. Tax-free. If you live longer than that, the policy expires, and no one gets anything (but you!).

How much? For a woman thirty-five or under, that's probably gonna run you somewhere between $500 and $700 a year (unless you're a smoker; then it's more expensive). Thinking that's a lot of money to spend on something you hope you'll never use? Well, if you own your home, that's probably about the same as your homeowners insurance. Certainly your life is as valuable as—if not *more* valuable than—your house?!

Anyway, if you break it down to fit in your monthly budget:

$500/12 months = $42 a month

I mean, that's the price of a mani/pedi. And this can ensure your family's future financial stability. Since you're going to (obviously) outlive the darn thing anyway, doesn't it feel better knowing it's there *just in case*?

Now, there's another kind of life insurance called *permanent insurance*,* or cash value. A permanent insurance policy is a lifelong policy with an added investment component to it; you can build up cash to leave your loved ones tax-free. But they also typically come with fees, commissions, and surrender charges—plus a higher monthly premium. These will set you back up to a few thousand bucks a year, but it pays out when you die, whether it's in seven days or seventy years. There's no "term" expiration.

And since a good bitch is a prepared bitch, you should consider getting long-term care insurance in addition to life insurance. Most health insurance policies and Medicare don't cover this kind of care, so you'll need this extra policy to pay for things like long-term rehabilitation or nursing care. You might think this is just for older folks, but you could bust a leg in a skiing accident and require physical therapy or other care for months beyond what your health insurance covers. The younger and healthier you are when you buy a policy, the less expensive it'll be, so get on it now to get you more when you need it later.

> **BITCH TIP**
>
> Don't wait to get life insurance until you really need it: older people and those not in the best of health pay steeply higher rates or may be turned down altogether, so buy as early as you can, but don't buy until you have dependents. Where do you get it? Start by deciding which type of plan, term or permanent, makes the most sense for you. Then go shopping to compare policies on a site like intelliquote.com; answer a few basic questions, and it suggests a variety of plans from leading providers. Voilà!

Lemme guess: you still think retirement and old age aren't your problem, so why worry about them now? I mean, you've got a career to build, a family to raise or plan for, dinners to eat and clothes to buy, right? You don't want *another* bill, right? Well, don't consider something like retirement payments "a bill." Instead, think of all the awesome things that the money you are contributing will get you down the road.

The future will sneak up on you before you know it. I promise you: you do not want to live out your golden years in a state-run nursing home because you ran out of money or be left on life support with tubes up your nose and down your throat because you didn't leave instructions. I think I've made my point.

BOTTOM LINE

Conventional wisdom: You should invest in a 401(k).

Maybe, but not if you don't have your financial house in order. 401(k)s are a good way to grow retirement savings, but you shouldn't do this in lieu of accumulating an emergency fund or paying down/taking on debt. Make sure your cash flow and debt situation can support 401(k) contributions. And, ideally, that your employer matches those contributions.

Conventional wisdom: Children first.

Parents will sacrifice just about anything for their kids, but funding a college education at the expense of your own retirement isn't doing your kid any favors if she's got to support you in your old age.

Conventional wisdom: Wills are for rich people.

You probably have some assets. Have a say where they're going to go. If you have kids, then you must provide for them in case you don't live until they reach the age of majority. Nobody likes to think about her own death, but not drafting a will doesn't mean you'll live forever. It just means that you didn't take care of business as a mere mortal. And not taking care of business is stupid.

STEP

10

MAKE IT GROW, BABY, GROW

Investing Is Just Not That Serious

At first glance, a title like Rich Bitch might make you think about bling-bling and jet-setting. But that's obviously not what this book is about. We Rich Bitches care about living rich, full lives that are powered by money but do not revolve around it.

Sure, the more money we have, the more we can do. But how do we get more? What do people who are just "rich" in the traditional sense of the word know that we don't? How do they grow their money—because they're obviously onto something? Short answer: they invest.

Now that you've tackled your debt, set up an emergency fund and set yourself up for retirement, it's time to make your money grow, baby, grow.

WHY YOU HAVE TO INVEST

You might be an A student in everything I've taught you so far. You may have followed all of the steps perfectly—but you will still struggle in the long term if you don't embrace investing. Why? Because of a little thing called "inflation," which basically means how much the cost of something today will increase in the future. (That's why a can of soda once cost a nickel and now costs a dollar.)

Let's say you invested $10,000 in a 1% savings account. In ten years, you'll have about $11,000. But in ten years, you will need more than $13,000 (accounting for an average 3% inflation) to get the same amount you got today for $10,000. So even though you thought you were doing a good thing by putting a decent amount of money in a savings account, that investment won't even help you curb the mean force of inflation. In fact, you would technically be "poorer."

Now, let's say you invested $10,000 at 7%. In ten years, you'll have almost $20,000. So not only did you show inflation who's boss, but also you made $7,000 after accounting for inflation.

"BUT, LAPIN, INVESTING IS SCARY!"

Oh, please. Spiders are scary. Investing is awesome. You're *making money*! How could that *not* be awesome?

Honestly, though, I'm tired of the studies and news reports that show how much less confident women are than men when it comes to investing. If you want a real reason why this should stop other than rah-rah girl power stuff, then here it is: women live longer than men (five years on average). A) Yay us. B) That means we're going to have a longer retirement, which means we need to have more money stashed away than men.

POP QUIZ: ARE YOU READY TO INVEST?

Getting into investing means you are ready to take your finances up a notch. But first, are all other parts of your financial house in order? You're ready to take it to the next level if:

- **You have an emergency fund set up** with the right number of months for your particular job (three to six months of living expenses; more if you have a precarious job like a real estate broker or actress).
- **You have all of your credit cards paid off in full.**
- **You're paying off all your other debt on time** and don't anticipate struggling.
- **You have a retirement system set** and you're maxing out the minimum contributions you can put in.
- **You have money saved** to start investing (typically the minimum is $500 to $2,500).

If you answered yes to ALL five of the above, then, you're ready to join the investors' club.

OKAY—SO, HOW THE EFF DO YOU INVEST??

You can read lots of books that tell you about stocks and bonds and strategies for investing in them. They will teach you, generally, how these things work. And that's great; I've read them, too. But after I put them down, I think, "Um, okay, but if I want to get a stock…where do I actually get it? Who am I gonna call?" (I could only rule out *Ghostbusters*.)

Here are 2 different options for starting to invest:

OPTION 1: DISCOUNT BROKERAGES

What they are: These are typically do-it-yourself operations (although some have offices in large cities where you can sit down, talk to a representative, and get help opening the account).

Who the usual suspects are: Examples of discount brokerages include E*TRADE, TD Ameritrade, Fidelity, Charles Schwab and Scottrade.

Typical cost per trade: $8-10

OPTION 2: FULL-SERVICE BROKERAGES

What they are: This is the expensive kind of investing, where you have professionals manage your account. You hope the advisor will add enough value to make up for the extra cost and thus not eat into your profits—but this is not guaranteed.

Who the usual suspects are: Examples of full-service brokerages include Morgan Stanley, UBS, Raymond James, Merrill Lynch and Wells Fargo Advisors.

Typical cost per trade: $150, plus possible commission

Whether you choose option 1 or option 2, here's what to look for and what to ask about when comparing accounts:

- What's the cost per trade (you want the lowest, of course)?
- Do you like their website and mobile functionality, if they have any?
- What are the quality of tools and research they offer you on their investment options (also, can you get a real live human on the phone when you call)?

- Is there a fee if your account falls below a certain amount?
- What's the minimum amount you can open an account with?
- Any perks or bonuses to opening an account?

HOW MUCH HEAT CAN YOU HANDLE?

The risk that you are able to stomach in your everyday life typically translates into the heat you can handle in the investment world. To find out what your risk tolerance is, take this quiz:

1. **Your friends would typically describe you as:**
    a. The designated driver.
    b. The life of the party.
    c. The thrill-seeking party animal.

2. **You win $100 at a friendly game of poker and:**
    a. Put it in your savings account.
    b. Use the money to go out for the rest of the night.
    c. Insist on playing another game so you can try to double your money.

3. **Your dream vacation would be:**
    a. Having a nice, well-planned staycation.
    b. Saving up to go somewhere you've always wanted to visit.
    c. Splurging on a far-off adventure or the buzziest exotic hot spot.

4. **The thought of investing in the stock market makes you feel:**
    a. Sick to your stomach. Obviously you are going to lose everything.

   b. Intrigued and excited to learn more.
   c. Awesome! You're going to make a killing, duh.

If you answered all or mostly As, you are not the riskiest bitch of the bunch. You're likely to be a more conservative investor, and you're okay with making less money in the market if the chance of losing is smallest.

If you answered all or mostly Bs, you'll likely be a middle-of-the-road investor with a healthy attitude to assess risk and reward objectively.

If you answered all or mostly Cs, you'll likely be an aggressive investor, seeking the highest possible reward without flinching at the possibility of losing money.

HOW MUCH HEAT *SHOULD* YOU HANDLE?

Now, you might consider yourself a thrillist, but *should* you act that way in the market? Maybe. Maybe not. That depends mostly on your age, but also when you need your money, how much money you can afford to lose and what you want to get with the money you invest. For some basic guidelines for the level of risk you *should* take on, let's take another quiz:

1. **How old are you?**
   a. 45+
   b. 35–44
   c. 20–34

2. **What is the next big purchase you are focused on?**
   a. Living a sweet retirement
   b. My kid's college education

    c. Nothing on the horizon, but a second house or car would be nice!

3. **When is your next big purchase?**
    a. 5 or so years
    b. 10–15 years
    c. 15+ years

4. **I expect my income to:**
    a. Decline in the next few years; unfortunately my job is on shaky ground.
    b. Stay the same. I'm tenured and have no worries that my salary will change significantly in the next few years.
    c. Increase! I am getting a raise or jumping to another job with a higher salary.

If you answered all or mostly As, you *should* be a more conservative investor because you are older, have a more of an urgent need for the money or have uncertainties with your future income.

If you answered all or mostly Bs, you *should* be a more moderate investor because you don't need the money too soon or you have a steady income stream.

If you answered all or mostly Cs, you *should* be a more aggressive investor because you have a long time horizon for your investments or are flush with cash to play with.

WHAT YOU WANT TO DO VS. WHAT YOU SHOULD DO

Reconciling who you want to be as an investor and who you should be as an investor is one of the biggest challenges in setting up your investment road map. Yes, you need to determine how aggressive you are going to be before you start so your investment options are narrowed down. There are a zillion options for investing. Determining a conservative, moderate or aggressive approach early on narrows the world down significantly. I find that doing that makes a foray into the investment world feel more manageable and less intimidating.

If you found you answered mostly As on both quizzes or strongly on the second one, you are a conservative investor. If you answered mostly Cs on both, then you are an aggressive investor. But if you answered mostly Bs on both or As on the first and Cs on the second, then you are a more moderate investor.

WHAT DO I INVEST IN?

The investment world can be broken down into two major categories: what you "own" and what you "loan." Before we go down the path meant for us—conservative, moderate, or aggresive—let's talk about the investing basics.

"OWN" INVESTMENTS

This category refers to *assets you actually own*, namely stocks. But what the heck is a *stock** anyway? A share of stock simply represents partial ownership in a company. You buy a share (stock) of a company, and that means you have partial ownership. You might hear about *equities*,* too—that's just a fancy term for a stock.

It's cool to say you "own" Apple or "own" the Green Bay Packers (they are a public company, BTW). You, as owner of the share, have (some) rights to the company's *profits*.* The money can come back to you in two ways:

1. **Many companies will literally pay you a portion of the profits they get.** These payments are called *dividends*.*

2. **The profits get put back into the business** or maybe are used to buy up shares of the business, both of which tend to make the stock more valuable, which in theory will give you more money…but only when you sell. Until then, remember, you've made money only on paper.

BITCH TIP

Stocks will drive you crazy if you watch them every day, and will cause you grief if you let them—especially if you fall in love with them. There's an old finance saying: "Falling in love is always expensive." If you can stomach the volatility and possibility of getting your heart broken, "own" investments will sweep you off your newfound investment-loving feet.

"Own" investments bounce around a lot but will give you a 10% return on average if you stick with them. This is important: 10% doesn't apply to short-term investments, only long-term ones. So if you power through the daily ups and downs, "own" investments will prove to be the best bang for your buck.

"LOAN" INVESTMENTS

These refer to *assets you don't actually own*, namely bonds. But what the heck is a *bond** anyway? When a government or a company wants to do something but can't afford to do it, it sells bonds. Bonds are kind of like IOUs. You buy the bond, essentially "lending" them your money for a certain period of time. Then, they give you back your money and then some. The extra is called *interest** or the coupon. In general, the higher the interest rate, the riskier your investment is. Makes sense, right? You wanna get paid more to lend your money if there's a chance you won't get it back.

You might hear bonds referred to as "fixed income" because you know what you can expect:

1. **You know when you'll get paid.** (Bonds typically pay interest twice a year.)

2. **You know how much money you're gonna get.** The interest rate is clear when you buy it.

3. **You know when you'll get your money back.** Bonds have a *maturity date,** or the point at which the bond pays you the final interest payment and gives you your principal back.

In general, "loan" investments tend to be less volatile but don't have the same stellar return as stocks do. Over the long run, bonds have historically returned about 5%. But they are more predictable and less likely to cause you to have a heart attack watching them.

GET A NICE ASS-ET ALLOCATION

"So, Lapin," you think, "You just said I make an average of 10% with 'own' investments and 5% with 'loan' investments, so if I just put all my money in stocks, I'll end up with twice as much money as I would if I invested in bonds, right?"

Nope, not so simple. Remember when we talked in Step 6 and Step 9? It's the amazing snowball effect called compound interest that we hate when it comes to our debt and we love when it comes to making money. This phenomenon occurs when the interest on your original investment keeps piling up. What makes it shoot up exponentially? Two things:

1. The earlier you put the initial investment in.
2. The higher the rate at which you put in your money.

Here's a quick example:

	"OWN" INVESTMENT	"LOAN" INVESTMENT
AMOUNT	$5,000 invested in stocks	$5,000 invested in bonds
LENGTH OF TIME	40 years	40 years
RATE OF RETURN	10%	5%
TOTAL AMOUNT	$225,000 after 40 years	$35,000 after 40 years

This example shows that, all things being equal besides the rate of return, "own" investments generate *a ton* more money because the money you are making from the interest grows along with the initial money you put in (it *compounds*). So, in this example, 10% versus 5% isn't double your return as it seems at face value—it's actually 6.5 times your money!

However, that doesn't mean you should throw all of your money into "own" investments like stocks. Investments are tricky, not like the easy example above, and, most importantly, not always a sure thing. The right combination of both those types of investments will give you your "asset allocation," which just means the amount of each you're invested in. The big question now is:

how much of each? Ah, and that's the big $64,000 question. The truth is, if I knew, I'd be a market psychic. Alas, I am not, and the fact is that even market wizards don't get it right all the time.

The dirty little secret is no investor has figured out exactly what to invest in and how much to invest. The best advice I can give you is that your "portfolio" (or, everything you own) must have both so that if one kind fails, the other can prop it up—that's just hedging your bets in the investment world in the same way you'd hedge them in the real world. As for how much of each, that will stem from a) what kind of investor we determined you would be, b) some standard rules of investing, or c) a combination of both.

First I'll give you the standard rules for "own" and "loan" investments, then some rules based on the amount of risk you will take on. This way, you can at least know what the rules are so you can break them if that's what's best for you.

"OWN" AND "LOAN" INVESTMENTS RULES

Taking stock of stocks: The rule for what percentage of your investment dollars should go into the stock category is *100 minus your age.* So, for example, this gives a thirty-year-old a portfolio that's 70% stock (100 - 30) and the rest, 30%, in "loan" investments like bonds.

Becoming a Bond Girl: The rule for what percentage of your investment should go into the bond category is *your age.* So, for example, if you are thirty, you would have 30% of money in bonds.

If you aren't interested in figuring out your risk level or factoring in your age or anything, consider using this simple rule: 60% in "own" investments like stocks, 40% in "loan" investments like bonds.

CONSERVATIVE PATH

Conservative bitches tend to be most of the following:

1. **Age:** Forty-five years old or older.

2. **Income:** Not totally certain.

3. **Time horizon:** You expect your next big purchase to be in the next five years and it's vital to your life, like retirement.

4. **Of a very cautious nature:** I wouldn't go so far as say you're scared of your shadow, but you're probably not personally willing to go out of your comfort zone.

General investment strategy: A conservative path is paved with more "loan" investments than "own" investments.

When it comes to the "loan" investments on a conservative path, *treasuries** are the usual suspect. They are the most common type of bond and are also considered to be the safest. When you invest in a treasury, you are basically giving the federal government money, and, in exchange, they are giving you interest. Treasuries are usually a safe bet because they are backed by the federal government which, in theory, is way less likely to fail than a public company.

When it comes to the "own" investments on a conservative path, *mutual funds** are commonplace. They prove that investments aren't only for the elite and supersavvy investors. A mutual fund gives you a ready-made portfolio that typically has a good variety and is also relatively low-maintenance. It's a communal investment of sorts in that a bunch of people (like you) buy into the fund so that y'all can pool your buying power together and get a better rate with your pooled purchasing power. You get in on a good smattering of assets that you wouldn't be able to get if you were just investing on your own. For example, famed investor Warren Buffett's Berkshire Hathaway stock is the most expensive of all time. I dare you to try to get into that one on your own. But mutual funds have more purchasing power than you do, which allows you to get in on stocks like Berkshire Hathaway for a rate you can actually afford. Everyone who owns a share of the fund owns equal bits of the investments within it. But you don't own any of the investments themselves. You'll profit (or lose money) depending on what all of the investments within your particular fund do.

Mutual funds are operated by money managers who routinely shuffle assets around within the fund so that you and your other fund friends (ideally) get the most bang for your buck. Just watch out for the high fees that can come along with joining one. There's no specific restriction on how much funds can charge, and they can be upward of 2%, which is a lot when it comes to investment fees. When you're dealing with precious percentages of return and compounding interest, you've got to watch the fees. It's just plain dumb to let them eat into your returns so much that the initial investment isn't worth it. I'm the first one to argue that investing is fun, but don't let it be just that. It's not pro bono. It's pro-profit.

MODERATE PATH

Moderate bitches tend to be most of the following:

1. **Age:** Thirty-five to forty-four.

2. **Income:** Pretty steady job situation.

3. **Time horizon:** You expect your next big purchase to be in the next ten years and it's of a recurring nature, like paying for a child's education.

4. **Of a very mild-mannered nature:** You are generally logical, rational, and responsible.

General investment strategy: A moderate path is more "own" heavy.

CONFESSIONS
OF A RICH BITCH

Baby's first portfolio

When I first started investing, I had a moderate appetite for risk. I didn't know a lot, but I was young, so even if I messed up, there wasn't much to lose. Here's what happened the first time I talked to the people at XYZ brokerage firm (no need to name them for the purposes of this exercise) and signed up for an account with $5,000 that I wanted to invest:

XYZ: So, Nicole, what kind of allocation do you want for your $5,000?

Nicole: I want to get aggressive with a 70/30 portfolio.

XYZ: Great. Just so you're clear, that means you're investing $3,500 in stocks and $1,500 in bonds.

Nicole: Correct. So, what are my options for different places to put my stock money and bond money?

XYZ: The simplest and easiest way is index funds. That means that you are buying into a little bit of all the stocks in an "index" like the S&P 500, which represents the five hundred biggest US stocks. Or a bigger index like the Wilshire 5000, which covers basically every stock in America, including smaller and medium-sized companies—probably around 2,500.

Nicole: So the Wilshire 5000 doesn't have five thousand stocks??! That's so crazy!

<awkward silence>

Nicole: Let's do $3,500 in the Wilshire 5000, please.

XYZ: And what about the last $1,500?

Nicole: Is there an "index" for bonds?

XYZ: The Barclays Aggregate Bond Index is the most popular.

Nicole: Sold. Let's do that for now.

XYZ: Okay, Miss Lapin, I will send you a confirmation.

Nicole: Thank you so much. This is so exciting.

<click>

Nicole: Hello?

A typical "own" investment for a moderate path is an index fund, which lets you buy one thing but get "exposure" to everything that's listed on the major indexes. You've heard of "the Dow"? That's just an index that tracks the thirty largest stocks in the US. The Wilshire 5000 and the S&P 500 are other options of *indexes** or a basket of stocks in which you can invest. I won't get into all of them here (that could be a whole other book!), but use the conversation I had setting up my account to ask your brokerage firm a bunch of questions and learn about the exact ones that make sense for you.

AGGRESSIVE PATH

Aggressive bitches tend to be most of the following:

1. **Age:** Twenty to thirty-four.

2. **Income:** Might be coming into a raise or more money.

3. **Time horizon:** All the time in the world, and the rewards are just gravy to your life.

4. **Of a very carefree nature:** You're the first person to raise your hand if the option to go skydiving presents itself.

General investment strategy: An aggressive path is paved with risky exotic investments that have the potential to yield the highest returns.

CONFESSIONS
OF A RICH BITCH

Baby grows up so fast

The next time I spoke to my friends at XYZ brokerage firm, I wanted to get a little more aggressive. So I added international investments into my mix. Just like with design trends that move west from Europe, sometimes greater exposure to up-and-coming investment trends that not all US investors are hip to yet can bring amazing returns over to this side of the pond (it could also be a disaster). Here's how that conversation went down:

Nicole: Hi, again! I'm interested in investing in some non-US companies. Can you help me?

XYZ: Well, Miss Lapin, there's something called the MSCI EAFE Index, which covers the developed world outside the US and Canada.

Nicole: Great, like Budweiser.

Nicole: Budweiser is owned by a Dutch company. Never mind. What about the buzzy countries I keep hearing about, like Brazil, Russia, India, China?

XYZ: The BRICs and others can be invested in via the MSCI Emerging Markets Index.

Nicole: So, let's do $3,500 in the Wilshire I had before, $500 in the Barclays and $1,000 in the MSCI EAFE Index. Rejiggering to go global, baby.

<awkward silence>

BITCH TIP

I hung up with a big takeaway that I learned after my next conversation with my representative friend from XYZ (we are besties; she just doesn't know it yet).

After my initial willy-nilly allocation, here are ways in which I became smarter about divvying it up. In hindsight, I shouldn't have done this all at once. It would have been better to invest this money over, say, six months, one sixth at a time. That is, in month one, you invest $750 of your stock money, the same the next, and so on 'til it's all invested. This is called dollar-cost averaging. It takes the mystery out of trying to pick the best time to put money in. It gives you more of an average of what the market is doing at that time. You *want* to buy in lower, obviously, but since the market bounces around a lot, there's also obviously no way to predict when it's going to be low. I mean, you could guess and hope to buy in low,

> but what if you buy super high? Whoops. That's why it's better to get an average of what the market is doing around that time. Some purchases will be lower, some higher, and that's okay. That's the point. You're spreadin' it around, and ideally it balances out to the average in the end.

A popular "own" choice in aggressive plans is international investments. Emerging markets have a lot of potential since those economies have room for growth. Still, they are more risky (they have a higher track record of failing) and are highly volatile overall. As you build wealth—and this is what investing's all about—you're going to want to stop being intimidated by going global. As a rule of thumb, let's say 20%-ish of your portfolio could be invested abroad. I'd say no more than that unless you're gonna get super into following the emerging markets. In that case, get it, girl. But you don't have to go big or go home. Just go abroad with a small suitcase. There's nothing gauche about that (*au contraire:* you don't have to check bags). That's smart and chic.

Other examples of aggressive investments you might want to consider include real estate and commodities.

REAL ESTATE

Real estate is either a great investment or a terrible investment, depending on who you ask. It all depends on what you are buying and where you are buying it. Whether you buy a property with hopes of selling it for a profit or renting it out as a commercial space, it's dicey as a business endeavor. There are a lot of X-factors in profitability; taxes and maintenance are but a few, like we discussed in Step 4. That's why it's an investment only for the bitch who knows a thing or two about it and has time to stay on top of it. Novices, go back to Step 4 to look at housing.

So, you don't want to be the next Barbara Corcoran, but you think real estate could work for you as an investment? It is possible to invest in real estate minus most of the X-factor of "what happens if there's a termite infestation that will cost me an arm and a leg?" There are investments called real estate investment trusts, or REITs for short, that trade like stocks on an exchange. The investment trust owns the real estate, manages it and passes profits (or losses) on to you if you're an investor. There are different kinds, like hotel REITs, apartment REITs, office building REITs, etc. If the REIT you are in does well, you get the income without the hassle of owning the physical property. Keep in mind, though, that you pay the REIT managers a fee for *their* hassle. And now you, as an investor, have another hassle: watching interest rates. When interest rates go up, REITs go in the pooper. Why? Because to buy the real estate within the REIT, the managers need to borrow money. If they can't do that cheaply, the REIT suffers. So while you aren't worried about fixing a water heater issue with a REIT, it's not all home, sweet home.

COMMODITIES

"Commodities" in the investment world also just means "stuff." They're not stocks or bonds. They are physical goods. In fact, commodities do well when economic times are bad (you know all those commercials telling you to "flee to gold"?) because while the value of stocks and bonds might be uncertain, we all know the value of "stuff." So, yes, gold is a commodity. So are the other metals, like silver and copper. Oil, timber, wheat, orange juice (yes, you can invest in that!), pork bellies (yes, you can invest in those, too!), cattle, etc., are all commodities.

No, you don't have to be a farmer to make money buying corn and grain or a baker to profit from cocoa or sugar. Commodities give you an investment in those things without the actual item (no, no one shows up with a bag of sugar if you buy "sugar futures"). When you buy a commodity "contract," you basically buy the right to the item at a certain price. So if you think sugar prices are going to go up, you can buy a sugar future and make a sweet profit by selling it when it does, indeed, go up.

The issue with commodities is that they are susceptible to weird swings. A bumper orange crop in Florida? Orange juice tanks. A diet craze causes people to eat chicken instead of beef? Well, cattle prices go down. Commodities are volatile and risky; that's why they are for the aggressive investor only. Also, investing in commodities requires a minimum amount to invest, usually around $5,000. And if that amount changes, you've got to be able to come up with the difference—and fast. Otherwise, if you're interested in commodities but not getting into the weeds (har har) too much, there are commodities mutual funds that can give your portfolio some exposure while also protecting you from the harsher elements.

KEEP CALM AND INVEST ON

If you've opened a brokerage account and invested/are investing your money, you've set up a portfolio. If you are actively looking at the best ways to take advantage of each option you have…you've officially become a "real investor." That's an awesome but also scary thing. So, let's go over a few what-ifs:

What if I become obsessed?

When I first started investing with a brokerage account, I found myself checking it 24/7 (just like I did when I first started selling stuff on eBay). I made myself nuts. I lost sleep over it. I stayed in on Saturday nights just to monitor my portfolio (kidding...kinda). RELAX. Your portfolio will be there making or losing money for you always, whether you are staring at the screen or not.

What if there is something really tempting to invest in?

You might hear about a hot new IPO or new investment guru or exotic investment that you just have to try, but stay true to your original strategy, especially if you don't know enough yet to veer off course. That "hot" IPO could be a dud, the "guru" a fraud and the "new investment" a crock of you-know-what.

What if I lose the money?

You will lose money. For sure. But it's all paper money. Until it's not. The only time you actually lose money is when you take it out (and that's the only time you are taxed on it, too). If your 401(k) doubled and then you lost it, you didn't actually lose any money; it just felt that way.

What if I want to bail when the market goes into the pooper?

Winners of the investment race (i.e., you) always take a deep breath and don't waver, no matter what. This will be you. So when the shit hits the fan, you're going to stay calm and carry on with the asset allocation you came up with. While everyone else is freaking out, you're going to know that this, too, shall pass, and start moving a little money from "loan" investments like bonds to "own" investments like stocks (because they are low, and that means you want to buy!). And when everyone is out partying like it's 1999 (that's a year that stocks were notoriously rockin'), you're going to be moving some of your winnings from stocks to bonds (because they are high, you want to sell!). There aren't a lot of certainties in finance but "buy low, sell high" is one of them (the other is "it's better to beat low expectations," if you're wondering). Remember it, and be active.

What if I become emotional?

There is probably no more significant hurdle that you or any other investor will face than emotion. We human beings are weak; we are prone to groupthink and irrationality. We panic together and become euphoric together, and the actions from these emotions make most of us crappy investors. Enough of that. You want to be emotional? Be that way about your man, your children, yourself, your shoes—anything but your money.

What if I missed out on buying or selling at the right time?

It's natural to be kicking yourself for selling too low or buying too high. It's part of the investing game. You've got to take some risk to get the reward, but don't take on more risk than you can handle. There's a Wall Street-ism that says, "Pigs get fed. Hogs get slaughtered." Think about it.

CONFESSIONS
OF A RICH BITCH

Five ways to outfox other investors

Some solid advice from my girl, Rachel Fox, actress on *Desperate Housewives* and seventeen-year-old day trader. Yes, you read that right—she's just seventeen!! (C'mon—if she can do this, you can do this.)

The first time I saw Rachel was when she was interviewed on CNBC. She was adorable and smart and I was totally smitten.

"What's this cute little fox (pun intended) doing on business news at such a young age?" I thought. "Oh, she's talking about day trading. Wait—she's talking about day trading?!"

She immediately became a girl after my own heart. I had never watched *Desperate Housewives*, but the graphics at the bottom of the screen said that she was an actress on that show. It also flashed a ton of other impressive acting creds, like playing Naomi Watts' daughter in the Daniel Craig film *Dream House*. Now, for most people, that would be enough of a swoon-factor, but what really gets me swooning is Rachel's weekly blog, *Fox on Stocks*, where she talks about being an avid investor (and a successful one too!). So here she is with some words of warning for would-be stock market foxes:

1. **Never take a stock tip.** This is true whether you are making a quick trade or a slow, long-term investment. Why? Because your timing may be different from when the "tipper" gets into and out of the stock. Trust your own research and judgment. The sooner you do, the more you'll understand how everything works and the better choice you will make.

   The one time I bought what someone suggested I buy, I lost my shirt…thousands of dollars. I bought several shares at $2/share. They told me the stock was definitely going to $10/share, and today it trades for a quarter of a penny/share. It's okay to laugh, but be sure to laugh *and* learn.

2. **Do not start trading with real money without first trying it out in a virtual (paper) trading account with fake money.** This rule is not hard and fast, but it is a strong recommendation. You will be so much more comfortable when you trade with real money if

you trade with fake money first, because questions will come up and you will not know everything. When you hesitate for a second and are trading virtually, it's no big deal. When you hesitate for a second because you don't know what you are doing and real money is at stake, that's a big deal.

3. **Do not get emotionally attached to a company whose stock you invest in.** You should be focusing on price only or other technical movements of a company. You should invest in stocks that you think will appreciate in price for one reason or another, but not just because you "love" the company.

4. **Don't watch your stock's price constantly after you've made your purchase.** It will drive you insane. Choose the price at which you will sell or buy and set those actions up to occur automatically.

5. **Do not put all your money into one stock.** Do not even get close. You can automatically diversify by purchasing mutual funds or *exchange traded funds (ETFs)*.* Whatever you choose, do not put all your money in one investment. If it tanks for whatever reason, you will lose everything.

BITCH TIP

There are lots of investing simulators online that give you tutorials and a bunch of fake money to play with, like MarketWatch Virtual Stock Exchange (marketwatch.com/game) and Investopedia Stock Simulator (investopedia.com/simulator). You can also sign up for a smartphone app, like iTrade Stock Market Simulator or 30 Second Stock Market, to play around with fake dollars before investing with real ones.

BITCH TIP

Now that you've gotten the hang of investing (and are liking it!), do you put any extra cash you get into a savings account or back into your investment account? A common question is this: am I keeping too much in savings when I could be putting it to work in the stock market?

To answer the question for yourself, you need to look at your cash strategically. We've already talked about having your emergency fund in Step 3. Don't EVER touch that. But beyond that, you shouldn't have a ton of cash hanging out, possibly losing money with crappy *interest rates*,* as we've discussed before, because of faster-growing *inflation*.* Keep any extra cash "on deck" (my subsavings account for this is literally called "investment account loading dock"). If there's a market opportunity, you want to be able to pounce. Remember the basic tenet of investing: *buy low, sell high*. If the market is "low" (or cheap), you want to have some cash on hand to buy. If you don't have that cash, you could miss out on the opportunity to boost your long-term results.

NO ONE PUTS UNCLE SAM IN THE CORNER

I know you're pumped to make some money. It's exciting and scary stuff at the same time. But remember: when you make money, you've got to give some up to taxes, which is beyond annoying. It makes me feel better to think that you *owe* taxes only if you've *made* money.

Capital gains* refer to the kind of profit you make from buying or selling something; same goes for any loss you make from buying or selling something. You'll hear a lot about "cap gains" in the investment world. You pay for profits only when you actually get that money in your pocket. So if you have a share of Apple's stock and it goes up by $500 but you just watch happily, you don't pay anything. It's only *when you get paid* that you have to pay a portion of your gain to the government. Remember that distinction: only when you cash out do you have to pay more tax.

But not all profit is treated the same. The variable is *time.* If you've invested in a stock for *less* than one year and you sell it to make $500 in profit, then that $500 is taxed as *ordinary income** (that's basically like you're getting it tacked onto your paycheck, so you'd pay the same tax rate you do with your paycheck, which is usually the highest). If you hold on to that stock for *more* than one year, then your $500 is taxed at a better rate. Moral is: longer is better.

An exception to this rule is if you invest in municipal bonds, which are bonds issued by local governments. That interest comes to you scot-free on the federal level and state tax-free if the bond is an in-state bond. It's basically the government encouraging you to invest in your 'hood.

WHAT ABOUT THE COSTS?

While I know it looks as if the lady at my fund and I are great pals, she's not my friend. She's not helping because she's a nice lady (she is that, too). She's gettin' paid.

Every fund has what's called an *expense ratio*,* which is basically what the fund charges to do what it says it's going to do. Expense ratios on index funds are typically very low, maybe 0.25% or less. An expense ratio of 0.25% would charge you $25 per $10,000 per year. A 1% expense ratio (typical for actively managed funds) would charge you $100 per year on $10,000. You don't write anyone a check; rather, the fee is collected from the fund assets. You never really see it; in the end, it just comes out of your return.

It seems like a super-duper small amount, but it adds up. Here's a quick example to show you how much it can add up. Suppose we have two funds: Fund RB1 and Fund RB2. Fund RB1 charges 0.25% per year. Fund RB2 charges 1.25% per year. Assume you invest $10,000 today for thirty years, and that the only difference in your return is the result of the expense ratios. Are you still thinking, "Lapin, that's such a baby amount. It's not that serious, what, like 1% of $10,000 is $100, times 30…" Wait, young grasshopper, you may be forgetting compound interest. Let's say RB1 gives you a 10% return, and RB2 gives you 9%. On that single $10,000 investment, the difference in fees is over $40,000, or four times more than your original investment! The little percentages seem nice and cute until you realize you could have bought a sweet car or down payment for a house with what they charged you.

WHEN CAN I GET AN ADVISOR?

First, this wonderful thing called the internet has a lot of good advice (and lots of bad advice, too). I would humbly recommend nicolelapin.com. There, you'll find a budgeting tool and plug-and-chug calculators (along with a ton of other useful tools, just sayin') to play around with the investments you are looking to make.

I realize that many people prefer to talk to a real, live person who will look after their money rather than do this online. Just know that you're going to pay for that. Advisors charge in a number of ways, but the two main ways are these:

1. Commissions, which can run hundreds of dollars per transaction

2. Management fees, typically in the 1% to 2% range

I know I sound like a yapping dog with the "watch out for fees" statements throughout this book. But now you're really going to understand why. It can get super expensive to pay for an advisor on top of the fees that already exist for investment funds (i.e., if your advisor charges 1% and a mutual fund charges 1%, you are on the hook for 2%). I'm not saying you shouldn't use an advisor; I am saying that if you're going to pay for one, you should get your money's worth.

Here's what to look for:

- **A good rapport.** Don't underestimate this. You want to feel comfortable talking to this person and confident that she'll take your call. Accessibility is one of the most important things you're paying for.

- **Good questions.** Does she ask you a lot of questions, and the *right* questions? You'll learn a lot from the questions your new advisor asks. If she doesn't include all or at least most of what we've already gone through in this book, that's a problem. Your long-term goals, your lifestyle desires, your current financial situation, your career and its prospects, your family, etc. Did she ask you about insurance and other important noninvest-y aspects of your financial life? Because a good advisor will. Good ones get a lot more touchy-feely/ borderline psychologist-y than you'd think. After all, your marriage problems cause you money problems, and if there's something major brewing behind closed doors, your advisor is going to want to/need to know.

What *doesn't* matter: The advisor's knowledge and skill at investing in specific stocks and bonds. Why? Well, because being able to pick a stock is not the role of a financial advisor. The most important thing an advisor does is develop a financial plan for you. Today, many advisors farm out their picks on stocks, bonds, and the like to people who do *only* that.

What *does* matter: Good advisors learn your desires and risk tolerances and devise a plan that meets your needs. They are like a singer's manager. The manager brings on a literary agent if the performer is going to write a book, an entertainment lawyer if the performer has a deal that needs to be signed, a makeup artist for appearances. Why? Because the manager can't do all those things alone but knows how to find people who can. In my little analogy, you are the performer and the advisor is the manager. All the experts report to the advisor. All the bills go to...you. If you like someone running the show and coming up with your own little financial planning team, excellent. Sometimes you gotta spend money to make money.

But other times, you don't have to spend money to make money. You've already learned a ton about your financial future yourself, so if you want professional TLC, look into it. Maybe it's right for you, maybe it's not. Even if it's not, you will at least have gotten it out of your system. I tend to think that figuring out what you *don't* want is just as important as figuring out what you *do* want. Just remember, in hiring a financial advisor, you are essentially bringing on a co-chief financial officer (the other one, of course, being YOU!). You will always be the primary chief, though. No one, not even the best advisor of them all, will care as much about you and your money as *you*.

BOTTOM LINE

Conventional wisdom: Only professionals can do this.

Oh, please. You know enough now to get going on your savings and to invest smartly. Sure, good professional advice is nice and worth having, but don't let the financial world's incessant (and obnoxious) attempt to complicate things paralyze you.

Conventional wisdom: You have to study stocks to invest in stocks.

Not really. You can achieve the right stock exposure at a low cost through an index fund or mutual fund without worrying whether Apple is going to sell a lot of iPhones or Exxon is going to move a lot of oil. What you're after is the overall return, and this you can achieve without reading the *Wall Street Journal* every day (although you already know my thoughts on that: you should!).

Conventional wisdom: Investing is for rich people.

If you do it right, you might become a high roller, but investing is truly democratic. You can get started with just the cash you'd blow on a lottery ticket, and with a much better chance of actually making money.

11

BEING UNDER, OVER AND ON TOP OF "THE MAN"

Rich Bitches in a Man's World

First of all: are men necessary?

No.

There, that settles it.

Well, let me be clear: I'm not saying there shouldn't be men in your life; that would just be crazy talk. What I am saying is that you don't need a man or anyone else for money. You know how to take care of yourself. Do not expect to be saved financially. You are your own woman. You've read this far, so I know you get it. Now, don't forget it.

So, let's talk about men: how to work for them, work with them, have them work for you; how to live with them and discuss money issues with them.

WORKING FOR THE MAN

Over the course of your working life—and we're talking forty or fifty years, unless you hit the jackpot and retire early—you're going to have male bosses, male colleagues and male underlings. Depending on your industry or field, there might be a lot of men around or a few. While things are changing for the better, there are some businesses that are still dominated by men, like finance, law, and sports or business journalism.

I've been in many male-dominated workplaces, and while there wasn't overt "lady discrimination," I found some standards and practices a little, well, not ladylike...like colleagues who like to woo clients by taking them to a strip club; they didn't tell me not to come along, but I don't think they would ever have imagined that I or another woman would want to. I haven't seen any overt *Mad Men* stuff like calling women "broads," but little things like having a tiny ladies' bathroom are subtly annoying.

CONFESSIONS
OF A RICH BITCH

The boss from you-know-where

When I first started in network news, I had a heinous direct boss. He clearly was not my fan. Supposedly, he was just in charge of my schedule: which hours I worked, which days I was off, when I could take vacation. But no. Instead, he took it upon himself to write me the most ridiculous emails about my appearance and presentation. One day, my makeup was looking too "draggy." Another day, my outfits were "not appropriate for relaying the news." I wish I made that up, but sadly it's true, and the last thing you want to read when you are on television. Another time—and this is my favorite—I was reporting on a story about a boulder falling off a cliff in California onto a car and I said, "Thankfully, the man wasn't killed." Okay, I kid you not, the a-hole sent me a note saying, "Don't editorialize by saying 'thankfully.' Just report the news." WTF?! I'm sorry,

I went to the best journalism school in the country, and I am a card-carrying member of the fourth estate (a fancy term for the "journalism elite"). But seriously, is anyone really going to argue with feeling relieved that a life was spared?! It's so ridiculous that I want to throw my computer against the wall just thinking about it.

His a-hole-isms weren't limited to email. He set up a five-minute "catch-up" meeting for the two of us. It showed up as an invitation on my calendar, and all I wanted to do was click the Decline button. But alas, I accepted it. We met at his desk (of course). He proceeded to tell me that I was too "cutesy and folksy and girly" and…"in the male-dominated days of news, of Morrow and Cronkite" (Burgundy?) "it is better to be respected than liked." Those condescending words are ones I will never, ever forget. Male-dominated? What decade was this dude in?? It is better to be respected than liked? Really? I wanted to scream. But instead, I hemmed and hawed and said, "Thank you for the feedback."

There's no right answer on how to deal with these things. But if I had to do it all over again, I actually don't think I would have said or done anything differently. I always think that it's best to minimize the ping-pong back-and-forth, especially when it is laced with vitriol. I am far from a saint; I've pushed Send on far too many emails that I should never have sent. But in this situation, all I wanted to do was focus on being more respected *and* liked. I worked harder than ever on "serious" projects and smarter reporting, but also on making more allies to outbalance the foe I had. But no, I drew the line at a sex change, which I'm sure was the only thing that would have placated him.

The only thing I regret about this situation is that I dwelled on it as much as I did (and still obviously haven't completely let it go). The other thing I half regret is that I tried to prove something to that guy. It was perfectly fine that I wanted to focus on being more respected and liked, but I shouldn't have done it for him—I should have done it for *me*.

I want you to know that you can be respected *and* liked. Just know that it's possible to be both. Don't overcompensate in either direction. You're undoubtedly going to work for some pretty difficult people throughout your career—men *and* women, too—but ultimately your aim should be developing your career for *you* and not letting their difficult personalities make your life more, well, difficult.

ASK FOR A RAISE (AND ACTUALLY GET IT!)

Men are four times more likely to ask for a raise than their female coworkers—and usually get one. So what gives? You've got to start asking, too.

1. **Timing is everything.** Set yourself up for success by finding a good time to approach your boss. At 5:30 p.m. on a crazy-busy Monday? Probably not the best time. The day after the company releases a dismal earnings report? Probably not the best time, either. After you've received a stellar performance review or praise from a client? GREAT time to make your move. Let your boss know that you want to speak with her "today at her convenience," which accommodates her busy schedule while putting a solid deadline on the conversation. And if you're scared you'll chicken out, asking for the time with her in advance will make it a *fait accompli* that the ask will at least occur.

2. **Do your homework.** Don't go into the conversation blind; studies show that women who approach a raise without a set, reasonable number in mind are less likely to climb

the pay scale. Talk to friends (both male *and* female) in similar industries to see what they're making, and find averages for your industry and level of experience on sites like Payscale.com and Salary.com. These sites allow you to search geographically, which is important as you decide what you need to live on in *your* area. And remember: the idea isn't to get a raise just to get by, but to have a little extra to dump into savings. So shoot on the high end of the averages you find. As my grandma used to say, "Reach for the moon; even if you miss, you'll land among stars!" (Or as one of my girlfriends amended, "Shoot for the moon and don't f--- it up. Earth is a long way down.")

3. **Gather your evidence.** Come prepared with specific examples of your stellar performance and positive feedback that you have received from colleagues and clients. You don't need an entire laundry list of the awesome things you've done at work, but a few key examples that demonstrate the qualities of a superb employee including professionalism, work ethic, creativity and cooperation (all good buzzwords to throw down in your convo, too). Cite a few important lessons you have learned during your time at the company, and express the desire to continue to learn and grow within that environment. Your employers will be more likely to invest in you if they see the raise as having long-term value. I know, it's awkward to talk yourself up/play your own publicist, so practice your little pitch and try for a warm but pointed delivery.

4. **Put community first.** It's important to respect your relationship with your boss and coworkers. After all, the numbers on your paycheck may change, but you're still going to be working with the same people. So frame the discussion around your role within the company. Think

of yourself not as a single moving part but as a valuable asset to the company at large. Demonstrate how your performance has positively impacted the company's performance. Finally, let your boss know that you respect her opinion by concluding with, "What do you think?"

5. **Get creative.** Sure, a salary bump is the most typical kind of raise, but there are lots of other ways to reward your performance, and some might be even more valuable to your current financial and personal situation. Perhaps it's a more robust health-care package, which will help mitigate your monthly health-care bills. Or you can ask for better stock options, or to be included in the company's bonus structure should they have one in place. Have a long commute or kids at home? Negotiate for one day per week of working from home. Whatever you ask for, the point is to know your worth and to make work *work* for you.

CONFESSIONS
OF A RICH BITCH

Working with the man

You may not be negotiating your salary and employment terms with a man, but it's crucial for you to know—and express—your worth no matter who your employer is. I'll never forget the first time I negotiated my own salary. It was the first time I had *two* competing offers, which basically made me feel invincible and out of control at the same time. On the one hand, I had *two* offers when I would have died to have just one working in a field I love, so I didn't want to mess it up. On the other hand, I had *two* offers, so I was bound to still have one if I played them off each other, right?

I was barely twenty and had only heard about women negotiating for themselves, but had no idea how it was done. I wasn't a hard-ass (and I really needed a job), so I just went back to each of them and said I had an offer from the other one. The money was basically the same: around $32,000 for workplace A versus $32,500 for workplace B.

The boss at workplace A wrote back and said that he could go up to $32,500 but the length of the contract needed to remain a strict three years with no outs. The boss at workplace B wrote back and said she knew workplace A wouldn't give me any more than what she was offering (she knew because she used to work there), so she wouldn't either, but she did gave me a flexible contract.

Now, the money was the same and I had heard that the boss at workplace B was a superstar woman in my industry who rose through the ranks quickly. She was a tough cookie, the kind of boss who smashed tapes and took names. So, naturally, I thought, "All things being basically equal, I'd rather work for her."

Now, just because we were both chicks powering it out in the industry together didn't mean she was easy on me. She made it clear, whether it was true or not, that there was another candidate waiting in the wings if I didn't accept.

I accepted the job at workplace B. I didn't want to go back and play "hardball" any more (even though what I did was basically "Wiffle Ball"). Also, I thought I would be "getting paid" by working for this new, awesome boss. She was extremely good at her job and everyone knew it—including her. I was pumped to work with her and see her in action.

A few months later, I was promoted (yay me) but I didn't actually get or even ask for more money for it. My boss then hired someone else for the same gig I had, but for more money.

Apparently, our mutual boss lady, who had a young family herself (yay her), offered to give the new hire more money because his wife just had a baby. Say WHAT? I found out that she had asked him: "Are you sure it's enough money for you and your family?"

So I had a bigger job but he made more money. That's right: because he might have a family to support, he got more money. Listen, I'm all about making more money to support a family, of course. I'm just not all about getting less money because I don't have one. I don't know what exactly it was that made a guy with less responsibility than me get more money from this ball-busting lady. It could have been girl-on-girl *Mean Girls* kinda hating, although I don't think it was (and hope that it wasn't). It was probably just a tale of not making my worth known enough and letting someone else assume that because I was young and hungry, I was also cheap labor. Whether I went home to feed twenty foster kids and ten cats or I went home to hang out with my boyfriend, I was still doing the same work—but I didn't have the guts then to make that clear.

If I had to go back and revisit my first negotiation, I would ask for more money at signing and at promotion. Obviously she had it to give, since she gave it to someone else. I was just too scared to lose what I had by asking for it. I will also never assume again that a woman has my back in business just because she's a woman. It's not a sorority. It's business, and I should have been better at it.

WHEN THE MAN WORKS FOR YOU

Some women feel like they have to overcompensate for being female by acting overly aggressive and abrasive. You want people to *want* to work for and with you, right? Right. Then who the heck cares if you're a woman? You can be feminine *and* professional. If you are good at what you do, that's all that matters.

Wanna know what the number one criticism I got was as I worked my way up in my career? People told me that I had to cut my hair. Yep, it was my *hair*. They said I needed to look more credible, so I needed to cut my hair. The more I think about it, the more I think it is as ridiculous as not saying you're thankful someone didn't die. I would always say, "What does my hair have to do with being good at my job?" Of course, it didn't have anything to do with it. I could (kind of) understand where they were coming from, but it stemmed from a place I hate: not rethinking convention. Just because anchorwomen up until that time had the "anchor bob" didn't mean I needed one. If I chose to have my hair that way, then cool. But, I didn't—ten years ago or today.

Fast forward to the present day and watch the news. You'll see long-haired anchorwomen wearing sleeveless tops (which was also taboo when I was starting out). Say it ain't so! How could it be that women who are bad at their jobs infiltrated TV news?? Instead, convention was finally challenged, and we've started to realize that you can bare arms and still be a respected anchorwoman (and, ahem, first lady).

I'm no trendsetter, but I had long hair back then and have long hair now. It's how I feel most comfortable. It's me. Every once in a while I think to myself, "I'm thirty. I own a business. Shouldn't I look a little more polished and professional?" And then I stop myself and say that I will only be more polished and professional if I feel those things. My employees want to work for me (I think and hope) because I am not pretending to be professional with some rigid hairstyle but because I have the experience to lead them and the ease to know that I do. These days I don't have time to analyze my hairstyle. And frankly, I wouldn't want to work for someone who did.

I have a poster in my office that says, "Look like a girl/Act like a lady/Think like a man/Work like a boss." I take that to mean look like whatever you want as long as you work your ass off like you run the place.

BITCH TIP

There's another thing in the work world of equal value to your skills and reputation: your Rolodex. That is, the contacts and connections you have collected and fostered over the years between family, friends, school, careers and beyond. You're a Rich Bitch, so I can guarantee that there are a few "winners" in there; contacts that are particularly valuable, not just to you but to others, as well.

Know their worth—and your worth, too. You could stand to make some actual money doing so. That's right, guys do this all the time. It's called the finder's fee, and it works like this:

1. **You have a contact of particular value** (such as a potential investor for a new company).
2. **You offer to connect your friend/colleague with said person** (either by offering to directly, or because they asked you to—it doesn't really make a difference who initiates).

> 3. **You make the introduction** and, as long as the meeting goes through, you charge a small fee for it (maybe 10% to 15% of the final deal, depending on the level of awesomeness of the contact and the work between them that comes out of the meeting). After all, they wouldn't have had that new bit of business without you.
>
> Feel a little used car salesman to you? It did to me the first time I heard about it, too. Get over it. Guys do this all the time. Your mad networking skills are not free, nor should they be. If friends/colleagues want to tap into your Rolodex, think about making 'em pay the toll.

ACT LIKE A LADY, WORK LIKE A BOSS

So you're finally in the boss's chair, huh? Whether you've moved up the ranks at work or are in a position to hire at your very own company, it's essential to take the time to foster relationships with your employees. Don't forget, you were there once, too, and happy employees mean a better work environment for all. Here's how:

1. **Get to know them.** I mean more than first names and hometowns. Your new employees may be anxious about what the change in leadership (that is, you) will mean for them, or what life might be like working at a small start-up, if that's the case. Put their fears to rest by showing a genuine interest in learning more about them. Make one-on-one meetings more than a one-time thing. Don't fall into the trap of being overly nice up front and then disappearing. Set regular check-ins to

revisit goals even after you're chummy with everyone in the office.

2. **Trust them.** It's easy to fall into micromanaging when overseeing people you don't know, but it won't make you very popular or effective. Plus, you'll only be creating more work for yourself. Instead, identify your employees' strengths and weaknesses and then plan semiautonomous tasks accordingly. Define the ultimate goal and deadline of each task, then set minideadlines for steps along the way. Regular check-ins will allow you to ensure that progress is being made without being overbearing; plus, these check-ins will allow you to adjust your approach as needed to get to the desired goal even faster.

3. **Dish a compliment sandwich.** Genuine praise can motivate a team to work harder; so can genuine criticism. Focus your feedback on behaviors and skills that you want to see more of while at the same time demonstrating why other approaches aren't as successful. If my employees fall behind, I talk with them privately. But I start with a compliment and end with a compliment. In between, I put in the zinger of what I think they need to improve on. It's not phony to compliment someone whom you are also reprimanding. I mean, you can find good in even the worst employees. A constructive way to motivate the improvement of the bad behavior is to relay optimism and respect. But if that doesn't work, compliment sandwiches work when you are firing someone, too.

4. **Be nice to your boss.** BTW: That boss is you now. I can tell you that being a boss doesn't mean all of a sudden you feel like a badass. In fact, it may be the opposite. When you first start to take on that responsibility of

being a boss, you might feel plagued with feelings of inadequacy and guilt. You might be overwhelmed with thoughts like, "Did I do enough at the end of the day?" or "I shouldn't have taken a break because now there's no one to blame but myself!" Don't assume just because your productivity matters to your business the most now that you have to be in front of your computer 24/7. Studies have shown that productivity works in cycles. So don't beat yourself up for stepping away. That time away from the computer could make you more productive when you return to it.

BITCH TIP

I have always been a girl's girl but not so much of a club/organized activity girl. However, some female employees and I started an ad hoc girls' club where we try new, unconventional workouts together every couple of weeks. Past adventures have included trampoline class, cheerleading, even sword-fighting—no joke. You don't need to join some stuffy Junior League type of club to develop a good "girl community." Your "professional group" doesn't need to be super organized, either. Mine certainly isn't. We just send a quick email saying we'll meet at the pole bar class or Beyoncé dance class (yes, there is one) or whatever sounds funny and fun. There's nothing better than bonding and laughing your ass off in the back of a trampoline class to make you want to have someone's back at work.

FOR LOVE OR MONEY: GETTIN' DOWN WITH A RICH DUDE

I'm not going to tell you how to snag a rich dude. That's lame. Instead, consider the term "Rich Dude" to be the male counterpart of "Rich Bitch" with the connotation of being driven to be smart and successful. I'd venture to say that you want that in a man. I do. And being driven to be smart and successful doesn't have anything to do with a guy's bank account. I was dating my high school wannabe hedge fund manager boyfriend while I was working (and making money) and he was a law school student (and not making any money). I couldn't have cared less that we lived off Chipotle burritos in his dorm room, which was so small that the bed had to be lofted in order to have space for a chair. He was brilliant and ambitious. But, as I told you at the beginning of this book, I apparently wasn't smart enough for him, because I didn't ask questions about finance when I didn't know. I never let that happen again.

My next boyfriend was also a law student. We were on and off and on and off and then on. We were the "looking at rings together" kinda serious. The offer he got for a summer job was rescinded, so he lived with me and I paid rent. I didn't mind the paying for stuff part, but his lack of drive after his job didn't pan out was a total turnoff. He wasn't a Rich Dude not because he had no money but because he wasn't determined to find something else to be successful at, even if it was a temporary job. At that point, I was cruising into the confident Rich Bitch territory, getting my three E's in check and my goals in order. I realized when he wasn't in those goals, he wasn't right for me.

I went on two interesting dates soon after my breakup. One was with a guy I met on a plane. Yep, that happened. He took me out to go beer tasting, which I thought was cool, and we started talking about work. I love talking about work; it's the thing I'm truly passionate about. And I'll never forget what he said: "I don't think women should work." Umm…"Check, please!"

The next one was with a guy who lived in my apartment building. Yep, that also happened. We went out to dinner and I was talking all about my day at work, and he said, "I really don't like to talk about work at the end of the day." Umm… "Check, please!"

Aside from physical and emotional chemistry, I think we all need professional chemistry in our love lives, as well. As you are going about shaping your big professional goals, you want a guy who can and wants to talk to you about them, someone to challenge those goals in a smart way, all the while being your biggest champion.

The right guy will want the same things. We want and need our own lives and goals, and you should want and need him to have the same. That's the only way for a strong "rich" couple to come together and complement each other, helping each other strive professionally *and* personally. Because really, your professional life and your personal life are just part of your one life. If you're not happy in either of the parts, you won't be happy in general.

THE TALK

Once you have found your Rich Dude, the time will come when you need to have The Talk. It's the time when the two of you come clean about money: what's important to you, what's not, what your financial situation *really* is, and of course the little secrets that may come back to haunt you (like money you owe to an ex, your credit card debt, or other forms of financial leprosy that, unacknowledged, could eat away at your relationship).

You're probably thinking that there's really nothing less romantic than The Talk. Here you are, falling in love, and you're going to start asking about credit scores and retirement accounts? Yuck.

Well, I'm sorry. The importance of The Talk cannot be overstated. You want to talk about your dream of designing and building your own custom house? He wants to talk about the car he wants to own or the sports memorabilia he's saving up for? Do it. Get it all out. Understand that money is the main source of conflict between committed partners. It's such an uncomfortable topic that half—HALF!—of all people have lied to their spouse or significant other about money. In fact, you're much more likely to argue with your spouse about money than anything to do with kids or who's doing the laundry or where you're going to take that long-awaited vacation.

Why is this? The answer lies in the beginning chapters of this book. Your approach to money is cultural, often acquired subconsciously, and incredibly personal. How you handle money is an expression of your desires and fears.

You need to have The Talk because just as you need to be on the same financial page with yourself, you need to be on the same financial page with your significant other. When should you do this? Soon. Okay, don't go all crazy and ask for a credit report on the first date. But also don't put it off forever. And certainly have The Talk before you shack up. By the time you're playing house together, you should have talked about the C-word (that's credit, you pervs).

GETTING DOWN TO BUSINESS

So where do you start with having The Talk? No, there is never really a "good time." Just make some time and get 'er done. Don't make it like an IRS audit. Be casual. Sit in a comfortable and private place, and talk it out. Pour a drink if that makes it easier for you. It shouldn't be confrontational; it should be aspirational. You're sharing, making plans together.

Having The Talk helps any relationship align your goals, your collective Endgame. Regardless of who makes more money (and if there is any weirdness if there is a big difference in your paychecks), your goals as a couple make you simpatico.

What does The Talk consist of? Well, a lot of what you've already done in this book. Ask your guy (or gal) what he or she wants out of life. Find out what's really important to the person. Sure, you think you know this already, but you probably don't completely understand it. You'd be surprised how money brings things into focus.

Here's a little cheat sheet of conversation starters:

- **Do you want to travel?** Does he? Do you both?

- **Buy a house?** Rent an apartment?

- **Get married?** Have kids?

- **What kind of stuff do you like to splurge on?** What would you buy if you all of a sudden came into a bunch of extra money?

Remember: your goals don't have to be perfectly in sync, just compatible. He wants to rent since his job might move him around; are you okay with that? Are you sharing rent? Are you both cool with that decision? What's important is that you share an understanding on the big money issues: buy Essentials, save for the Endgame, spend a reasonable amount on the Extras. And just because one person might not be contributing to the team financially doesn't mean he or she doesn't have an important role. Consider your relationship (or family) like a business, too. There are different roles, like a chief operating officer, who doesn't focus on bringing up the numbers but makes sure things run smoothly, and is equally as valuable as the partner who takes on the role of chief revenue officer.

Next comes what will often be the most difficult part of The Talk: what is your current situation? This can get really uncomfortable. Maybe you have to admit to a bunch of bad money habits. Maybe he does. Maybe you have to point out those bad habits, which is probably the most difficult talk of all. Whatever the situation, face it head-on. As tough as it seems now, it will only get tougher later if you sweep it under the rug. Ask the hard questions, and be honest yourself.

Here are some topics to hammer out, in no particular order:

- **Get your credit reports.** It might feel like "getting tested," but it's not that serious. Yeah, this seems like distrust, but hey, he may not even know what's on his. You're helping him understand his situation. You should go first. Your mission should be to hold nothing back and demand that nothing is held back.

- **Talk about your budgets.** What does your own personal balance sheet look like? Your assets? Your liabilities? Your cash flow for the month? Where is it all going?

- **Work out a financial plan together, just as you've already done for yourself.**

- **Talk about your money secrets.** It might not strike you as all that sexy, but neither is arguing about money or nasty little financial surprises down the road.

The Talk will probably take place in different sections at different times. Don't try to boot camp this conversation all in one night. It will just end up in a fight. Work at your own pace. Also (brace yourself): The Talk doesn't happen just once. Or at least it shouldn't. It should happen all the time, especially as your lives and financial situations change. As with the other parts of your relationship, the better you communicate, the better off you'll be.

And just as you might divide and conquer the household chores, so should you divide and conquer the financial chores. No one is dying to be the bookkeeper (well, almost no one), but if you can and will do it and he won't, then do it. Or, if he's the bookkeeping type of guy, let him do it. Delegate. It's hard to do when it comes to money, but too bad. Welcome to adulthood. That doesn't mean you shouldn't know what the bills are or how they're paid. If the designated bill payer is for any reason unavailable—traveling for work, in an accident, whatever—the other partner should be able to step in seamlessly.

So if you've had The Talk and been honest with each other, delegation and the sharing of responsibilities will be easier than it might seem right now, for one simple reason: trust. It's a big reason you're together in the first place. Where there's truth, there must be trust. And trust is sexy.

SHACKIN' UP

You understand that moving in together is a big step. But have you considered how big a *financial* step it is? You should.

If you're married, then there are rules of how assets and debts are divided up if things go south. But if you're not married, it's more of a free-for-all. So have an honest discussion up front, and try to put what you decide in writing. It's awkward as heck, but so is having your name on a lease when he splits. Or, what if you're supporting him while he's going to school? How would you feel if your relationship ends when he graduates and he goes off and makes a fortune? Sad, sure, but how about "owed," too?

So here's what to hammer out before shackin' up:

- **What would it look like if you divvy up what you have acquired together**, including furniture, cars and even money?
- **Will you use credit cards?** Will you have joint bank accounts? What are the rules of engagement?
- **Whose name is on the utility bills?** Lease? Mortgage? Car? (Remember: if your name is on it, you're responsible for its getting *paid*.)
- **Who gets the dog?** No joke, this is one of the things couples who are living together and break up argue about most. (And dogs are awesome, but they ain't cheap!)

There's nothing that says you can't change the agreement as your situation changes, but get something down first. That's the hardest part.

Remember that your rights in the eyes of the law depend on whether or not you and your sig-o have made it official. Domestic partnership laws vary greatly from state to state, but here are a few things you can expect:

If you are unmarried:

- **No federal or state tax benefits at all.** The best ones go to married people who file jointly. Boo.

- **You'll have to name each other as beneficiaries in your wills,** on your financial accounts and on your life insurance policies if you want your sig-o to get your stuff when, God forbid, something happens to you.
- **You'll have to designate your partner as your health-care proxy** (free forms found online) or power of attorney (forms available online but need to be notarized). Otherwise, your parents or other immediate family will have the power to make decisions for you if you're unable.

If you and your partner have a civil union:

- **The federal government does not currently offer civil union benefits,** but several states do to varying degrees.
- **You'll need to secure Health Care Power of Attorney** (HCPOA) or Health Care Representative (HCR) status to ensure hospital visits. There are free forms available from each state's government website.

WHAT'S MINE IS MINE

"He's the one," you say. You're totally in love, I gotcha. Even with all that, don't go all lovey-dovey and overly trusting with everything you've worked so hard for.

At the start it may be best to keep your finances separate, especially if you're contributing equally to household expenses. But then, you'll probably want to look into having some sort of joint account. You can divide your accounts up into "Yours," "Mine" and "Ours." Here's what I suggest keeping in the "Mine" account under your name, at least in the beginning:

- Bank account
- Credit card
- Car

The first thing that's usually melded as an "Ours" account is a bank account, into which you each put an agreed-upon part of your pay and from which household expenses are paid. In practical terms, someone will likely take the lead in writing most of the checks or paying the bills online. Still, you're mixing your money and your lives in a similar way, and this will usually cover your Essentials and sometimes Extras, depending on what they are.

You should always keep a "Yours" and "Mine" Endgame. There isn't a joint retirement option, and even if there were, I wouldn't suggest that you use one. No matter whom you're living with and/or how committed you are, you should never shortchange your Endgame.

MARRIAGE

Do I need to say this is a big step? Of course it is. And how awesome that same-sex marriage is now recognized by the federal government and more and more states every year. Still, few women consider the financial ramifications of getting hitched. The most obvious one is that not only your emotional fates are tied together but also your financial ones.

If you're good boys and girls, you've had The Talk several times already. Now comes what I like to call The Advanced Talk:

- **You'll have to determine whether to file your taxes jointly or separately**; typically filing jointly will be cheaper, and there are often tax breaks.
- **You'll have to decide whether to insure each other's lives,** a.k.a. get life insurance.
- **You should both write up a will.**
- **You might also want a pre-nup.** Yes, women can get pre-nups to protect themselves, too. Women I've spoken

to who have made their man sign one feel pretty
damn empowered.

These feel like icky things to talk about in the midst of the time
you've dreamed about since you were a little girl, but part of living
out that dream—often a big part—is planning, for better or worse.

I'VE GOT YOU, BABE

In the end, it doesn't matter if you work for a man, are the boss
of a man, have a man or leave a man. It's not about men. Period.
Nothing makes me want to throw stuff against a wall more
than hearing a woman talk or even joke about getting a "M-R-S
degree" (as in, going to college for the sake of finding a husband).
Not to get all feminist on you, but guess who you knew before
all these guys? Um, *you*. That's the only thing you've got that's
certain, toots. The guys in a professional and personal capacity
come and go. You are your own CEO, and as such you are always
going to be the boss of you—through sickness and health, 'til
death do you part.

BOTTOM LINE

Conventional wisdom: Men are a pain in the ass.

Actually, this one is true.

Conventional wisdom: Women aren't as respected in the workplace as men.

This one is up to you. It's a fine line between standing your
ground and standing up for yourself and becoming a she-
monster. Have confidence in your abilities, your vision and
your voice to speak up. After you've figured out what you want
(remember all the way back in Step 2), ask for it.

Conventional wisdom: Love conquers all.

It doesn't when it comes to money. Have The Talk and continue to have The Talk. Relationships are always changing, as are financial situations and even desires, so keep the lines of financial communication open. This way, money doesn't get in the way of love.

12

BRINGING IT HOME
Your Life Is Your Business

The most powerful topic to me, which like much of what we've talked about in this book doesn't feel like a typical, traditional business topic, is the business of *you*. Newsflash: you are your own business. You are your ultimate business card. If you don't take care of yourself and treat your life like a business, you won't be good in any other kind.

So, as we are bringing this twelve-step program home, let's tie up some odds and ends: things in your life that seemingly have nothing to do with personal finance but can actually have *everything* to do with it.

YOUR HOME IS A BUSINESS

Your home isn't always where your heart is—but your home can be where your stress starts. If, first thing in the morning, you are thrust into chaos from the disaster that is your closet, to the pile of bills on your desk, to the roomie/boyfriend/husband who is pissed off because you give him zero attention, to your dirty car and your disorganized purse—what do you think your day is going to be like? One word: crap-tastic.

So learn to run your home like a business. Here's how:

- **It sounds trite, but if your space is organized, you'll have a better chance of being organized in your professional life.** Low-hanging fruit: color-coordinate your closet. Set up your hanging clothes to go from whites to yellows to reds to purples to blues to blacks. It will save you time getting dressed in the morning and temper that age-old "I have nothing to wear" complaint, too.

- **Donate clothes, shoes, bags, accessories, old makeup, etc.,** that you haven't used in years and that are now just contributing to the clutter. If it's hardly worn or valuable, sell it on eBay and make some extra dough. Or do something good for the world and donate it to charity—plus you can take a tax write-off.

- **Have a system to organize and tackle your bills, junk mail, invitations and letters.**

- **Carve out time to tend to your partner so that you make him (or her) feel like a priority.**

- **Pick a couple of flowers from your garden (or grab some from the corner store) and place them in a vase by your bed so that you see something that makes you smile first thing in the morning.**

- **Do you keep tripping over the same end table in your living room?** Does the color of your bathroom walls annoy you? You can give your home a facelift just by rearranging the furniture or adding a coat of colorful paint to make your home feel new without spending a pile of dough on new furniture or decor.

- **If you have to call in a professional, such as a plumber or electrician or babysitter, use your Rich Bitch negotiating skills.** Shop around for the best price and highest quality service. Do a little research on AngiesList.com or Care.com or even Yelp.com for customer ratings and recommendations.

- **Keep a little folder for all of your household stuff: appliance warranties, service providers, maintenance calls, etc.** That way you'll know whom to call when something goes haywire.

Once you have a system down, you will feel at peace in your home, and it will help you recharge when you are stressed and overextended. Transform your chaotic mess into your own domestic sanctuary and you will find that you are happier and even better at doing your job, whether you work from home or elsewhere.

YOUR BODY IS SERIOUS BUSINESS

It's not all about having a rockin' bod—although sure, it's a great asset to have. Your health is your most important asset. After all, you are your own brand ambassador, and you have to be healthy in order to shine, inside and out.

The reality is that if you are starting your own business, you likely have to pay for your own health insurance and doctors' appointments. You no longer have paid sick days. Taking days off may be easy since you are your own boss, but every day that you're not working, you're also potentially missing opportunities.

If you get really sick, that's going to suck, whether you work for someone else or for yourself. Not just from a financial stand-point, but from the career momentum standpoint of having to cancel hard-earned meetings and having to take a break from your purpose-driven pace.

Make your health a priority. I should practice more of this than I preach, but let's all try to do more of this: schedule annual checkups with your primary doc, even if you think you don't need it. Even bare-bones insurance policies will pay for these. And this is one I actually like doing: an annual dental cleaning! Not only does it make your teeth feel so fresh and so clean, but it's an investment in your dental health, too; a little maintenance is better than getting hit with a huge bill (and a lot of pain) for a root canal—the cost of which most dental plans do not fully cover.

Schedule your workouts as you would meetings. Even beyond the health-promoting benefits, when you exercise regularly you are happier, you think more clearly, your confidence is boosted, and endorphins are pumping through your body, giving you that extra injection of enthusiasm that you need to push just that much harder. A lot of people think they are too busy and that they have no time, and the first thing to go is exercise. I'm so guilty of this. I hate working out, but I do it because I know it's good for my body, my health and, ultimately, my business. Even President Obama—the leader of the free world, for cryin' out loud—manages to hit the gym *six* days a week, and that's not including those well-known basketball games with his staff. First Lady Michelle Obama gets up at four-thirty in the morning three times a week to get her workout in. If those two can find the time, we all can.

BITCH TIP

When things get really crazy around the office, my production company cofounder and I hit the streets of New York for a run. I kid you not. She's a marathon runner (like a serial one); I'm a runner who looks like she is power-walking as she "runs," but we both benefit from the fresh air and change of scenery. It's amazing how something as simple as working up a sweat can help put things in perspective and get the creative juices flowing; we often come up with new story ideas, solutions to problems we've been working through or plans for world domination while out pounding the pavement. And it's my favorite kind of two-fer: getting some good work done and also squeezing in a workout so we don't have to stress about making it to the gym on top of everything else. Don't think for a second that you have to be chained to a desk. When in doubt, sweat it out!

PHONE A FRIEND

I'm not going to hunt you down and make you do any of the things we've talked about in this book. That's on you. Develop a community of other women (or men, of course) who've admitted that they have a financial problem. Ask them for help, too. In fact, help each other. Create a support system. Agree to go on a spending freeze together. Make it fun:

- **Instead of having a girls' night out at that new bar on Friday night for $12 cocktails, have an even better girls' night in.** $8 wine from Trader Joe's, some snacks, and some good company go a long way!

- **Flirting with a new designer bag?** It's in your hand, you know it's wrong, but you're walking up to the salesperson to ring it up—now phone a friend and have her talk you off the ledge. Take a picture of the bag and text it to your group to show them what you had the willpower to pass up.

- **Create friendly competition around who is doing best at cutting expenses: think The Biggest *Debt* Loser.** Share how you were able to talk your cell phone provider into giving you a reduced rate, or how you played your credit card companies against each other to cut your interest rate in half.

- **Have a clothing swap where you shop in each other's closets; one woman's trash is another woman's come-up.**

No good bitch is an island. As money issues become more intense, a like-minded community will keep you sane and moving in the right direction.

CONFESSIONS
OF A RICH BITCH

Missives from a girl crush

Girls creator Lena Dunham grew up as the ultimate fangirl of iconic filmmaker Nora Ephron (*When Harry Met Sally*, *Sleepless in Seattle*). So you can probably imagine how thrilled Lena was years later to get an email from her self-professed hero, complimenting her first film (*Tiny Furniture*) and inviting her to lunch. (I'm sure she would have been even more excited if she had known that it was just the first of many lunches the two would have.)

Nora went on to teach Lena about not being labeled as a "woman writer," how to talk to the film crew, how to make a shot list, even which fleece jacket to wear on set. But

Nora also shared with Lena her wisdom on self-respect, which dessert to order, how to find the right apartment, the best contractors, the best doctors, and a man who appreciates you, famously telling her that "you can't meet someone until you've become who you're becoming."

Lena was still living with her parents when she met Nora. As their friendship grew, Lena's career took off. Her girl crush became a support system not only for her career but also for living a richer life than she ever could have imagined.

CHECK YOURSELF

Life is weird and unpredictable. Even after you've gone through all these steps, something will likely change, and you might have to start all over again, rejiggering your Spending Plan and your goals. Keep calm and budget on.

Check in with your inventory on a monthly basis and add in any additional expenses so that your Spending Plan is a real-time reflection of what you have to spend (and to save). This includes medical bills, relocation costs, a new pet, etc.—expenditures that you didn't necessarily count on when you first made the plan. Chances are that as your career blossoms and you become a savvier investor, you will be adding additional income to the mix, too.

As you grow and accumulate greater wealth, your Spending Plan is going to become more complex. But that's a *good* thing. This isn't a race. Pace yourself. You're not a firework, so don't go big at the beginning and burn out. Remember why you are doing this in the first place. Celebrate the *little* things that can lead to really *big* victories.

CONFESSIONS
OF A RICH BITCH

I knew I made it when…

You probably have one of those moments in mind, when you will finally know you have "arrived." If you don't, you should, because it's the best, most personal motivator—and sweetest reward once you get there.

Mine was avocados. Yes, avocados. They're expensive to buy at the grocery store and I used to say to myself, "I'll know I've made it when I can buy as many avocados as I'd like."

My BFF Nicole told me, "I remember starting out my career with tens of thousands of dollars in student debt—some of which I still have—and having to walk a mile in my heels with my girlfriends in order to save money on parking when we'd go out to a restaurant or bar. I used to say, 'I'll know I've made it when I can afford to valet park my car.' I still think of my former self and those sometimes painful, always long walks every single time I pull into valet."

Other friends of mine have told me that they knew they made it when they could have a mani/pedi at the same time or stop mixing the last bits of conditioner with water to make it last longer. Celebs have been quoted as saying they knew they had made it when they were featured as a crossword puzzle clue or parodied in a skit on SNL. For Oprah, it was when she could afford to buy nice towels and linens.

So what's your motivator? It can be as big as a house or as small as an avocado. Just have your "I made it" moment. And, when you get there, cherish the moment and don't forget the struggle.

DON'T RELAPSE

We aren't crash dieting. We are shifting our lifestyle. Not just today, but for the long term. How much or how little money you have right now is no guarantee of what that amount will be next year or even next month. A financial diet is like a regular diet in a lot of ways. When people who are overweight become thin, they don't just want to be thin; they want to *stay* thin. So the lifestyle changes they made to get to their goal weight don't just evaporate once they get there; they continue to work out and eat healthily every day, forever, in order to *maintain* those results. If you go on this financial diet for just a few months in order to extract yourself from debt, then go back to your old ways of thinking and spending that got you into such a pickle in the first place, where do you think you'll be in another year? In even more big, fat debt. This book is about changing the way you look at money. Change your mindset, and your finances will follow.

EVERYTHING WILL BE OKAY IN THE END; IF IT'S NOT OKAY THEN IT'S NOT THE END

So, I think you've gotten to know me by now. I've told you stories I've never told anyone before. And why? Because I wanted to show you all of it, and mostly my flaws. I'm far from perfect. I've f---ed up a lot in life, especially with money. I'm flawed, just like we all are. I might have taught myself everything I could about money, and I want to teach you everything I know, but I certainly don't know *everything*. I haven't come at you like the "financial voice of God." I'm still learning, because no matter how much we know, when we stop learning...we die. The passion to learn more keeps us alive. Sure, learning stuff we are scared of makes us feel as though we *want* to die, but it's pretty much the secret to having a great, fulfilling life.

The only way I knew to tell you my stories was to tell them honestly. So there you have it, my stories to inspire you, gross you out, make you laugh, but most of all to let you know that we are *all* still figuring it out. The truth may not set you free, but it will get you moving in a better direction. I believe the only way to get yourself on the right track is to tell your honest story.

So, it's your turn, bitch.

GLOSSARY

want to (finally) give you a money dictionary that doesn't require a dictionary to understand the word's definition. That doesn't exist...so I made my own. You know how you explain a term to a friend who doesn't "get" it? That's the way it's written here. Let this glossary be your go-to guide for definitions with a practical perspective whenever you need a little cheat sheet. Some stuff changes over the years, but these basics never go out of style.

401(k): A popular retirement plan offered by an employer. The coolest thing about it is that you can put money in tax-deferred. That means you are able to save a bigger chunk of your paycheck up front (since you're using money you've made before taxes are taken out), let that grow, and only pay taxes when you take it out, in other words, when you are ready to retire. It's meant to help you when you're old, so the IRS tries to hook you up with that tax incentive because you're not supposed to use it until then. If you do there's often a 10% penalty (on top of any taxes you now have to pay). [*See also: Roth 401(k), IRA, Roth IRA*]

529 Plan: A college savings plan that allows your money to keep making money tax-free as long as you do one thing: use it to pay for college. You can use it for whichever college your little heart desires, but if you use it for something else, then taxes and penalties will come your way.

A

AAA: Refers to a credit rating (not roadside assistance), and it tells you if a company, a state or local government, or even a country is likely to repay its debts. The grades help you decide if you want to take your hard-earned cash and invest in those places. The AAA is the best grade there is and it goes down from there, AAA-, AA+, AA, AA-, A...you get the point. Anything with a BB+ grade and below is so risky that it's actually called "junk." But this can sometimes be a good thing—"the higher the risk, the greater the reward." In finance it might be good to have a little junk in the trunk. These grades help you make the choice to play it safe or take a gamble.

AGI (Adjusted Gross Income): AGI is literally the bottom line on the first page of your tax return (if you file your taxes yourself). It's your gross income, or money you've made from all sources during the year, minus big deductions like educational expenses or losses from selling your home. Lenders care a lot about this number because it's viewed as the most accurate report of your income.

Amortization: This is spreading a loss out over a fixed period. It has two meanings: 1. The breakdown of your payment between interest and principal when you pay off debt on a specific schedule. This applies mostly to home or car loans. In the beginning, you'll mostly be paying off the interest. Then, as the payments near the end, they will eat mostly into the principal until (ideally) you're all done repaying. 2. When you talk about depreciating something intangible (copyrights, patents, intellectual property, franchise rights) on your taxes evenly over the time you expected to use it for but didn't (because it wasn't as valuable as you thought). For example, "In order to pay off the enormous debt she incurred securing a patent for making milkshakes out of chicken (for which she realized there was zero market), Nicole will amortize her loss over the next few years."

Annuity: A steady stream of payments. It's anything that pays you something at regular intervals, whether monthly, yearly, etc. An annuity can be a "life annuity," which is like an alternative retirement program for yourself. Or, you buy an annuity as an investment, like you would buy stocks or bonds. Either way, annuity plans (there are millions) work like this: you put money in, you can let it grow tax deferred (so you pay tax only when you get the payments) then get a series of checks back. (*See also: Variable Annuity*)

Appreciation: The amount something increases in value over time. The opposite is depreciation, or the amount something decreases in value over time. Obviously, you can appreciate anything (I appreciate you for reading this book), but in finance it mostly refers to "capital" like stocks, bonds, homes or other property like fine art. (*See also: Depreciation*)

APR (Annual Percentage Rate) or APY (Annual Percentage Yield): The interest you will pay or receive for the entire year. APR is a simple calculation for the year, whereas APY (*synonym: EAR*) takes into account compounding interest, which makes it a more intricate (and, typically, more accurate) calculation. That's the only difference. As you know, companies sneakily market interest rates all the time. If APR is 10% and APY is 10.5%, it would make sense that a bank that wants you to use its credit card will use APR (it appears lower) and then use APY (it appears higher) for savings accounts. Both essentially refer to the same thing. They are just different ways to present it.

ARM (Adjustable Rate Mortgage): A loan for a home that has an interest rate that will bounce around. Unlike traditional fixed mortgages, ARMs will reset to "market conditions" (they'll get better or worse) after a stated period of time, usually three, five, seven or ten years. Think twice about signing up for an ARM just because the initial monthly payments look good. All that can change. A 3/27 mortgage is an ARM that stays fixed for three years, then bounces for the next twenty-seven years. (*See also: Mortgage*)

Asset: Anything you own that has cash value. Assets aren't limited to what's in your bank account. Your home, your car, your stamp collection: all assets. Assets that are cash or can be turned into cash quickly (like cash or stocks) are called "liquid assets," whereas the ones that are difficult to turn into cash quickly (like a home or a boat) are called "illiquid." (*See also: Liquidity, Liability*)

Asset Allocation: The breakdown of where you're putting your money. The three main asset classes—equities (stocks), fixed-income (bonds), and cash—have different levels of risk and reward, so depending on what your goals are for investing you want to balance the risk/reward by investing in varying amounts of each. For example, an aggressive investor may have an 80-20 asset allocation, putting 80% in stocks, which have greater potential for earnings but also greater risk, and 20% in bonds or cash, which have less earning power but are safer investments. The older you are, the less aggressive you're likely to be since you'll have less time over the long term to recoup any losses should any of your investments tank. (*See also: Diversification*)

B

Balance Sheet: The state of your financial union. It lists assets on one side and liabilities on the other. It's called a balance sheet because assets must "balance" with liabilities. Assets - liabilities = net worth. So if your liabilities are greater than your assets, you have a negative net worth, which is bad.

Bank Account: Where you stash your cash. At the most basic level, there are savings accounts and checking accounts. Savings and checking accounts at your local bank or online bank will usually require a minimum deposit to open the account and a minimum monthly balance. Since checking accounts are used only for transactions like deposits and withdrawals, they offer no interest. Savings accounts, however, will give you a teeny tiny bit of interest each month. (*See also: Money Market Accounts, Certificate of Deposit*)

Bankruptcy: This is what happens when you can't pay your debt. Filing for bankruptcy, also known as bankruptcy protection, stops your creditors from coming after your assets. Both people and corporations can avail themselves of this option. This might sound like a quick get-out-of-jail-free card, but be warned, your credit rating will go down the toilet for years.

Basis Point: A fancy way to talk about decimal points in finance. "One basis point" is 0.01; "10 basis points" is 0.10; "100 basis points" is 1.00. I know what you're thinking: Why not just say "one" instead of "100 basis points"? Well, once it gets down to little numbers every tenth and hundredth counts, and if you want to put your money where your mouth is, you don't want it to be a mouthful.

Beneficiary: The person who stands to gain, or benefit, from a financial transaction. For example, the person you assign to inherit your money or the person who gets medical benefits from your health insurance plan.

Blue Chip: A nickname for high-value companies (like the actual blue chips if you've ever played poker). "Blue chips" are the big guys, like McDonald's and Nike. They are considered the biggest, strongest, most robust stocks of the bunch. They are often considered trendsetters: where the blue chips go, so goes the market. Examples of blue chips are the thirty stocks that make up the mighty, mighty Dow Jones Industrial Average, or "the Dow." (*See also: The Dow, S&P 500*)

Bond: When a company or government needs to raise money for, say, a shiny new machine or fancy bridge, it borrows money by selling bonds. Bonds have durations of ten years or more (durations of one to ten years are technically called "notes"). There are different kinds of bonds—typically government or corporate bonds—but generally speaking, if you invest in a bond, you'll get paid back the full value (or "principal") at the end of the bond's duration ("maturity date") plus interest payments (called the "coupon"). Bonds are considered safer investments than stocks, but have lower earning potential.

Bond Fund: An investment option that gives you exposure to a bunch of different kinds of bonds at the same time. There are millions of types of bonds, including municipal, government and corporate. With a bond fund, you can profit (or lose money) from a variety of them, depending on the exact one you sign up for. Remember, you don't actually own all of them—the fund does. You are just buying a piece of the proverbial pie. (*See also: ETF, Mutual Fund*)

Book Value: The value of a company based on the numbers on the "books." It's the estimated worth of a company if the business were shut down and everything sold. Book value is the opposite of market value, where companies feel more valuable than their books would suggest. Buzzy tech companies like Apple experience a higher market value than what the underlying business is doing. The concept is analogous to valuing your car by Kelly Blue Book. There's a value based on stats of age and mileage. But if, for some reason, Brad Pitt was seen in your car, what you could get for the car would go way up. (*See also: Valuation*)

Bottom Line: Refers to the last line on a balance sheet which reflects—and is synonymous with—an individual's or corporation's net worth. This is the money left over after all expenses have been accounted for.

Broker: A company or person who executes your financial transaction for you. No, regular folks like me and you aren't allowed to actually buy, sell or trade assets, like stocks and bonds. You can place orders for them, but then you need a broker to execute them for you. For that, they will charge you either a fee per transaction, or a fee based on a percentage of your assets. There was a time when only the rich could have a broker. These aren't those times. Today, there's no lack of options for discount brokers who charge very small fees, allowing everyone the option to trade. (*See also: Financial Planner*)

Brokerage Account: Also called an investment account, it's the place where you hold financial assets. Examples of brokerage accounts would include your 401(k) or IRA, as well as nonretirement accounts.

Bubble: In finance, a bubble is not something that can be made from soap, but it's about as durable. Bubbles form when a lot of market players chase a particular asset (for example: tech stocks in 2000, real estate in 2007), pushing prices up to unsustainable levels. Then something pricks the bubble and prices come crashing back down.

Budget: A plan for how much money will be made and spent over a certain amount of time. You're not the only one with a budget. Governments, companies, families, countries, etc. have budgets. Being on budget means you meet your plan's expectations. Being off budget can be good or bad: you could have a surplus or a deficit. Understanding what you're making and, especially, planning how to allocate your money, is the key to staying on budget. (*See also: Balance Sheet*)

Buffett, Warren: I wouldn't say that you have to know about many people in the finance world, but Warren Buffett is a must. He is one of the greatest investors of all time. Oh, and one of the richest men in the world, too. His nickname is the "Oracle of Omaha," which speaks to his ability to pick great value investments, whether choosing stocks or buying companies (from his home in Omaha).

Bulls/Bears: In the finance world, bulls are aggressive and bears are skeptical. "Bulls" are people who believe a market or stock is going up (they are said to be "bullish") and "bears" believe a market or stock is going down (they are said to be, you guessed it, "bearish").

Business Plan: It's a written roadmap that describes in detail what your business is and does. It outlines what the goals for your business are, how you're going to achieve them, and a basic timeline for doing so. Typically you also include some ideas for marketing, hiring, and, of course, the nitty-gritty numbers of projected revenues and expenses. Having a business plan helps start-ups raise money because they can show potential investors their vision for the company. (*See also: Seed Money, Venture Capitalist*)

C

Capital "Cap" Gains: It's exactly what it sounds like—you are gaining on capital (money). So, when you buy something (a stock, a mutual fund, a house) and then sell it for a profit, you have a capital gain. (If you sell it at a loss, you have a capital loss.) If you sell before the year is up, it's called a short-term capital gain, and you usually *don't get any* tax love. Investors want to be taxed at the long-term cap gains level (more than a year) for money they make because it's way better than ordinary income (as in, if you just added that amount into your regular salary). The highest personal tax rate is 35%, whereas the highest cap gains tax bracket is 20%—so by getting as much of their profits into this lower tax category bracket as possible, they keep more of them.

Capitalism: It's a system of economics, where people have the freedom to buy and sell whatever (legal) stuff they want. Unlike communism, in which the government determines how you make money, capitalism lets people figure out how they want to conduct business. Above all, capitalism breeds (and thrives on) competition. That's why we see so many different companies selling essentially the same thing: they're fighting for your business—because they can. It's economic survival of the fittest.

Cash Flow: You probably already know that money can flow out of your hands like water. Cash flow measures how much cash you do—or don't—have on hand. You can measure a company's cash flow or you can measure your own, with cash inflows being things like your salary or alimony, and cash outflows being things like your expenses and credit card bills.

Cash Reserves: Your emergency fund, or cash you put away and can easily access for known near-term costs and also (perhaps more importantly) unforeseen problems and expenses. You should have six to nine months of cash reserves in a place you can get at when you need it, typically in a savings account, money market account, CDs, etc. Companies should have cash reserves, too—and if they don't, just like you, they can face bankruptcy.

CEO: The chief executive officer runs the whole show; all of the other C-level executives report to her. (*See also: C-suite*)

Certificate of Deposit: Also called CD, it is a step up from your regular ol' savings account. You still open it at a bank, and it pays you interest for a set amount of time (three months, six months, one year, five years, etc.), after which you get your initial money back. You can't pull your money out before that time, or you'll lose the interest—and that defeats the whole purpose of getting it in the first place. It's worth using only if the interest rates are better than your savings account, because you won't be able to touch the money while it's in the CD.

CFO: The chief financial officer runs all of the company's finances.

CMO: The chief marketing officer is in charge of the company's communications and marketing.

COBRA: A temporary health insurance plan that allows you to continue on the plan you had before, either through an employer or parent, after your circumstances have changed (e.g., leaving the company and becoming self-employed or graduating from college but not having a plan of your own yet).

Collateral: Something you use to back up yourself and your investments. It's like when you go bowling and give the alley attendant your driver's license in exchange for your bowling shoes; he knows that, since he has your license, you're not going to walk out of there and take the shoes with you. So he feels more than safe giving them to you. When it comes to money, you might offer up your car or house as collateral for taking out a loan, or cash to get a secured credit card.

Commodities: Things you can see, touch, feel, and/or use for which there is a price. Some are old standbys (gold might fit the bill), some are modern necessities (oil, natural gas, and other energy commodities would fall into this category) and some are things you'd never think could be traded (like pork bellies, from which we get bacon). BTW, investing in, say, pork bellies doesn't mean you actually get that object (ew), but you own stock in it that's traded on one of about a dozen special exchanges for commodities like the Chicago Mercantile Exchange and the New York Mercantile Exchange. (*See also: Stock Exchange*)

Common Stock: This is what most of us call stock, which is simply partial ownership in a company. But, just because you own some common stock in the company doesn't mean you have a say in anything; the "common" part denotes that you're on the bottom of the totem pole. In fact, if the company goes out of business, you'll be among the last in line to get your money out. Likewise, if the company makes money, you'll be the last—only after everyone else—(employees, vendors, bond holders, preferred stockholders) to see a piece of that profit. (*See also: Preferred Stock, Stock*)

Compound Interest: A.k.a. the "snowball effect." We know that interest is the money you make off an investment (or the money you are charged for a loan). Compound interest is the money you make off the interest on the money you are investing. That means it's really "interest on interest" which will make an investment or loan grow at a much faster rate than regular ol' interest. The exponential growth cuts both ways. On the investment front, it's the most powerful force for increasing your wealth the fastest. In the race to make your money grow, if interest is a Vespa…then, compound interest is a Lamborghini. On the borrowing front, it can drive you into debt despair the fastest, too. For example, if you loan your friend $10 at 10% interest, compounded annually, she'll owe you $25.94 after ten years. Don't be naïve and think it's just the simple percentage; compounding interest doesn't just add up—it multiplies exponentially.

Corporate Bond: Debt (a.k.a. "paper") issued by a corporation. You're helping them do something they couldn't do otherwise. So, they say "thank you" by giving you interest back. Corporate bonds typically have a higher rate of return than government bonds, because there is a greater risk that a corporation will fail than a government—so they make it worth your while. (*See also: Bond*)

Corporation: If you're starting a business, you can do that without incorporating. But as your business grows, you don't want to be held personally responsible should you-know-what hit the fan. You form a corporation (or "incorporate") so that it's your company—not you, as an individual—that is held responsible. A corporation is its own living, breathing thing: it can enter into contracts, hire employees, borrow and loan money, and pay taxes—all of that fun stuff you can do, but without dragging your personal name and assets along (that's a good thing especially if it gets dragged through the mud).

CPA (Certified Public Accountant): The numbers pro who will help you file your taxes and may assist in other areas of your financial life, like investing and retirement.

CPI (Consumer Price Index): A number the government puts out based on how expensive basic things like milk and bread are compared with past prices to show how well or how poorly the economy is doing. If the CPI is high, this indicates inflation, which means you have to spend more dollars to get the same amount of stuff; if it's low, you guessed it: deflation, which means you have to spend fewer dollars to get the same amount of stuff.

Credit Card: A card that allows you to buy things before you actually pay for them. Provided that you pay off your credit card balance in total every month, credit cards offer you convenience, a short-term, interest-free loan, and typically other perks in the form of rewards. Trouble arises when you don't pay off that balance and find yourself getting socked with compound interest and fees. (*See also: Debit Cards*)

Credit Report: Your credit report is your financial report card. It breaks down your payment history into nitty gritty detail—every successful or missed credit card and loan payment—and then spits out an actual grade: your credit score. Lenders and landlords (sometimes even employers!) use this report to gauge how financially responsible you are. You can check yours for free once per year at annualcreditreport.com. (*See also: Credit Score*)

Credit Score: If your credit report is your financial report card, then your credit score is your actual grade. A credit score is a measure of how reliable you are at paying your bills. If you are looking to borrow money, your score will determine your interest rate, or whether you can borrow at all. It measures how much debt you have versus how much debt you could have (so if your credit cards are maxed out, your credit score will be lower). Scores range from 300 to 850; 700 and above is considered a good score. (*See also: FICO Score*)

Credit Union: It looks like a bank; it smells like a bank; but it is NOT a bank. A credit union is owned by its members. It's basically the mom-and-pop version of the national banks. Instead of trusting your money to a huge national bank, you're pooling your money with your neighbors. You don't get all of the same bells and whistles as with a national bank, but you might get better interest rates and loans: after all, the lenders at these community banks know where you're coming from (literally) and are therefore more willing to help you out.

C-Suite: The top executives (C = chief) of a company, which can include the CEO, CFO, CMO and others.

D

Debit Card: Looks like a credit card but allows you to spend only money that you actually have in your checking account.

Debt: Also known as borrowed money. Not all debt is created equal. You can take on debt for legitimate reasons—to buy a home, to finance a business, to go back to school. But it's also easy to borrow money for things you just *want*, like swiping your credit card out on a shopping spree or taking out a car loan. If you are responsible with your debt and make your payments on time, it can be a great way to live the life you want. But if you are irresponsible with it and make late payments (or don't pay at all a.k.a. default) you can end up with interest payments, a bad credit score, and even bankruptcy. (*See also: Default*)

Deductible: The amount of expenses (usually set) that you pay out of pocket before your insurer jumps in to pick up the rest of the tab.

Deduction: Any item or expense that you can subtract from your gross income to reduce the amount of money that Uncle Sam can tax you at the end of the year. These are good when it comes time to file as they typically mean more money in your pocket. The most common deductions are charitable contributions, anything related to running a business, home mortgage interest payments and medical expenses. (*See also: Gross Income, Itemized Deduction, Standard Deduction*)

Default: Failure to make payments on a loan. You'll likely get charged big penalties and, if the loan was for a particular item like a car or a home, you could lose it. Seriously. Those loans are secured loans, where the item is collateral that the bank takes if you don't pay up. Defaulting on unsecured loans can lead to wage garnishment.

Deferment: Financial procrastination, or delaying a loan payment. You might defer on, say, a student loan payment if you are still in school, or graduated recently but haven't found a job yet. But it's not a good idea to keep kicking the can down the road, as you're getting hit with interest the whole time.

Dependent: Someone who depends on you financially; usually a child, but it can also be another family member, such as an elderly parent.

Depreciation: When something loses value over time. Something that depreciates is typically an actual item like a car or computer—it loses value/relevance soon after you purchase it. (New cars depreciate 15-20% the second you drive them off the lot, and we've all felt the burn of buying a schmancy new gadget only to have a newer one come out a few months later.) (*See also: Appreciation*)

Diversification: Helps you to avoid putting all of your eggs into one basket, only to drop the basket and break them all. Like in the proverb, distributing your "eggs," or investments, around into different "baskets," or investments, reduces your risk of breakage, or in this case—breaking the bank! For example, let's say you put 80% of your investing money into stocks. Don't go all in on one stock; instead, invest in a variety of them, so if that one stock tanks it doesn't tank your entire portfolio. (*See also: Asset Allocation*)

Dividend: One of the things a company can do with its profits is give them to the shareholders in the form of cash; this is called a dividend. Getting cash is nice and thus so are dividends. Even better, as earnings grow, companies can give out more dividends, which is even nicer. They can also cut them in bad times (which sucks). What do you do with that cash the company sends you? Best to reinvest it. Over time, reinvested dividends are a major source of stock investor returns.

Domestic Partnership: So you share your house, your car, your dog, your bank account, your LIFE—but you're not technically married: you're in a domestic partnership. It's a legal and/or personal relationship between two people who share the trappings of marital bliss without the official title.

Dow, The: The Dow Jones Industrial Average, an index of the top thirty "blue chip" stocks, like Apple, Microsoft and Wal-Mart. It's an index that is usually a good indicator of how the overall stock market is doing. If you hear "the market is up today" on the news, they are usually referring to The Dow. (*See also: Index, Blue Chip*)

E

EAFE: Another one of those financial acronyms, pronounced EEE-fee. The EAFE (the letters stand for Europe, Australasia, Far East) is a stock index that covers the major markets of the industrialized world, excluding the US and Canada; think of it as the S&P for the rest of the world. And while we're on foreign stock indices, let's mention the MSCI Emerging Market Index, which covers emerging markets like China, India, Brazil and the like. Some other country-specific foreign indices you might hear mentioned on the news include the TSX (Canada), DAX (Germany), CAC 40 (France), FTSE 100 (or "Footsie," Great Britain), Nikkei (Japan), Shanghai (China, obviously), and the Hang Seng (Hong Kong).

Earnings: Not to be confused with revenue, this is the amount of profit that a company takes in over a given period of time after taxes. So, it's effectively the amount of money the company actually makes. Earnings are typically the main factor determining a company's stock price, because they serve as a good litmus test for whether the business will be successful in the long run. (*See also: Revenue*)

EBITDA: Stands for Earnings Before Interest, Taxes, Depreciation and Amortization. EBITDA is essentially profits. It's a saying you'll hear a lot if you are starting a business. The better the number is, the better the company is doing.

Equity: Another word for stock. If you have equity in a company, it means you own shares in that company. You can have equity in a public or private company. (*See also: Stock, Bond*)

Escrow: An account that is set up such that you can't touch the money in it. When two parties are conducting a transaction, an escrow account is usually held by an impartial third party. If you buy a house, for example, you'll be asked to deposit a certain amount of money into an escrow account until you and the seller have satisfied all of the terms of the sale.

Estate: All of your stuff. All of it: your house, your car, jewelry, all of your money, and legal rights—minus anything you owe (debt and liabilities). "Estate Planning" is a nice way of saying how to plan for what happens to your estate when you die, which includes setting up a will, power of attorney and tax planning for everything in your estate so that you leave your heirs with the best financial situation possible.

ETF: Exchange traded funds are like mutual funds but they trade on a stock exchange. They are also cheaper to buy than mutual funds because they aren't managed by professionals. It's a way to get exposure to a bunch of different stocks by buying just one thing. So, you want exposure to technology stocks? You can get an ETF for that—many, actually. There's an ETF for almost any type of investment you want to make. (*See also: Mutual Fund*)

Executive Compensation: What it sounds like—how much the big boys earn in salary, bonuses and stock or stock options.

Exemption: A reduction to the amount of your gross income that would otherwise be taxed. The amount of the reduction is the same for everybody. There are two types of exemptions: personal and dependency. For example, if you are filing your own tax return and have two children, you have one personal exemption for yourself and one dependency exemption for each kid = three total exemptions. At the current amount of $3,900 per person, that's $3,900 x 3 = $11,700 that you can take out of your gross income. (*See also: Deduction*)

Expense Ratio: The fee that a fund you invest in charges to do what it says it's going to do. Expense ratios on index funds are typically very low, maybe 0.25% or less. An expense ratio of 0.25% would charge you $25 per $10,000 per year. So if you have $10,000 invested in that fund, think of the $25 as a service fee for the broker managing the fund to work it for you. A 1% expense ratio (typical for actively managed funds) would charge you $100 per year on $10,000.

F

Fair Market Value: What something is worth, or its essential value, were it to be sold in the open marketplace right now (not what you paid for it initially).

FDIC: The Federal Deposit Insurance Corporation. You've seen their stickers at the bank. The FDIC insures your bank deposits up to $250,000. It's a corporation wholly owned by the federal government. Provided that you keep your balances under the insured amount, even if your bank fails you can sleep easy knowing that you will get your money back (at some point).

Federal Reserve: The Central Bank of the United States; call it "the Fed" for short. The Fed sets interest rate policy (also called monetary policy) in the country. Its mission is to promote both full employment and low inflation, two often contradictory goals. In order to shield the Fed from short-term political influence, its members are appointed by the executive branch—yep, POTUS himself. The current chair (or "head") of the Federal Reserve is Janet Yellen, the first woman ever to hold the position. (*See also: Monetary Policy*)

FICO Score: Another name for your credit score. Named after Fair Isaac Corporation, the data company that dreamed up the equation for calculating the score. (*See also: Credit Score*)

Financial Planner: Someone who gives you financial advice and guidance to help you meet your long-term money goals. Financial planners may be certified or just have been at it a long time, but either way remember that you're paying for their advice; it's not free and unfortunately not always in your best interest. Typically, financial planners are specialized and knowledgeable in all of the different aspects of your financial life including taxes, estate planning and retirement. But at the end of the day, the most important thing is that you have a good rapport and they have your best interests in mind. (*See also: CPA, Wealth Management*)

Fiscal Policy: The way in which the elected federal government manages its money. Spending and taxing are the most common kinds of fiscal policy. When you hear talk on the news of the government's budget, or a new tax plan, what you're hearing is a discussion of "fiscal policy." Don't confuse it with monetary policy, which is executed directly by the Federal Reserve and deals with setting interest rates. "Fiscal" and "monetary" are not synonyms.

Fiscal Year (FY): It's the special twelve-month calendar that a company or government uses for preparing financial statements and drawing up their accounting. Where the calendar year runs the same year in and year out (January 1 to December 31, duh), the fiscal year in the US runs from October 1 to September 30 of the following year. The fiscal year is written as the year in which it ends; so, FY2016 will begin on October 1, 2015, and end on September 30, 2016.

Fixed Income: A set amount of income that doesn't change, and that you can always rely on. The most common type of fixed income is a bond (corporate or government). Fixed income durations vary. For example, for US government fixed income, called treasuries, the shortest is a bill (under a year);

then a note (1-10 years); and finally a bond (10+ years). (*See also: Bond*)

Foreclosure: When a bank or creditor takes away your house because you can no longer make payments on it. Typically, they sell the house and then use the proceeds to pay off the outstanding loan.

FRM (Fixed-Rate Mortgage): A loan for a home in which the rate you're paying the bank doesn't change. A fixed-rate mortgage is amortized over a certain amount of time so that each of those "fixed" payments goes to paying back some of the principal and some of the interest each time. For example, a thirty-year, fixed-rate mortgage is one in which the borrower makes 360 (one per month) equal payments, after which the loan is paid off. (*See also: ARM, Mortgage*)

Funemployment: No, it's not making the most of an unexpected layoff from your job. It's when you say, "I love my job. I love my life"—and you're totally in control of both things. You might be making a little less money, but you're being paid in happiness.

Futures: A contract for the right to buy or sell something at a later date by making the actual transaction today. A bakery, say, might want to lock in a price for the wheat for cookies they will need to make. The owner might buy a wheat futures contract today, so that there are no surprises in the price when she needs to buy it a year from now. She might spend a little bit to buy that contract, but it's acting as insurance in case the price skyrockets. Futures can be used for commodities, like wheat, but also for stocks. In fact, S&P futures (futures on the S&P 500 index) are among the most actively traded.

G

GDP: Stands for gross domestic product and is a way for economists to measure the strength of a particular economy. For example, US

GDP looks at the total market value of all goods and services produced within the US, from cars to appliances to clothes to shoes. When US factories produce a lot, it usually means the economy is healthy because they have buyers for their products, and GDP will increase. When factories slow down production, it means there are fewer buyers, and GDP will decrease.

Green Mortgage: A mortgage that sets money aside for home improvements that will increase the energy efficiency (and ultimate resale value) of the home. You can get one of these when you are buying a new house or refinancing a house you already own. A certified home energy rater visits your house and suggests improvements to make it more energy efficient; once you have made the improvements, the mortgage lender repays the expenses back to you. (*See also: Mortgage*)

Gross Income: How much you make before taxes. The salary your company offers you is typically in gross income, so before accepting a job offer, you should factor in taxes to get the amount you will *actually* be taking home. (*See also: Net Income*)

Growth Stocks: These stocks tend to be new and buzzy, and are growing faster than the average company. Growth companies tend not to pay dividends, as they're re-investing their earnings back into their growing businesses. While you don't get your money back right away, the long-term money you stand to make is typically pretty good. Growth stocks are especially common in certain industries (like technology and biotech). An example would be Twitter, which tends to bounce around a lot, versus a value stock like Johnson&Johnson, which is more reliable. (*See also: Value Stocks*)

H

Health Savings Account (HSA): A health savings account allows you to put away pre-tax money to pay for medical expenses.

Hedge Fund: Hedge funds are pools of money collected together for investment purposes. They're not regulated by the government, so they're even riskier than publicly traded stocks, and they're not open to everyone, usually only "qualified investors," a term that most of us would define as "wealthy." Hedge funds can and do invest in just about anything, and can be both long and short at the same time—hence the term "hedging," or protecting yourself from the risk involved with that investment.

Home Equity Line of Credit: This is like a home equity loan, but instead of giving you a lump sum, the bank holds onto it, allowing you to draw on it as you need it up to the maximum amount. (*See also: Home Equity Loan*)

Home Equity Loan: Also known as a second mortgage, this type of loan allows homeowners to borrow against the value of their home. The amount of the loan is based on the difference between your equity in the home and the home's current market value...so basically you're borrowing the amount that you could hypothetically stand to pocket by selling it.

I

In the Black: "In the black" means your company is profitable. The opposite is being "in the red"—or in the negative earnings zone. The term Black Friday is typically the day that retailers hit their numbers, bringing them out of the red (negative earnings) and into the black (positive earnings = hooray!).

Index: A means to measure a particular market, or section of a market. In the United States, the best-known stock market indices are the Dow Jones Industrial Average (DJIA, or Dow) and the Standard & Poors 500 (S&P 500 or S&P); the former contains thirty large-company stocks, the latter, five hundred. Other US indices include the Wilshire 5000 (pretty much every stock), the S&P Midcap 400 (medium-sized companies), the Russell 2000 (small companies), and the Barclays Aggregate Bond Index (the bond market). You'll often hear newscasters talk about the Dow or the S&P because indices give us a quick look at what's going on in the market. (*See also: S&P 500, Dow*)

Index Fund: A type of investment designed to match or track the types of stocks found in a market index, such as the S&P 500. Instead of buying each stock in an index individually, it's one-stop shopping that gives you exposure to the whole index by buying one share of the index fund. So when you hear commentators say "The S&P is up"/"The S&P is down" and you are invested in the S&P index fund, then you're up or down for the day. (*See also: S&P 500, Dow*)

Inflation: The slow and steady upward creep of prices for goods and services, and, as a result, the decline of purchasing power. Stuff gets more expensive over time, and therefore people can't buy as much. Inflation is expected to grow 3% per year, which is why making more than that by investing is so important; otherwise, your money will be worth less tomorrow than it is today.

Initial Public Offering: An "IPO" occurs when a company sells stock to the public for the first time. It's essentially the debutante ball for a private company announcing that it will let anyone buy into it. The buzzy ones tend to be well-known consumer platforms ("B-to-C," which is business to consumer) like Facebook, but all sorts of companies go public that you haven't heard of ("B-to-B," where businesses sell to other businesses). It's also a time when founders make actual bank and not "paper money" or equity that hasn't been liquidated.

Institutional Investors: Unlike mom-and-pop investors, the big boys, by which I mean the folks who run mutual, pension, hedge and insurance funds (basically the people who move around large sums of money) are lumped into this category. When you invest money in a mutual fund, or an index fund, there's someone on the other end managing the money. (*See also: Mom-and-Pop*)

Interest: It's what you pay when you borrow and what you receive when you lend. Interest rates are determined by market conditions and the condition of the borrower. The better the condition of the borrower, the lower the interest rate—which is why your credit score is vitally important when you want to do something like take out a mortgage.

Investment Bank: A bank that doesn't take deposits but raises capital for businesses (often through stock and bond offerings) and sets up trades for institutional investors. Goldman Sachs and Morgan Stanley are the two prime American examples.

IRA: Stands for individual retirement account. The money you put in is tax-deductible now, but you will have to pay income tax on it when you make a withdrawal. Unlike a 401(k), which is offered through your employer, an IRA is yours—and will always be yours—wherever you go. [*See also: 401(k)*]

IRS (Internal Revenue Service): Your favorite guy: the Tax Man. The IRS is the government agency charged with collecting and enforcing taxes and coming up with all of those crazy rules and regulations. This is where your tax return goes on April 15 each year.

Itemized Deduction: This is what you save all those receipts for during the year. If your expenses amount to more than the standard deduction, then you'll want to "itemize" your taxes (you can only do one or the other). Eligible expenses include mortgage interest; state, local, and property taxes; medical expenses; business travel and entertainment; home office equipment and supplies and charity donations (this all appears on Schedule A of your federal Form 1040). (*See also: Deduction, Standard Deduction*)

J

Joint Account: If you're looking to pool your finances with a significant other or business partner, a joint account is what you will need. You can get a joint checking or savings account through a bank, or a joint brokerage account through an investment company. It goes without saying that you should trust the person with whom you're sharing a joint account, since you'll both have access to the money.

K

Key Rate: It's the rate that determines what banks charge on loans. You like low key rates when you're borrowing money for investing in starting your own business or paying down your credit card. Conversely, you actually prefer high key rates when you're being more responsible with your spending and putting your money in a savings account because that means you'll get more interest on the money you put into the bank.

Knowledge Capital: This is a way companies describe the value each individual employee brings to the table. For example, your own personal knowledge capital is made up of your experience, professional skills, knowledge of a particular industry, your ability to work with a team, your amazing ideas, etc. Obviously as a business you want the most knowledge capital as possible, so you hire the most skilled employees that you can find—and afford.

L

Liability: Something you're on the hook for. You might think of liabilities as obligations that will need to be settled at some point. Spent a hundred bucks on your credit card? Well, you know you've got to pay it someday. That's now a $100 liability. Take out a mortgage? That's a liability, too. (But the house you bought with it is an asset, even if it might not feel that way.) (*See also: Asset, Balance Sheet*)

LIBOR: It stands for the London Interbank Offered Rate, but don't be confused: it's not just a London thing. It's the basic interest rate, or bare minimum, that you can borrow money for.

Life Insurance: How much is your life worth? No...really. Life insurance is an insurance policy that you take out to protect your loved ones in the event that you die. Your beneficiaries (typically your spouse and children) stand to receive the proceeds (tax-free) in the event that something happens to you, thereby helping to ease the financial impact (if not the emotional one) of your absence. (*See also: Term Life Insurance, Permanent Insurance*)

Liquidity: Your ability to pay *now*—having liquidity means you have cash. Note that even the wealthy can sometimes be illiquid if they own an illiquid asset (real estate, say) that can't be turned into ready cash.

Loan: Money you borrow, usually from a bank or other financial institution. In exchange for giving you the money you need, you will need to pay them a percentage of that money as interest (on top of giving them back what you borrowed). Common types of loans are student, mortgage, auto and home equity.

Long: When you're long, you own something—a stock, perhaps—and are hoping that it will go up in price, when you can then sell it at a profit. It's the opposite of short, where you think something will go down in price. (*See also: Short*)

M

M & A: Stands for mergers and acquisitions. A merger is like a marriage in the business world. Sometimes two companies will merge to form one large company; it's wanted by both parties, rarely arranged and mutually beneficial. An acquisition can be friendly (when management approves) or hostile (when management can't agree on a merger or takeover and things get ugly. Either way, an aquisition is when a company takes over, or aquires another company). There can also be divorces, like the high profile one between AOL and Time Warner.

Macroeconomics: The study of economics that focuses on the performance of the economy in general, from unemployment to GDP to inflation. For example, macroeconomics looks at price levels of stuff like milk over time to come up with overall spending trends for the entire country. (*See also: Microeconomics*)

Maturity Date: When a bond you've purchased pays you the final interest payment and gives you your principal back. At that maturity date, you essentially get repaid for the loan you gave to the company or municipality you invested in, in addition to the interest you received.

Microeconomics: The study of economics that looks at individual household or company spending or saving data to gather overall trends, like determining what types of things people are buying. (*See also: Macroeconomics*)

Mom-and-Pop: You and anyone else who isn't an institutional investor. Sometimes called "mom-and-pop retail," the term refers to the average folks in the street and their actions in the market, and is often used to differentiate the actions of normal people from more sophisticated investors. (*See also: Institutional Investors*)

Monetary Policy: Policy that sets and controls interest rates. In the US, it's the job of the Federal Reserve. Don't confuse this with "fiscal policy"—it's not the same thing and the terms aren't interchangeable. "Fiscal" policy refers to the actions of the government (taxes, etc.), not the Fed.

Money Market Account: It's similar to a regular savings account, but it usually gives you a better rate because you are letting the bank be more aggressive with what they do with your money. With a regular savings account, the bank can't invest your money, but they can with a money market account. For that privilege, they give you a bit more interest in return.

Mortgage: A loan used to buy real estate in which the real estate is collateral for the loan. Interest is typically paid monthly. In the US, the standard, plain vanilla mortgage is the thirty-year-fixed, in which the borrower makes 360 (one per month) equal payments. After that, the loan is paid off. This kind of loan has a fixed rate for the life of the loan and is amortized—that is, each payment contains some principal repayment, so that the loan balance declines to zero over time. In practice, most thirty-year borrowers pay off their loans early, usually because they sell their houses. (*See also: ARM, FRM*)

Municipal Bond: A bond issued by a city, county or state. "Muni" bonds (as they're often called) are popular investments with individual investors, because in most cases the interest they pay is not subject to federal income tax. Within the state of issue they're also not subject to state income tax, so many muni investors opt for homegrown bonds.

Mutual Fund: Instead of just buying individual companies, a mutual fund is a basket of a bunch of different securities: stocks or bonds. Anyone can buy into a mutual fund, and it has a low barrier to entry compared with a hedge fund. It's basically built-in insurance for investing because it's diversified, so if one stock fails, you are (usually) propped up by another company in the fund to keep your returns slow and steady. And because you are pooling money with other people, you get exposure to a bunch of different investments you wouldn't have the opportunity to buy into on your own.

N

NASDAQ: Short for National Association of Securities Dealers Automated Quotations, the NASDAQ is a stock exchange, like the New York Stock Exchange. But instead of having a trading floor, the NASDAQ exists in the ether. It is tech heavy and welcomes up-and-comers.

Net Income: An individual's or a company's actual, total income after deductions, credits and taxes are factored in. In a few words: it's the amount of bacon you're actually bringing home. (*See also: Gross Income*)

Net Worth: A snapshot of what you're worth on paper by subtracting your liabilities (everything you owe, like credit card debt and students loans) from your assets (everything you own, like cash and investments). A positive number is nice; a big positive number is better. (*See also: Bottom Line*)

New York Stock Exchange (NYSE): Also known as the "Big Board," the NYSE is considered the largest stock exchange in the world. Based in New York City (duh), it used to be an actual exchange featuring a trading floor and a loud, crazy, open outcry system to buy and sell stocks. It still looks like that on TV, but the dirty little secret is that it's just for show and more than half of all NYSE trades are conducted electronically.

Nonqualified Account: An account that gives you interest that you have to pay tax on. The most basic type of nonqualified account is an individual checking or savings account.

O

Opportunity Cost: The amount of money you spend (on a swank new car, for example, or paying down debt) that could be doing something else potentially more valuable for you over time (like going back to school or investing in your business).

Ordinary Income: Income that is taxed at ordinary rates (as opposed to capital gains) and is usually made up of salary, wages, commissions and interest from nonqualified accounts. (*See also: Capital Gains*)

P

P/E Ratio: Stands for price-to-earnings ratio. It's a way to measure stock value and is calculated by dividing the current stock price by earnings per share. The higher the P/E ratio, most likely the better the investment.

Permanent Insurance: This kind of life insurance has level premiums and pays a fixed amount of money to the beneficiary when the insured dies. But it also has an investment feature, which grows in value, which the policyholder (who is not necessarily the insured person, since you can buy a policy on somebody else's life) can withdraw or borrow against. Unlike term life insurance, this kind of policy never expires. (*See also: Life Insurance, Term Life Insurance*)

P&L Statement: P&L stands for "profit and loss." We like the P but hate the L. It's also called an "income statement." Companies have P&Ls to show how much money they've made and how much money they've spent. Your online bank statement is like your very own P&L. Sometimes it can be very good or very bad. P.S. Sometimes people will confuse the abbreviation and say "PNL." That doesn't exist, so don't be that person.

Portfolio: The whole shebang of all your investments: stocks, bonds, mutual funds, CDs and all that good stuff.

Preferred Stock: This is stock that gets more perks than common stock. Preferred stock dividends must be paid before dividends are paid to common stockholders (hence the name "preferred"). And, in the case where a company goes out of business, preferred stockholders get their money first. (*See also: Common Stock*)

Premium: Refers to your monthly insurance payment, typically for health insurance. Unless you change your plan or the insurance rates go up (which unfortunately happens all the time) then it's the same amount every month.

Principal: The total amount borrowed on a loan, and/or the amount you still owe on that loan, separate from interest. So if you have taken out $10,000 in student loans at an interest rate of 4.66%, your principal for that loan is $10,000. A few years down the road, when you have paid off some of the loan and have $6,000 remaining, then $6,000 is your new principal.

Private Equity: This is when investors (usually institutional rather than individual) put money directly into a company rather than buying shares on a public exchange.

Profits: Repeat after me: profit = total revenue - total expenses. Once you have overcome the expenses, costs and taxes needed to sustain your business, the rest of the money coming in is profit. (*See also: Revenue*)

Public Company: In short, a company that anyone can buy into. This company has already had its "coming out" party by joining the stock market via an initial public offering (IPO). The biggest advantage of "going public" is the ability to sell stock (which can make the company, its employees, and its shareholders a lot of money). But the downside is that it opens the door to increased regulations and less control for the company's founders and majority owners.

Purchasing Power: How much stuff can you buy with $1? Purchasing power is the value of a dollar in terms of the amount of goods or services that one dollar can buy at a specific time. It's heavily influenced by inflation, because inflation typically decreases the amount of goods or services you'd be able to purchase with that dollar. (It's why $15 used to be able to get you a ticket to the movies, but that $10 could maybe buy you one third of one today.)

Q

Qualified Account: An account that allows for a tax break on the contributions you make to it. Qualified accounts, like a 401(k) allow you to funnel a portion of your paycheck each month into the account, which reduces your overall taxable income— meaning you pay less in taxes at the end of the year. (*See also: Nonqualified Account*)

Quarter: In finance, quarter refers to a quarter year. Companies tend to report earnings on a quarterly cycle. That's why you see Q1, Q2, etc. when talking about the health of different companies. When quarterly earnings reports roll around, the stock market often gets edgy. It also gets edgy when the government releases certain economic statistics every quarter, like GDP.

Quarterly Earnings Report: Publicly traded companies tend to release information about their performance on a periodic basis, sometimes quarterly. A quarterly earnings report discloses information about the company's net income, earnings per share, net sales, and more. This information helps industry analysts and investors to understand the overall health of a company better. Quarterly reports tend to be issued at the beginning of January, April, July and October and reflect past financial information. (*See also: Quarter*)

Quote: You'll usually hear the word "quote" being used in reference to a "stock quote" or "quoted price." Stocks and other securities that are traded on an exchange trade at different prices throughout the day. At any given point, the "stock quote" or "quoted price" is the most recent price at which a buyer and seller agree to acquire and sell the asset.

R

Ratios: Wall Street loves ratios, as you already know if you read the entry on the P/E ratio. Besides the price-to-earnings ratio, there's price/book, which measures a company's value in the marketplace relative to its book value, debt/equity, a measurement of how indebted a company is, and many more.

Rebalancing: Buying or selling securities to maintain or change your asset allocation. Let's say you had an 80/20 allocation of 80% stocks and 20% bonds and you wanted to play it a little safer and switch to 70/30. You would sell some of your stock and invest the money in bonds...thereby rejiggering or "rebalancing" your portfolio.

Refinancing: The process of transferring debt from a high-rate loan to a lower-rate loan. It's like switching from overpriced cable service to something more manageable if you have the opportunity to do so. You still have to pay but it's not nearly as pricey. Not everyone can do it, though. You have to have a good payment and credit history.

A big reason for doing this is to have a little more cash readily available by reducing your monthly bills.

Revenue: A term for the gross amount of money a business receives before expenses are deducted. Because a profit and loss statement starts with revenue, revenue is sometimes called the "top line." (*See also: Bottom Line, Profits, P&L Statement*)

Risk Averse: Means apprehensive about taking chances. If this is you, you'd rather take a long walk than go cliff diving, and you're more likely to invest your money in something safe like CDs or bonds rather than in the stock of a new internet start-up.

Road show: If you owned a company, and you decided you wanted to start selling shares of your company to the public, you would take your "show" on the road to try and "sell the sizzle" and look for money for the company. Typically, companies engage in road shows before an initial public offering, or "IPO." It helps to spread the word about your company and get investor support.

Rollover: If you leave a job where you have a 401(k), you can take the money with you—that's right, "roll it over"—either to a 401(k) at your new job, or to an IRA. [*See also: 401(k), IRA*]

Roth 401(k): It's just like a normal 401(k) in that it's a retirement plan offered by your employer, but you pay tax on the contributions when they go in so you don't pay taxes when you take the money out. [*See also: 401(k)*]

Roth IRA: Like a regular IRA, it stands for "individual retirement account." But, unlike traditional IRAs where you are taxed only when you take your money out, Roth contributions are taxed up front but not later on. It's a great deal if you qualify. The catch is that if you are lucky enough to make $125,000 if you're single, or $183,000 if you're married, it's too much money to play the "Roth" game. (*See also: IRA*)

Rule of 72: A nifty party trick and a good way to get a feel for compounded returns. Take 72 and divide by your expected return and you'll get the approximate number of years it will take your money to double. Going to get an 8% return? Expect to double your money in 9 years (72 divided by 8). It's a simple trick.

Russell 2000 Index: An index measuring the performance of around 2,000 smaller companies in the Russell 3000 Index, which is made up of 3,000 of the biggest US stocks. Because it reps the "little" guys (who actually aren't so little: the average market capitalization for Russell 2000 companies is between $300 million and $2 billion), the Russell 2000 serves as a benchmark for small, or "small-cap," stocks in the United States.

S

S&P 500: The Standard & Poor's 500 index of America's 500 largest stocks. Some say this is the best indicator of the true pulse of the US economy. (*See also: Index*)

Sarbanes-Oxley: Also known as "SOX," the *Sarbanes-Oxley Act of 2002* was named for two lawmakers who aimed to create new standards for boards, management, and accounting firms of public companies. The regulations are like "checks and balances" over companies the public can invest in. They are supposed to have your back if you're an investor.

SEC: Stands for the Securities and Exchange Commission. It is a federal government organization that is supposed to be the good guy. Their sole purpose is to "protect investors" from the bad guys (like shady brokers or fraudulent trading schemes). They put in regulations for "securities" markets or anything stock related. Investors feel like the SEC has their back while companies often think they are a thorn in their side.

Secured Credit Card: A credit card for people who have little or no credit, or the most dreaded of all: bad credit. They're backed by a savings account, which serves as collateral on the credit available on the card. You deposit money into the savings account and it remains there, thereby backing the card and easing the lender's fears about your credit-worthiness. The card's limit is based on two things: your credit history (if you have any) and the amount you deposited into the account. So why would you get a card of this type? If you want to build credit, or rebuild bad credit. (*See also: Credit Card, Debit Card*)

Secured Debt: It's the kind of debt you get when you take out a loan and back it with collateral, like your house, to reduce the risk associated with lending. For example, you could use your house as collateral to take out a mortgage. But if you don't pay, the bank takes your house, instead. They will then sell it and use the proceeds to pay back the debt. The "security" for their debt will always win over your security. Ouch. (*See also: Unsecured Debt*)

Security: A general term to describe a position of interest in a company, such as a stock (ownership), a bond (a creditor position), or a derivative (the right to buy a stock, say). Think of a financial family tree where "security" would be the name of the family, and stocks, bonds, and derivatives would be types of securities underneath.

Seed Money: A.k.a. "seed funding," or the money to help you get your small business off the ground. You'll likely get your seed money from friends and family who believe in you and your dream (that's why your first round of fund-raising is called the "friends and family" round). If you're not lucky enough to have a supportive community around you, you'll probably turn to your savings or your credit cards for money to make your company grow, baby, grow.

Share: The amount, or "stake," that you have in a company where you own stock; also the unit used to measure stocks. For example, if you own 1,000 stocks in a company, you own 1,000 shares. (*See also: Shareholder, Stock, Stock Market*)

Shareholder: The owner of stock in a company. If the company does well, shareholders stand to make money—and sometimes big money. But if the company does poorly then shareholders have the potential to lose money, too. Your stake in the company as a shareholder depends on how many shares in that company you own. (*See also: Share, Stock, Stock Market*)

Short: "Going short" basically means you're trying to make money off of something that you think won't do well. It's the opposite of "going long" or just buying a stock outright which is a vote of confidence in that company. It's a more advanced trade because there is way more risk. If you buy the company outright, the most you can lose is 100% of the value. If you short it and it goes up more than 100% you can lose an unlimited amount of money—so be careful, and make sure that you think it's going to go way down because you make the difference if you are right. You lose the difference if you are wrong. (*See also: Long*)

Social Security: The big daddy of social welfare. The Fed rolled it out in 1935, and we've been living with and around it ever since. The program's benefits include retirement income, disability income, Medicare, Medicaid, and death and survivorship benefits. Based on the year you are born, you can start getting retirement benefits as early as age sixty-two or as late as age sixty-seven. (That number is likely to get higher in the coming years, so you might not start collecting until age seventy or even older.) The amount of income you get from the government is based on the average wages earned over your lifetime. Spouses are also eligible to receive Social Security benefits, even if they have worked only part time or not at all. It's been around for a long time, but factors like longer life expectancies, a large baby boomer population currently entering retirement age, and inflation have put it in serious danger in current times.

Standard Deduction: A flat amount you can take out of your taxes. You can either choose to take a "standard deduction" or an "itemized deduction" to reduce your tax bill (but not both). If you choose the "standard deduction," it makes doing your taxes a whole lot simpler because you don't have to save every receipt. You just write the amount down ($6,200 for single people in 2015) with no questions asked. This might be for you if you don't have a mortgage or have a lot of medical or business expenses that would act as good "itemized deductions." *(See also: Itemized Deductions)*

Stock: A share, or stake, in a company. As a shareholder, you own part of the corporation's assets and earnings—so you're (technically) a part owner! Your stake in the company depends on the number of shares you own relative to the number of total number of shares (so, sadly, your one hundred shares of Apple probably won't get you into the next shareholders' meeting…). Stocks are also the "meat and potatoes" of most investment portfolios and have outperformed most other investments historically. Publicly traded stocks have a ticker symbol to identify them and trade on—you guessed it— the stock exchange. *(See also: Equity, Security, Stock Exchange)*

Stock Exchange: Where stocks are traded. It can be a physical place, like the New York Stock Exchange, or a computer system, like the NASDAQ, or any of the many other systems used to trade stocks. Overall, billions of shares of stock are traded every day. Once upon a time, when someone said "the stock market," she meant the NYSE. But now there are many more exchanges where stocks are traded. *(See also: Share, Shareholder, Stock)*

Stock Market: This represents all companies investors can buy into, sell or trade. To actually place a trade, investors use different stock exchanges, like the NYSE or NASDAQ. So when you hear on the news, "The stock market crashed after the President's speech," it's referring generally to all stock trading. *(See also: New York Stock Exchange, NASDAQ)*

Stock Split: This is when companies divide existing shares to lower the share price so that more investors can join the party. For example, let's say that The Lapin Corporation of America has

10,000 shares selling at $100 a pop. The maximum capitalization is $1,000,000. If the stock split two for one, that means there are now 20,000 selling at $50 a pop. (The share price goes down, but the max capitalization stays the same.) The lower price can be more inviting to more investors. If you already owned one share of this company at $100, you would now own two shares at $50 each. A stock may split two for one, three for two, or any other combination. A reverse stock split is when a company lowers the number of its outstanding shares, which would be, for example, a one for two split. (*See also: Stock, Share*)

Sweat Equity: It's the best advice in business: outwork everyone. It's how much you and only you invest in your company by working at it, not just taking cash from the outside and looking pretty. It's said that your "sweat equity" will pay off most in the long run. It's kinda like if you own a home, and you decide to go to Home Depot and redo your kitchen yourself before selling the house for a profit. You've added value by working at it.

T

Tax Credit: Unlike deductions and exemptions, which reduce the amount of your income that is taxable, tax credits reduce the actual amount of tax owed. So yes, you would be correct: They. Are. Awesome. Sometimes the government will offer a tax credit to encourage certain behavior, like a credit for first-time homeowners to encourage people to buy a house and boost the housing market, or a credit for replacing older appliances with more energy-efficient ones that are better for the environment. The amount of the credit depends on what it's for, and credits don't necessarily apply to everyone: they can be offered to individuals or businesses in specific locations or industries.

Tax Day: Any day you owe tax, typically thought of as April 15 of each year. Of course, providing you pay in almost all of what you owe, you can file your taxes as late as October 15. Corporations also have tax days, three months after the end of their fiscal year.

Tax-Deductible: These are expenses like health insurance and contributions to tax-deductible retirement plans like an IRA or 401(k) that are not subject to taxation. If you deduct those payments from your taxes, you are essentially lowering your total tax liability, or amount of money you are on the hook to pay taxes on. (*See also: AGI*)

Tax-Deferred: An investment that lets your money grow unhindered by Uncle Sam. You pay the taxes on the returns only at a later date, instead of having taxes take a chunk out of the investment while it's still growing. IRAs are the most common tax-deferred investments. (*See also: IRA*)

Tax-Exempt: Sometimes the US government will give a company "tax exempt" status, meaning that they are not subject to any tax from the government or regulator. Usually religious organizations, schools, social clubs and public charities are tax exempt—but they don't get off totally scot-free. They have to adhere to special rules and regulations that go along with that privilege.

Taxable Income: Income that is subject to tax; just as bad as it sounds.

Term Life Insurance: A life insurance policy for a set amount (say, $1,000,000) for a fixed amount of time (say, twenty years). If you die within those twenty years, your beneficiary gets the money. Tax-free. Jackpot. If you live longer than that, the policy expires and no one gets anything (but the joy of you being alive). (*See also: Life Insurance, Permanent Life Insurance*)

Ticker Symbol: An abbreviation of a company's name that represents its stock on an exchange. FYI, stocks traded on US exchanges like NYSE have three or fewer letters (Wal-Mart = WMT) in their ticker and NASDAQ stocks have four letters (Google = GOOG). (*See also: Stock Exchange*)

Trade: Pretty simple: selling, buying, or exchanging goods, services, and, in financial terms, stocks, bonds and the like. Buy a share of a company? That's a trade. Sell it? Ditto.

Treasuries: Bonds issued by the United States federal government. When the federal government needs to borrow money—and it needs to borrow money all the time—it issues Treasuries, which are backed by the full faith and credit of the United States (and not subject to state income tax; you still have to pay federal tax on the income, though). There are several types of Treasuries: T-bills (maturities of one year or shorter), notes (maturities of two to ten years), bonds (maturities of ten to thirty years). Note: people tend to refer to all three of these types as "bonds," but know that there is a difference based on duration.

Trust: "Trust" is the most important ingredient in a relationship, right? Well, a financial trust is just that: a relationship. Only it's one comprised of money. A trust is formed when one party "trusts" property or assets to another party (typically a bank) for the benefit of a third party or beneficiary. For example, a parent might leave a trust for children under the age of eighteen, or for children who have mental disabilities that impair their ability to take care of their own finances. There are two types: a living trust, which is in effect during the trustor's lifetime; and a testamentary trust, which is outlined in the will of someone who has died. Once the beneficiary is deemed able to manage the funds on their own (for example, when children turn eighteen) they get full possession of the trust and use of whatever's inside it.

U

Underwater: That's when the amount of a loan is more than the thing you borrowed it for is worth. For instance, if you get a $300,000 mortgage loan, but the real estate market crashes and your house now has a market value of only $250,000, your mortgage is considered underwater.

Unsecured Debt: This is the kind of debt that isn't secured by any goods that can be repossessed if you fail to pay, like a car. Student loans and credit cards are examples of unsecured debt. (*See also: Secured Debt*)

V

Valuation: A valuation measures how much something is worth, now or in the future. There are different ways to value companies. Some are tied to profits, while some are tied to other metrics like users. In the tech world, you often see companies like Facebook or Twitter valued in the billions of dollars with no profits because their valuation is based on a strong user base.

Value Stocks: These are stocks that don't have great earnings growth potential, but that trade at low valuations (low P/Es, for example). Value stocks tend to be more mature, settled, old-school companies like Coca-Cola or General Electric with steady earnings. They also tend to pay dividends.

Variable Annuity: This is a type of insurance product generally sold to those who are preparing for retirement or are in retirement. An investor buys an annuity at a set price and then holds it without taking payments (though she can make additional investments) during a period known as the "accumulation stage." Money is invested in open-ended mutual funds offered within the annuity and grows on a tax-deferred basis. After the accumulation stage, the holder of the variable annuity is able to withdraw money from the annuity or to "annuitize" it, in which case the insurance company sends the investor monthly income for life. For this reason VAs (as they're sometimes called) are generally used for those seeking retirement income. The size and scope of these annuitized payments depend on the performance of the portfolio in which the variable annuity is invested, as well as the age of the investor and the current level of interest rates. (*See also: Annuity*)

Venture Capital: This comes after seed money. And if you need it, you will have to give up some control of your idea and company to the venture capitalist (vc) or a venture capital firm giving you the money. The VC will give you the money you need only if they think you have potential (i.e., ability to make them money). (*See also: Seed Money*)

W

Wage Garnishment: If you owe money on a credit card or a loan, and don't pay it back, the lender can go to court to get an order that allows them to take a chunk out of your paycheck until the debt is repaid. This is called a "garnish" (I know, not cute like the other meaning of "garnish" as in to decorate). This is how bill collectors get paid whether you want to pay them or not.

Wall Street Journal, The: Also known as simply the *Journal*, it is one of only two national newspapers in this country (the other is *USA TODAY*). If you want to know about the financial world, the markets, or anything business, you want to get a subscription pronto.

Wealth Management: This is kind of a one-stop-shopping financial services deal. You can get help with your taxes, investments, and estate planning all under one roof—for a fee, of course; usually a percentage of the value of the assets they are managing. Keep in mind, there is usually a minimum to get this service, which can be six figures. That's why they call it "wealth management" and not just "money management."

X

X: Mutual funds all have ticker symbols that end with X. That way you can distinguish them from other stocks. It's good for them because they have more ticker options—lots get snatched up by other companies and you can't have two the same! (*See also: Ticker Symbol*)

Y

Yield: The interest rate you get paid when you buy a security, expressed by percent. With a bond, you'll notice it has something called "YTM," "yield" or "yield-to-maturity," which tells you the rate of return you will receive if you hold the bond until maturity. For example, if you buy a ten-year $10,000 at 6% "yield," you'll receive $600 per year for ten years, on top of the $10,000 you originally invested. Stocks also have yields, often called dividend yields. Invest $10,000 in a stock with a 3% dividend yield and you'll receive $300 per year in cash.

Z

Zombie Debt: This is a debt you've had so long you may have spaced that you still owe it, and chances are the company you owe it to has given up on ever seeing it, too. But it can still come back to bite you if the debt gets turned over to a debt collector; those guys will hound you relentlessly until you pay up.

ACKNOWLEDGMENTS

It's always been a dream of mine to write a finance book for an audience who would have never picked one up before. I knew it could be done, but, just like anything worth doing, it certainly wasn't easy. These rock stars helped make it happen:

Steve Troha, my whip-smart (and devilishly handsome) agent at Folio Literary Management for believing in me and my ability to share my story in my own sass-tastic voice. You will always be the *original* rich bitch.

Becca Hunt, Shara Alexander, and the entire (female!) Harlequin team, for throwing your energy and passion behind championing the Rich Bitch cause. I'm beyond grateful for your TLC through this entire process. Thank you for always embracing me for me, potty mouth included, every step of the way.

Jaime Cassavechia and Jenna Spector and the EJ Media Group for tirelessly promoting this book and always supporting my belief that money topics can be entertaining to a mainstream audience (and for troubleshooting the aforementioned potty mouth).

Ashley Mills, my brilliant agent at CAA, who is always one step ahead of me, rooting and ringleading ceaselessly for Team Lapin. For learning and growing together over the years and never dreaming small.

Judee Ann Williams, my CAA foundation agent, for being the OG leader of my wolf pack and for throwing down your southern spice like no other.

Tom Repicci, my jack-of-all-marketing-trades, for always going way beyond the call of duty. For your belief that there's no limit to what I can do and calling me at midnight and five o'clock in the morning with your ideas to reinforce just that. I'm always amazed at your thoughtfulness, thoroughness and unyielding support.

Carolyn Conrad, my dear friend and entertainment lawyer (in that order) who regularly busts balls on my behalf, delivering the classiest smackdowns I've ever seen. For being my biggest confidante and fan and the most thoughtful gift giver I know. I'm so lucky to have you in my life.

Robert Flutie, Shab Azma and Danielle Iturbe, my dauntless managers who risk their lives every day trying to tame their most unmanageable client. You had me at "hello." You complete me and you know it.

Elizabeth Stephen, my producing partner and the wisest woman I know, for pushing me to aim even higher than I already did. For making me strive to be the Helen Gurley Brown for a new generation. I will never fully understand why you care so much about me, but I'm beyond thankful that you do.

Ellen London, my sidekick, partner in crime and everything-in-chief. For being the only person who can make sense of my crazy stream-of-consciousness emails and handling every task with grace, creativity and chutzpah. For being fiercely loyal and always seeing the best in every situation. I would play in traffic for you and would be dead in a ditch without you.

Randi Zuckerberg, the woman to whom I could listen sing or lecture forever and who is still the best sounding board a girl could ask for. I don't know how you defy the space-time continuum as often as you do and still have time to listen to me kvetch. You serve up the best compliment sandwich I've ever had. And, if I could come back as anything in my next life, it would be as your roomie, obviously.

Nicole Wool, you will always be the #1 Nicole in this relationship. You are my rock, my soul sister, and the strongest woman I know. You've taught me all the best, most important things I now know. You are the only bestie I ever want to know.

The Rubin family, for putting up with me writing, studying, and riffing on my new ideas and big dreams on family vacations. For watching every media clip I send around and being the foundation for me to believe I can accomplish anything.

And, to Michael, my better half, for pushing me further than I knew was possible (even when I resisted). For always wanting me to be *great*, not good.

INDEX